AIR RAID WARDENS WANTED

A RESPONSIBLE JOB FOR RESPONSIBLE MEN

ARP

APPLY TO YOUR LOCAL COUNCIL NOW !

NATIONAL SERVICE

We would like to thank the following: the Royal Society for the Prevention of Accidents, and in particular their Senior Press Officer, Jo Stagg, for allowing us to use their posters, Annie Falconer-Gronow, for doing her usual magic with the design of the book, Ian Bayley for his amazing patience, and to our very patient editor Anne Bennett, and, as ever, our families: Jonathan and Isaac, Ian, Charlotte and Michael, and William and Ralph.

All the recipes, tips and other suggestions in this book come from contemporary publications and government leaflets. I can take no responsibility for case of food poisoning, explosions, fires or other disasters which might ensue if you try any of them out!

AIR RAIDS
&
RATION BOOKS

Life on the Home Front in Wartime Britain

CHURCHMAN'S CIGARETTES

THE CIVILIAN RESPIRATOR—HOW TO REMOVE IT

First published in the United Kingdom in 2010
by Sabrestorm Publishing
90, Lennard Road, Dunton Green
Sevenoaks, Kent TN13 2UX

www.sabrestorm.com

British Library Cataloguing in Publication Data
A catalogue record for this book is available from the British Library.

Designed and typeset by Annie Falconer-Gronow

ISBN: 978-0-955272363

Printed by Tien Wah Press

AIR RAIDS & RATION BOOKS

Life on the Home Front in Wartime Britain

Mike Brown & Carol Harris

A Sewing Machine can be almost as much a weapon ... as a Spade

The comfort and quiet

distinction of a Humber

CONVERT YOUR OWN
GAS-MASK CONTAINER

INTO

A COMPLETE EMERGENCY OUTFIT!

+ FIRST AID OUTFIT.

"IRON"

★ ★ ★ ★ ★ ★ ★ ★ ★ ★ ★ ★

HOUSEWIVES OF BRITAIN

You are fighting one of the war's most important battles— by keeping your homes running smoothly and your families in good health

★ ★ ★ ★

This
DOMESTIC FRONT
EXHIBITION

is here to help you

★ ★ ★ ★ ★ ★ ★ ★ ★ ★ ★ ★

Come in and see how many of your wartime housekeeping difficulties can be overcome when you know how to set about them. The experts are here to help you, and their advice is free

introduction

When we think of the Home Front, many of us immediately picture 1939, the Second World War, air raid shelters and rationing. Yet the concept of warfare where the civilian population itself was 'at the front', a prey to enemy bombs, and shortages caused by an aggressive attack on the nation's larder by the U-boat assault, actually goes back to the First World War. The concept of war from both the air and beneath the sea had at that time only recently been seen as belonging in the pages of fantastic literature, like that of Jules Verne and H. G. Wells, yet now it became grim reality. The inventiveness which created those concepts now had to be employed in devising responses to them, and air-raid shelters, anti-aircraft guns, public warnings and searchlights were evolved to combat bombing, while the Women's Land Army, wartime recipe books and rationing were employed to counter food shortages.

By the end of the 'Great War' people were sick of warfare, and printed stories of the war were rare. As time wore on the slaughter in the trenches of France, and in places like Gallipoli, began to be recounted, but compared to them the privations of the home front seemed small, and were rarely mentioned in print. With so few still alive who remember the Home Front in the First

World War, it comes as no surprise that most people today know very little about it.

Just one generation after that war ended, a mere twenty-one years after the 'war to end all wars', the simmering discontent of its unjust settlement exploded into the Second World War. Now the legacy of Britain's Great War home front came to the fore. Measures against enemy aerial raiders, devised and perfected during the First World War, were renamed Air Raid Precautions and recycled. The Ministry of Food, first created in the First World War, was reborn, and rationing, brought in against kicking and screaming opposition as late in the earlier war as 1918, slid smoothly into place after just over three months of war in January 1940.

These measures did not appear from nowhere, any more than the war was a result of a sudden madness in September 1939. The conflict had been brewing almost since the end of the previous war; certainly there had been discontent, even resentment, but the extremists in Germany had been marginalised as prosperity and jobs had come to the majority

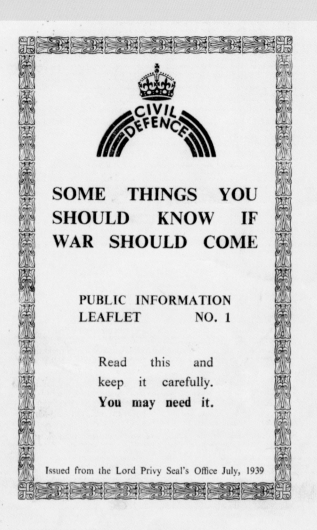

CIVIL
DEFENCE

SOME THINGS YOU
SHOULD KNOW IF
WAR SHOULD COME

PUBLIC INFORMATION
LEAFLET   NO. 1

Read   this   and
keep it carefully.
You may need it.

Issued from the Lord Privy Seal's Office July, 1939

Above

If War Should Come leaflet. These were sent to every house in Britain in July 1939, giving advice and directions on what to do in the event of war. (HMSO)

were taking place, with the formation of the ARP Department of the Home Office in April 1935, and the Food (Defence Plans) Department in 1936; the latter would later become the Ministry of Food.

The Munich Crisis of September 1938, when it appeared that Europe would once again be plunged into war, as gas masks were issued and trenches dug in public parks, awakened all but the most die-hard optimists to the threat. The next twelve months were taken up with rapid shelter-building and planning, while the government issued mountains of advice on all aspects of the home front: the blackout, gas masks, rationing and evacuation among others.

When Prime Minister Neville Chamberlain announced that 'This country is at war with Germany' many, of course, were alarmed, but few were surprised.

Perhaps because the scale of the bombing was so much greater this time round, or because so many more people were involved in the various civilian services, or due to the more widespread nature of the media – magazines, the press, cinema and the 'wireless' – or maybe because of the huge social shift that had occurred between the wars which meant that the 'common man' was celebrated, and that history was no longer seen as just the deeds of the great and the good. Probably because of all these things, the home front in the Second World War was widely covered, and consequently is generally known of today, yet still in a sort of one-size-fits-all kind of way.

People's experience of the home front differed greatly. These were mainly regional variations, most marked between the towns and the country-

through aid plans. However, economic downturns often bring dissatisfaction to the surface, and this is exactly what happened, with many turning to those offering political 'quick fixes', such as the Nazis. Thus the road to conflict was well signposted for those who were prepared to look, and from the mid-1930s onwards in Britain, preparations for war

side. In rural areas, raids were far less frequent, a fact which often added to the 'townie's feeling of superiority over his country cousins. Richmal Crompton describes this in **William and the Bomb:** *'She was not even affected by the bomb snobbery that the inhabitants of the village found so exasperating in most of its London visitors. She did not describe her methods of dealing with "incendiaries", her reactions to "screamers", her shelter life, the acrobatics she performed when taking cover at various sinister sounds.*

The village was sick of such descriptions from evacuees. It was perhaps unduly sensitive on the subject from what might be called bomb inferiority complex. For, though enemy aeroplanes frequently roared overhead during the night watches, and a neighbouring AA gun occasionally made answer, providing the youthful population with the shrapnel necessary for their "collections", no bomb had as yet fallen on the village.'

As well as this, food shortages were usually far less acute in the country; there was often a little extra to be had if you knew a farmer, or someone who knew a farmer, and there was always wild food: mushrooms, berries, and of course, rabbits, pigeons and other wildlife. There were drawbacks to country living however, as many urban evacuees found to their cost. Few country areas had the luxury of connection to all the amenities, electricity, gas, water and sewerage, and many a wry smile was caused by newspaper advice on how to do without gas supplies or electricity, or water, after an air raid. Transport problems, caused by petrol rationing, were a headache in the town, but could be a nightmare in the country.

For those living on the urban home front, everyday life was dominated by specific concerns. Death from the air was the obvious one, although even in the towns and cities, for most people raids in their immediate area were a fairly rare occurrence. Air-raid warnings and the need to take cover were frequent, but these most often led to boring and uncomfortable periods spent in the Anderson or Morrison shelter rather than sheer terrifying danger.

Below
Cartoon by Fougasse. The government issued swathes of advice and instructions but, as the cartoon shows, some people still complained that no-one was telling them what to do.

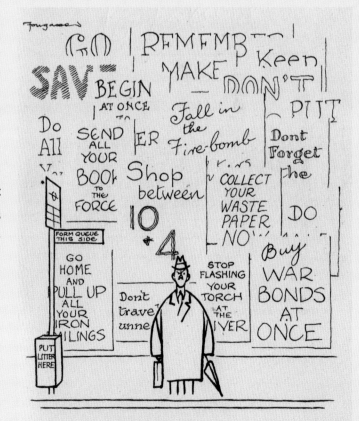

" If only they'd tell us all what to do."

Most of the time life in the suburbs was about adapting everyday life to the problems which war brought, first among them a flood of official and semi-official instructions and advice. The leaflet *War Emergency Instructions and Information,* issued in September 1939, included: *'Information and instructions will be given to the public by means of broadcast announcements. These announcements are of vital importance to everyone. Listen carefully and have a pencil and paper ready so that you may make a note of anything that concerns you, and inform other persons in your household who have not heard the broadcast.*

Announcements will be made in all news bulletins and at special times which will be announced beforehand.'

The start of an increasing official involvement in everyday life began for most people on Friday 29 September 1939, 'National Registration Day'. Every householder in Britain was required to register everyone resident in their house as the official registration notice stated: *The return on the schedule herewith will be used not only for National Registration but also for Food Rationing purposes. It is to your interest, therefore, as well as your public duty, to fill up the return carefully, fully and accurately. Help the Enumerator to collect the schedule promptly by arranging for him to receive it when he calls. Do not make it necessary for him to call a number of times before he can obtain it. When the Enumerator collects the schedule, he must write and deliver an Identity Card for every person included in the return. Help him to write them properly for you by letting him write at a table. If the whole household moves before the*

schedule is collected, take it with you and hand it to the Enumerator calling at your new residence or to the National Registration Office for your new address. The address of this office can be ascertained at a local police station.'

As the leaflet explained, registration entailed the immediate issue of identity cards, and in

Below
In September 1939 everyone was registered, and issued with an identity card. This is a first pattern card for an adult – new cards had to be issued later as these were so easily forged, and could be used to obtain precious ration books. (HMSO)

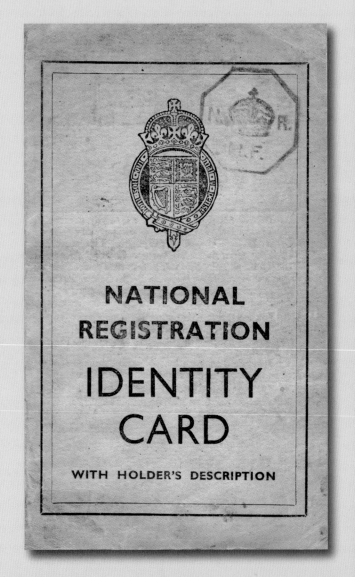

NATIONAL REGISTRATION

IDENTITY CARD

WITH HOLDER'S DESCRIPTION

October the first food ration books were issued, followed eighteen months later by clothing ration books and points ration books, and eight months after that by 'personal points' cards for sweets. These led to further instructions and tips for saving or making the most of rationed goods, or for substitutes.

Virtually from the start of the war, the government took control of the supply of scarce resources through a series of 'Limitation of Supply Orders', under which manufacturers of specified items could only produce a fraction of their previous total. This was 66% for most items, falling by the end of 1940 to 33%, and just 25% of 'fancy goods' such as combs, umbrellas, lighters and toiletries. By the end of 1941, with the loss of much of our rubber supply to the Japanese, a long list of rubber items was no longer allowed to be made.

As with rationing, people sought alternatives, and advice on these was freely given by government, magazines, newspapers and books, yet this created a domino effect as many of these substitutes themselves became scarce, and substitutes were sought for the substitutes, and so on.

Several of the chapters in the book are concerned with the rationing or shortage of certain goods, and with advice from many sources. Sometimes inventive, sometimes hilarious, sometimes even revolting, but almost always interesting, these give us a wonderful insight into the trials of everyday suburban life in the Second World War as well, perhaps, as a few ideas for today's conservation-minded and economy-conscious age.

Below
Even in the Phoney War period, the various restrictions of war could be a headache, as this advert for Wincarnis at the beginning of March 1940 suggests. Soon the blitzkrieg would begin, and restrictions would be the least of your worries.

Restrictions **YOU MUSTN'T LET** Blackouts **WARTIME GET YOU DOWN** Rationing Worries

Almost every woman is in real need just now of a wartime pick-me-up, something to safeguard her health and nerves and give her extra resistance to cope with wartime's worries and problems. It is dangerous to get into an overtired and overstrained condition. Start to fortify yourself *now* with Wincarnis, the stimulating, restoring Tonic Wine. There's no waiting with Wincarnis. One sip and you think — Ah, that's good, that's cheering! One glass and you set about your job of work with new heart and will. For Wincarnis pours iron, rich beef and malt extracts and two kinds of vitamins into your system—starts building up your stamina right away. *Wincarnis,* THE QUICK ACTION TONIC, *is backed by over 26,000 medical recommendations.*
"*I am glad to say I have quite recovered from my illness and am now perfectly well again. I took the Wincarnis as a final pick-me-up.*"
H.E.B., LIVERPOOL

ARE YOU: TIRED, OVERWROUGHT, ANXIOUS ?

Feel better, more cheerful **IN ONE MINUTE** *after one glass of Wincarnis*

Health is priceless

WINCARNIS

Costs only 6/6 & 3/9

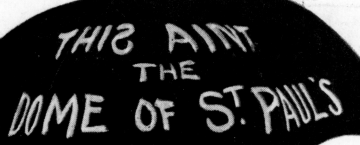

air raids

Air raids had first come to Britain on Christmas Eve 1914, when a German aircraft dropped a bomb in a cabbage patch near Dover Castle. It broke windows and blew a man out of a nearby tree, but otherwise no serious damage was done. The following month two Zeppelins, massive dirigible balloons, crossed the coast in Norfolk. One of them dropped bombs on King's Lynn, killing two people and injuring thirty. These were to be the first of many civilian air raid casualties in Britain.

Over the next year this Zeppelin raid was followed by others, spread as far afield as Edinburgh in the north to Portsmouth in the south, which would leave 556 dead and 1,300 injured. In 1916 the raiders changed from airships to aeroplanes. Due to their limited range, raids were now concentrated in the south-east, leaving 857 dead and 2,000 injured.

Measures were introduced to combat the assault, measures more commonly associated with the Second World War – anti-aircraft guns, searchlights, air-raid warnings, given by factory sirens or policemen blowing their whistles. Public buildings were employed as air-raid shelters, using places such as police stations, churches and, in some areas, natural features such as caves, or man-made equivalents such as tunnels, or, in London, the Underground.

Left
Postcard from the First World War. Air raids were not new to Britain in 1939, though when they did come they would be far bigger than in 'the last war'.

Right
Woman reading an ARP notice. Such advice as what to do in a raid would become deadly serious for many people. (HMSO)

Tube stations were felt to be so safe that several of the least courageous started to set up home in them, much to the authorities' annoyance, and in 1917 a Cabinet Committee recommended a policy which they named 'dispersal', that is encouraging the public to rely on the protection offered by their homes rather than to gather in crowds in a public place. This policy would continue to be the official line between the wars.

During the 1930s, with war approaching, the threat of air raids was ever present in the public mind, but now, with the rapid interwar improvements in aviation technology, so graphically demonstrated in the Spanish Civil War, the expected raids were anticipated to be massive, their death tolls hugely inflated by that other weapon of the First World War, poison gas.

gas masks

During the 1930s there was a general expectation that poison gas would be used against civilians in any future war. In 1934 the British Government set up a committee to examine the use of gas masks, or respirators, for the general population. They reported that most people would not be prepared to buy a gas mask on the off-chance that war might come, and that many would be unable to afford one; it was therefore decided that if an effective mask could be produced sufficiently cheaply, the country should build up a stock of masks to be provided free to all members of the public in the event of an emergency.

It was found that such a mask could indeed be produced, and in October 1935 the government

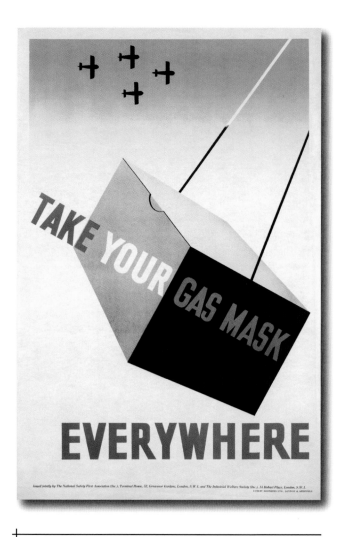

Above
Government poster – 'Take your Gas Mask Everywhere'. Despite such exhortations, within a few months less than a quarter of the population would do so. (HMSO)

agreed on the production of 53 million masks, beginning the following year. The Civilian, or General Civilian Respirator, as they were officially designated, was designed for members of the general public from the age of about four upwards, who were not expected to remain for long periods or to do strenuous work in an atmosphere affected by gas. They came in three sizes, large, medium and small; later an extra-large mask was produced.

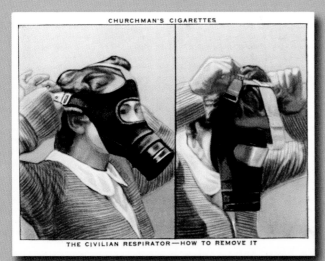

CHURCHMAN'S CIGARETTES

THE CIVILIAN RESPIRATOR—HOW TO REMOVE IT

Above

Cigarette card from 1938, showing the correct way of removing the civilian mask.

The first, and by far the most common, version was made of a single sheet of thin rubber, sewn under the chin, with a single oval eyepiece, or 'window', made of cellulose acetate. In 1940 a second version was introduced, with the stitching around the window and along the join 'luted', or sealed, with a self-vulcanising latex solution, although the original version continued to be produced. A moulded variation of the civilian mask was produced by the Avon Rubber Company.

The soft rubber of the civilian respirator meant that no outlet valve was necessary, as the air would be expelled from under the sides of the mask on breathing out; however, this was a problem for people who, through age, weak heart, asthma, hay fever and other conditions found even the slight effort of expelling the air past the cheeks too great a strain. The Avon moulded-rubber design was adapted for this purpose by the addition of a 'flutter' outlet valve fitted like a nosepiece. These were

Other Gas Masks

Not all civilians wore the civilian mask. Some members of the ARP, the Fire Brigade, the Police and the Home Guard were issued with far more robust masks, originally designed for members of the armed forces. Unlike civilian masks, which were to be worn by people sitting sedately in their shelter or refuge room, the service mask had to be tough enough to enable the wearer to move around, run, and even fight while wearing it.

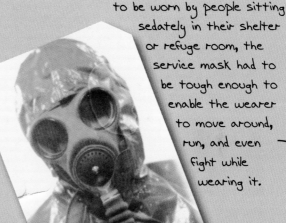

The Service Respirator had a thick moulded face-piece with replaceable glass eye-pieces. Connected via a corrugated rubber tube, a detachable heavy filter was carried in a bag hung around the neck.

CHURCHMAN'S CIGARETTES

CHARCOAL

THE SERVICE RESPIRATOR

Most people carried their service masks all the time. This school teacher is wearing his civilian service mask to the obvious amusement of his pupils.

issued on production of a medical certificate approved by the local Medical Officer of Health.

It was realised very early on that a different type of mask would be needed for children below the age of five, as the shape of a developing child's face was unsuitable for the general mask, and another was required for babies. Designs were produced, including cardboard boxes fitted with pumps, a kind of oxygen tent, and a hood fitted to prams.

By the end of 1937 an anti-gas helmet for children up to two years old had been developed, but a gap between two- and five-year-olds still remained. At the time of the first Czecho-slovakian crisis in May 1938 there had still been no design passed for such a mask, while the babies' anti-gas helmet design had gone through several modifications; the final design for this age group would not be accepted until August of that year.

Respirators were first issued to the general public at the time of the Munich Crisis in September 1938 to people living in government-designated 'danger areas'. During the last weekend of September fitting stations were hurriedly opened in schools, town halls and other buildings, and the public were exhorted through adverts, posters, loudspeaker vans, and announcements at churches, public meetings and sports events to go to be fitted out with a gas mask. By now the government had stocks of 40 million adult masks, but none of the 1.5 million children's respirators, or the 1.4 million babies' anti-gas helmets required, causing deep concern, and more than a little protest.

One week later the crisis was over, but the government decided to leave those masks which had been issued with the public for a trial period of six months, and to issue protective cardboard cartons designed to double up as carriers. By March 1939 stocks of both masks and cartons had been issued to most local authorities. Wholesale distribution began again during the summer of 1939, and in July the government issued a set of Civil Defence Public Information leaflets to be delivered to every house in the country, the second of which included *Your Gas Mask – how to keep it and how to use it.* At the end of that month, as the international situation worsened, the government asked local authorities to complete distribution immediately. Already there was a need to replace previously issued masks; some had been lost or damaged, and some had even been sold to American tourists as souvenirs of the Munich Crisis!

By the end of 1937 the babies' gas helmet or hood (known as the baby-bag) had been developed. The final design consisted of a hood, made of impervious fabric, fitted with a large, curved, plastic window. The hood enclosed the baby from the waist upwards, and was closed around its waist by a draw band. The hood was enclosed in a metal frame with an adjustable tailpiece, turned up at the end to prevent the baby slipping or wriggling out. Air was supplied by a set of bellows on the right-hand side of the hood; being, in effect, a small iron lung, it was stated that the mask contained enough air to keep a baby supplied for five minutes should pumping stop, thus enabling its adult operator to take small breaks or deal with some other emergency. The Ministry of Home Security booklet, **ARP at Home,** gave instructions for its use: *'First give at least 12 sharp strokes on the pump to clear the air out of the helmet. Then continue to pump slowly*

and steadily; 35 or 40 strokes a minute is fast enough to keep out poison gas, and to provide plenty of air for a child even three or four years of age. If you pump too fast you will tire yourself out.'

The small child's respirator had at last been agreed on. The problem had been that the shape of a young child's face, and their unpredictable and sometimes unruly behaviour, made a mask similar to the soft rubber civilian mask unsuitable for them. A moulded rubber mask was designed to answer these problems. It had an elastic harness which allowed for growth without the need for adjustment, and a hook-and-eye at the back to prevent children removing it themselves. The mask was usually made in bright colours – a red face-piece, and a blue filter – to make it a thing of fun, thereby encouraging children to wear it. These colours were reminiscent of Technicolor, used especially for cartoons, so they were often nick-named 'Mickey Mouse' masks. As a rough guide it was suitable for children between the ages of about 18 months and 4 to 4½ years.

The second distribution of masks in July 1939 encountered two problems. First, being midsummer, many people were on holiday, so extra stores had to be diverted to seaside resorts. Second, supplies of baby-bags and children's respirators were still low, and in some areas non-existent. To fill the gap, the government issued extra supplies of the small-size adult masks for use by children from two years old, and suggested the use of the baby-bag be extended to two-year-olds, but this hardly helped as there were often too few of these.

When war broke out, the distribution of adult civilian gas masks was virtually complete. This

Left
An early illustration of a baby's gas helmet, or baby-bag, as they were commonly known. These were issued to children up to about 18 months; most hated being inside the helmet.
Above
An air-raid warden displaying the baby-bag (right) and the small child's mask, better known as the 'Mickey Mouse' or 'Donald Duck'.

A·R·P
GAS

WARNING SIGNAL   Sounding of Hand Rattles

"ALL CLEAR SIGNAL"   Sounding of Hand Bells

Some gases look like mist, some are almost invisible, others appear in liquid form. Colour ranges between Dark Brown and Yellow.

How you can detect the presence of Gas

BY SMELL

       Musty Hay.
       Bleaching Powder.
       Garlic or Onions.
       Mustard or Horseradish.
       Geraniums.

or

BY PHYSICAL EFFECTS

       Flooding and running of the eyes.
       Irritation to the eyes, nose and throat.
       Pain in chest, nose or mouth.
       Inflammation and blisters on skin.

ACTION

Immediately put on your Gas Mask. Put on your hat, coat and gloves, and await instructions.

Oilskins for coats and hats are the best protection— alternatively, rubber mackintoshes.

If you have skin irritation or pain of any kind, report to your nearest A.R.P. Warden or First-Aid Post.

Above

An ARP gas notice, describing how to detect the various types of poison gas that could be used in war.

Right

Advert for the 3S gas-mask container. Many people bought or made covers or containers for their masks, to replace the cardboard boxes in which they were issued.

Far Right

A child's gas mask, issued to children between the ages of about 18 months and five years.

3.S GAS MASK CONTAINER

SIMPLE — SAFE — SANITARY

Waterproof

Attached Lid

Easily visible in Black-out

Space on lid for name and address of owner

Clean outside of tin with damp cloth

INSTRUCTIONS FOR USE OVERLEAF

compared favourably with Germany, where only about 12 million had been issued. By mid-September the British Government could report that distribution of the adult mask was complete, and by late October, to everyone's relief, the issue of baby-bags was also virtually complete, while stocks of the child's mask had grown to the extent that mothers of children older than 18 months were encouraged to exchange the baby-bags they had been issued for children's masks. By the end of January 1940, the issue of both was at last complete.

There was no law obliging people to carry their mask, although at first many cinemas and dance halls refused admittance to anyone not carrying one, and several firms sent home employees who arrived for work with no mask. Police and wardens would deliver stern lectures to people found without one. It became a matter of much concern that, in the event of a gas attack, those without a mask were unlikely to submit quietly to their fate and that vicious fighting might ensue as people who did not have masks tried to grab them from those who did.

Gas mask practice was encouraged by the government through short films and other media. *'Do you practise wearing your mask once a week? You should practise regularly and see that your family do so too, even the small children.'* Children could be a particular difficulty. **Toys in Wartime** suggested: *'Particularly children under six should be accustomed to wearing their gas-masks through play. If you wait until there is an emergency (which we hope will never come) it is going*

to be very difficult indeed to get them to wear them for any length of time. They will complain that they cannot breathe in them and then you will have extreme difficulty in making them keep them on until danger has passed. . . .

Many schools are taking the advance precaution of teaching the children to sit for long periods in their masks, but as far as I can see this is very seldom being done in the home or with very young children. If you make it a game they will be much more inclined to lose all fear of the mask and they will be willing to wear them for longer and longer periods, so that should an emergency arise, they will not be so completely unaccustomed to them. Of course, it is an unpleasant subject to have to teach a child, but that is better than being unable to get him to wear a mask when there is real or possible danger about. Tell them that there are times when we have to wear masks so that we can get clean air to breathe. Whenever you get a child to wear his mask, be sure to wear yours at the same time. That will make it

imitative play and they will feel that they are being "grown-up" in wearing one. Make the periods short at first and let them take them off when they begin to feel real discomfort, explaining each time that this is only a game and there may come a time when they will have to wear them until they are told that it is safe to remove them.'

The Ministry of Home Security booklet, **ARP at Home**, also dealt with this subject: *'Do you have trouble in getting your child to wear its mask? If you do and you have tried in every way you can to coax it to wear the mask and failed, try to get a small playfellow, who does not mind wearing its mask, to come in when you are next trying to get your own child to practise. This very often does the trick, for children hate to be made to look ridiculous before their little friends.'* If this did not work you might resort to: *'Another way is to leave the child alone with other children. Children have their own methods of dealing with playfellows who are reluctant to do some special thing, and they will often succeed where you would fail.'* For some, however, even this could not sort out this very real worry: *'If, however, all efforts fail, take your child to the ARP Department of your local authority and explain the situation before the child and ask for a baby helmet to be issued instead of the Mickey Mouse. These helmets can often be issued to larger children.'* In the end, should even this fail, the one remaining alternative was to have them evacuated to a safe area, where the wearing of masks would be unnecessary.

The necessity of carrying your gas mask with you all the time brought with it its own problem – forgetfulness. Tens of thousands of gas masks were

left on buses, trains and so on, and were piled up in railway lost property offices and police stations. Under the Civil Defence Act of 1939 members of the public could be fined £5 for failing to use reasonable care in preserving their mask, and in March 1940 the Ministry of Home Security introduced charges for the replacement of a mask lost due to negligence. These were 2s 6d for an adult's mask, 3s 6d for a child's mask, and 25s for a baby's helmet, plus pro rata charges for repair of damage. However, this did not apply to masks lost or damaged during air raids, or to people who were unemployed or in receipt of public assistance, while officially evacuated children who lost or damaged their masks during evacuation had them replaced free of charge.

One of the biggest concerns about gas masks was the wearing of spectacles while also wearing the mask. For the thicker, moulded-rubber Civilian Duty and Service masks, special respirator glasses had been designed; these had hyper-thin, flexible arms, which would be sandwiched against the head by the respirator, while still keeping the whole thing airtight. These would not work with the normal, far thinner, civilian respirator. The government advised that you should take off your glasses for the short period that you would be expected to wear your mask, but many people were reluctant to do so. As with so much else, private manufacturers filled the gap, producing various gas mask spectacles, usually held on with a band of elastic which passed round the head, or over the ears and under the chin. The government refused to authorise any of them however, arguing that the elastic would form a furrow in the skin, allowing the gas to enter the mask, or that the spectacles themselves would distort the shape of the mask, with the same effect, or that they might puncture the mask.

"You can take your gas-mask off, Sir, the 'all clear's gone!"
"What d'yer mean? I havn't got it on!"

A debate sprang up in the pages of **The Optician** about the best solution, including one suggestion that lorgnettes were the answer; the eventual outcome was advice that those who could not do without their glasses should buy a Civilian Duty mask, price 16s 6d from the manufacturers, Siebe Gorman, and a pair of respirator spectacles from their optician. Several people took a cheaper route and wore their glasses over the mask.

Left
Sarah Churchill (the prime minister's daughter) poses for a publicity photograph with her gas mask, watched by Commander E. J. Hodsal, director of the ARP services.

Above
Gas-mask glasses advert. The civilian mask was not designed to be worn with glasses, and the official advice was to leave them off when wearing one, but many were not happy to do so.

The wearing of gas masks posed other problems. There was a debate in the letters pages of **The Times** over whether it was necessary to shave off a beard in order to be able to put on a mask. One suggestion was that *'the beard should be tightly rolled up and tucked under the chin, four curling pins being used to secure it'*. The **Daily Mirror** reported that *'Hair-dressers in the West End of London report the latest coiffure – the Gas Mask curl. Idea is to leave a centre-parting for the main strap. Clusters of curls stand out on either side.'* Wearers of wigs had particular difficulties as the mask tended to dislodge the wig as well as creating heat and discomfort. One reader wrote to the **Hairdressers' Journal** with his solution: *'I have a small rubber-lined sponge bag which I keep in the box along with my gas mask. My private drill consists of taking off my scalpette, putting it into the sponge bag and then slipping the latter with its closed outlet downwards into my hip pocket. I then fit on my gas mask and on the top of my head I put a beret which I keep handy in my coat pocket.'*

After a brief flurry, the carrying of gas masks fell off rapidly. In London the Mass Observation organisation carried out a gas mask count; the figures showed that 75% of people carried their masks in the first month of the war, dropping to only 30% in November, and by February 1940 only one person in twenty had their masks ready. Figures fluctuated in response to events in the war, but never again rose over 30%. The Mass Observation report went on: *'Gasmask carrying is much lower*

"We had Harricot beans for dinner to-day"

in provincial towns and rural areas, and in many recent counts has been below 1% (e.g. Cardiff, Letchworth, Worcester, Bolton). It is difficult to move about in Britain today without seeing the most pressing appeal to carry your gasmask as a matter of urgency. A number of gas exhibitions are now being held. Inside such an exhibition in Shepherd's Bush, under 5% were carrying gasmasks.'

Even Herbert Morrison, the Minister of Home Security, admitted that if the carrying of a gas mask *'was conclusive proof of the good citizenship of the men and women of this country, we should have to come to the conclusion that there were not many good citizens'.*

In October 1940 the government submitted to the inevitable and announced that it was no longer necessary to carry a mask every-where in reception areas, although mask carrying in danger areas still stayed low; even the London Fire Service dropped the compulsory carrying of gas masks after the first year of the war. Reception areas were those places where the likelihood of raids was considered low and these would receive evacuees, such as Wales and the West of England.

Early in 1940 the government was told that the Germans had perfected a method of using arsine gas. Only the existing Service masks could protect the wearer against this so an extension filter called a Contex (short for container extension) was added to all civilian and civilian service respirators. The mammoth job of fitting these green extensions was carried out by the wardens' service by the simple means of adding them on to the end of the existing container with sticky tape. One side-effect of this was that certain of the commercially produced gas mask cases were too small to accommodate the lengthened filter box.

With the entry of Japan into the war in December 1941 things took a new turn. The loss of the rubber plantations in the Far East meant that rubber had to be conserved, and that meant gas masks. On 30 July 1942, Herbert Morrison announced the government's decision that in order to reduce wear and tear and conserve supplies of rubber, respirators should not be carried by the public at all times, but should be left at home so long as they could be reached easily in case of need, and that anyone sleeping away from home should take their respirator with them.

To the very end of the war the government tried

Above

Advert for a joint gas-mask container and first aid kit. Many firms cashed in on the war, selling gas-mask cases or similar items.

to keep everyone prepared for a gas attack with renewed poster campaigns, arguing that as Germany became ever more desperate, so the chances of such an attack, delivered by aircraft, or later, by V-weapon, became more likely. On VE-Day, as the bonfires sprang up, one of the most popular, or rather unpopular, additions to many a fire was the hated gas mask!

passes filtered air through the kennel. Hundreds of these kennels are at present on order; the demand is so considerable that delivery cannot be promised within any specified time.'

Alternatively, they suggested that you get hold of a wooden box as large as possible, then in each side cut holes about the size of 'half a crown' (about the size of a 50p piece), place the animal

So much for people, but what of animals? **The Times**, on 8 September 1939, carried an article on this. *'The People's Dispensary for Sick Animals of the Poor has produced a gas-proof safety kennel which it recommends as the best protection for dogs, cats, and other small animals against gas attack. The kennel is a gas-tight box with windows. It has a floor so hinged and sprung that every movement of the animal works a bellows that*

inside, and then completely cover the box with *'a woollen blanket soaked in a solution of chloride of lime (two tablespoonfuls to a gallon of water), which is obtainable at any grocer or chemist. The animal may be uncomfortable, but it is receiving the best protection you can give it.'* It has to be concluded that the box should have had a lid too, as no doubt the dog or cat would soon have tired of sitting in a box and left!

Bird cages should be hung off the ground in a gas-proof room *'below the level of any gas light jets. If no gas-proof room is available, completely wrap the cage in a wet blanket. (This method should only be used as a last resort.)'*

The makers of Bob Martin pet products later gave directions for the gas proofing of a kennel, which they described as *'a simple and inexpensive matter. Fit a door which will completely cover the entrance, overlapping for two or three inches on all sides. The normal vents should be left untouched for ventilation purposes, but if the kennel does not possess any the roof must be modified so that one or two slats can be removed, and the resulting space protected by wire netting. Take care that the sharp ends of the netting are outside the kennel so that the dog will not injure himself. When an air raid warning is sounded, cover the entire kennel with an old blanket soaked in a solution of one teaspoonful of glycerine, one teaspoonful washing soda and one pint of water, and tie round the lower edges with a piece of string. Gas proofing a kennel in this fashion will give a dog complete protection against most of the gases likely to be encountered. The solution of glycerine, washing soda and water should always be kept ready against emergencies.'*

Interestingly, they stated that *'Generally speaking dogs are immune to the effects of nose and tear gases, but if liquid gases, such as Mustard or Lewisite, which can be recognised by their smell of onions and geraniums respectively, have been used, then the dog should not be allowed out of his shelter until contaminated places have been cleared. If a dog is gassed, and particularly if he is affected by liquid gas, obtain expert help immediately the air*

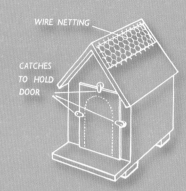

raid is over. If help is likely to be long delayed a contaminated animal can be given first aid treatment.'

For cats, they suggested that *'It is advisable that a gas-proof box be made for your cat. It should be proofed against gas in the following manner:- First fasten the lid securely, then cover completely with a blanket which has been soaked in a solution of one teaspoonful of glycerine, one teaspoonful of washing soda and one pint of water. It is most important that all joints and crevices be properly sealed and made proof against gas. The box should be provided with straw or washable cushion. On no account should a cat be released from his shelter until all traces of gas have been removed.'*

The RSPCA pamphlet, **Animals and Air Raids,** referred to gas-proof boxes or kennels: *'We are against these. Some of them cost £4 each. Some have to have air pumped in for small dogs. All are open to the objection that, if the owner becomes a casualty, the animal may be overlooked and die of starvation. If gas is used, put your dog or cat in their sleeping basket. The sleeping basket should be covered with another of similar size inverted over it and the blanket put over all and held down. Take both into your shelter and put over the animal an* *ordinary woollen blanket that has been soaked in plain water or in a solution of permanganate of potash. The solution should be a dark wine colour. Only do this when the rattle warning for gas attack has been given. Do not allow the dog to chew the blanket because when the permanganate gives off its oxygen a poisonous solution results. Do not use a solution of chloride of lime (bleaching powder). If you do, your cat may suffer and die. Chloride of Lime should only be used by an expert for the protection of dogs and cats.'*

the blackout

The first lighting restrictions, as a measure against air raids, were introduced in areas around harbours in August 1914, and were extended to the whole country one month later. Like other early anti-Zeppelin measures, they were to remain a feature of ARP schemes throughout the 1920s and '30s.

In 1936 the Home Office prepared a Draft Order (to be implemented in time of war) banning exterior shop and advertisement lighting and motor vehicle headlamps, and requiring the screening or extinguishing of all interior lights, these proposals being approved in November 1937. Local authorities were informed of the 'black-out' proposals, as they had become known, in February of 1938.

In the event of the blackout being brought into force, householders had to ensure that no light escaped from their premises; illuminated advertising and shop-name signs were banned and street lighting was to be replaced by white lines on kerbs, trees, telegraph poles and down the middle of roads. Motor vehicle headlamps were to be masked as were interior lights on buses and trains.

Throughout 1939, a series of blackout exercises took place across the country. Street lighting was found to be a problem; each lamp-post had to be switched off individually, usually by

removing the bulb. In many inner-city areas this would take up to six hours, while extinguishing adverts, shop signs and so on could take up to twenty-four hours. By June 1939 plans had been set to mobilise about 3,000 electricity and gas concerns to shut down all street lighting. Mobilisation of their teams would commence with the message, 'Street Lights Message Black'.

The blackout regulations came into force on Friday 1 September 1939. The following instructions were issued at this time by Sussex police:

'Precautions to be taken immediately by all concerned
Private Dwellings
All windows, skylights, glazed doors, or other openings must be completely screened after dusk, so that no light is visible from outside. If blinds are used alone, they must be of stout material and dark in colour and must cover the window completely. If curtains are used they must be dark and thick.

Dark blankets or carpets or thick sheets of brown paper can be used to cover windows temporarily. Special care must be taken to cover completely skylights and other windows directly visible from the air.

All lights near a door leading outside the building must be screened so that no light can be seen when the door is opened.

Keep your house dark.
If a raid takes place remain indoors.'

The government leaflet *War Emergency Instructions and Information*, issued that month, gave very similar advice: *'All windows, skylights. glazed doors or other openings which would show a light at night must be screened with dark blinds, curtains or blankets, or with brown paper fixed on to the glass so that no light is visible from outside. All lighted signs and advertisement lights and other outside lights must be turned out. All street lighting will be stopped till further notice.'*

Left
The blackout without the raids was soon seen as romantic, and became the theme for several songs, such as this one.

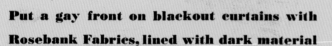

As with most ARP measures, the blackout was based on the experience of the First World War, when aircraft were far slower, and often flew very low. Thus, at first, the rules were extremely strict, and people were prosecuted for lighting a cigarette in the street, as 'experts' insisted that this could be seen by pilots. Perhaps in the string-bags of 1916, travelling at 60 miles an hour at 100 feet, but at 2,000-plus feet, and at 150-plus miles an hour? The complete blackout in force at this time became a source of, at best, humour, and at worst real danger as deaths on the road shot up, but for people in general they were a source of intense irritation and confusion. In **Let George Do It** (1940), George Formby gets on the wrong train in the blackout, and finishes up in Norway instead of Blackpool!

In the **Civil Defender**, a magazine for ARP members, readers were asked to comment on various facets of the war. Two responses to the blackout were *'Tolerable, but only just',* and one that summed up most people's view, *'a necessary evil'.*

The blackout produced a storm of letters to newspapers, containing complaints and advice, like this one from **The Times** in November 1939: *'When walking in the blackout, whichever side of the pavement they take, walkers are involved in unexpected risks: on the one side Belisha beacons, lamp-posts, pillar boxes and sand bins; on the other, sandbag promontories. The middle of the pavement is the only safe place and . . . I suggest that the better rule at night would be that walkers northwards should use the west and those walking southward the east pavement . . . It does not matter much at night which side of the street one walks* since there are no shops or other attractions.'

A writer to **Picture Post** that December complained that *'In order to make themselves more visible in the blackout, people are wearing white hats, gloves, scarves, stockings, buttons, etc., and even using white umbrellas. Would you print the following warning in large print – White walking sticks are the sign of a blind man!'* Dog walking was a also a problem in the blackout, as this letter to **Picture Post** pointed out in April 1940: *'You would be doing a public service if you did a pictorial feature teaching dog owners to keep their animals under proper constraint, and to have some consideration for the sensibilities of others. In particular they would be well advised not to air their dogs on a lead in the blackout. Wartime life is difficult enough without being tripped up and bitten by a frightened animal in the dark.'*

The makers of Bob Martin's commented that: *'exercise always presents a more difficult problem in Winter, and during blackout nights the question becomes more difficult than ever. Wise owners realise that it is a necessity for good health and that there is no adequate substitute for it. Where the curtailing of exercise is unavoidable, dogs need Bob Martin's Condition Powders more than ever to provide and maintain a supply of pure, rich blood. During blackout hours it is advisable that dogs are exercised on the lead and that they be fitted with a white coat or collar. Wherever possible dogs should be exercised during the hours of daylight throughout the duration of the war.'*

If this was not possible, there was another

Left
The blackout later became synonymous with gloom, but as curtain producers pointed out, this did not have to be the case inside the house.

Above
Another way to make the blackout less gloomy was to fit blinds, as this advert shows.

answer, as this advert claimed: *'Seeing is believing – Luminous dog leads and collars, the real blackout safety for yourself and your dog – Demonstration at the Pet's Arcadia, 60 High Street, Dover.'* The only real problem was that many of these luminous answers to the blackout did not work, and those that did were radioactive!

Under no circumstances should pets be allowed to wander. In November 1940 the RSPCA advised: *'From two points of view it is wrong to allow cats and dogs to be in the streets where simple precautions are possible to confine them to the house. An animal*

Left
All sort of aids to being seen in the dark were sold, including white walking sticks, but this caused some confusion as people assumed the owner was blind.

Below
Walking your dog in the blackout could cause all sorts of problems, which this coat was supposed to prevent.

roaming the streets at night in these times stands an excellent chance of being run over. From the motorists' point of view, too, the danger of accident is vastly increased. It is surely within the ingenuity of every animal lover to see that the household pet is exercised in the daytime and is safely inside four walls when darkness descends.'

Even negotiating your doorstep in the blackout could pose difficulties. **1001 Household Hints** recommended that you *'Melt ½lb of glue in 1½ pints of water. When dissolved, stir in 1lb powdered whitening. Apply to your doorstep with a brush and only a very hard shower of rain will remove it.'* Or *'To whiten edges of steps, etc., for black-out purposes, mix common whiting with milk to consistency of cream. Paint on. It will keep white for months.'* And finally *'Stitch a piece of elastic to the lining of your handbag and attach your door-key to the other end. In the blackout this will save you time and temper by preventing that desperate fumble in search of the door-key.'*

In mid-September 1939 the rules for both road and rail travel were slightly

relaxed; masked headlights could be used in the former, and dimmed carriage lights in the latter. A month later people were allowed to use suitably masked hand torches in the street. **The War-Time Lawyer**, published in 1940, gave details: *'Hand torches are permitted after dark, if obscured by two layers of tissue paper, but must be put out and kept out when an air-raid warning has been sounded, and in any case may only be used if the amount of light shown does not exceed what is permitted by Home Office Regulations. At present this is one candle-power.'* In the 1944 film **A Canterbury**

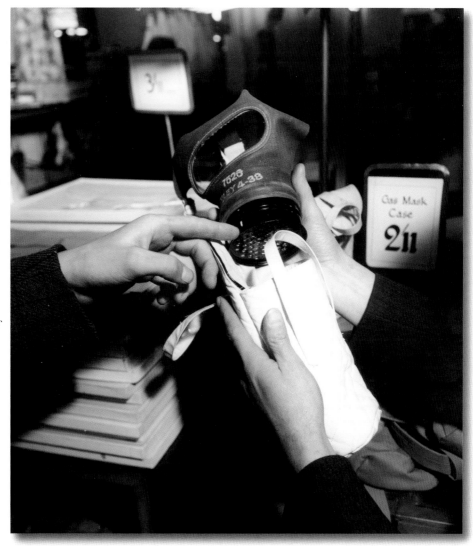

Right
A double precaution: a white gas-mask case would help you to be seen in the blackout.

Tale, an American serviceman is unimpressed by the somewhat pathetic beams of the locals' torches. *'Call that a flashlight?',* he says, and is then shouted at by figures of authority when he uses a powerful torch in the street.

Manufacturers began to produce special black-out torches: *'The Lucas No. 68 Black-out Lamp has been specially designed for ARP and Civil Defence activities, but it also has many advantages for household use during the black-out. The long, slanting hood is white enamelled inside, and there is no reflector, so that the light is diffused downwards and there is no upward or direct light. It is fitted with a sliding handle for carrying, and a strong loop clip at the back by which it can be attached to the belt or to the pocket, leaving both hands free. The price is 3s 11d.'*

This did not, however, save you from the police or, later, the Home Guard for committing the cardinal sin of inadvertently shining your torch upwards – the action, of course, of a fifth columnist signalling the Germans! For this there was the 'Legalite'. *'Everybody should know by now that the law frowns on anybody who flashes a torch upwards in the black-out. The trouble, however, is that it is such an easy thing to do in an absent-minded moment. Now, however, a device about the size of a coat button has been put on the market which can be fitted to any torch and which definitely excludes the possibility of such untoward happenings. It is known as the "Legalite", it can be obtained through dealers and garages, and the concern responsible for its introduction is L. G. Hawkins and Co., Ltd., 30-36, Drury Lane, London, W.C.2.*

HOPING TO SEE YOU SOON !

The "Legalite", as we have said, is about the size of an ordinary coat button. It is made in only one form at a cost of 1s. All you have to do, say, in the case of a cylindrical torch, is to unscrew the cap and insert the button so that it makes contact with the lower end of the battery, then screw the cap into place again. It can be fitted equally simply to any other form of torch. The effect is instantaneous – almost magical. The torch is switched on, and when pointing downwards it functions normally, but lift it towards the horizontal and the light instantly goes out. Direct it vertically downwards towards the ground and the light comes on again. You simply can't make a mistake. The secret is a mercury switch contained within the button. We do not, as a rule, become lyrical over inventions, but on this occasion we think we are justified in describing the "Legalite" as one of the simplest yet one of the most useful inventions of the age' (from The **Light Car** magazine, March 1940).

From November 1939, blackout times were cut back to half-an-hour after sunset until half-an-hour before sunrise, while during the summer months, these periods were extended by fifteen minutes. British Summer Time, which had been due to end on 8 October, was extended to 19 November and then brought back in February 1940 for the rest of the war. In May 1941 Double Summer Time was introduced, adding yet another hour on from May to August 1941, and from April to August 1942 to 1944.

By December 1940 places such as churches, markets, theatres, cinemas and shops were allowed partial illumination, which had to be extinguished

Far Left
As with so many other wartime necessities, the blackout became the butt of jokes, and many humorous postcards like this one, which clearly shows some of the many aids to being seen in the blackout, including a white gas-mask case, were available.

Left & Right
The advertising agents for light bulbs had to work hard to use the blackout to help sell their products, but those of Ediswan bulbs managed it!

FORGET THE BLACK-OUT SIDE

Let's see! —
ROYAL "**EDISWAN**" LAMPS

Obtainable at all electrical suppliers.   L. 1.

When they sound the last 'ALL CLEAR'

BY HUGH CHARLES   &   LOUIS ELTON

RECORDED & BROADCAST BY
DONALD PEERS

1/-

Irwin Dash Music Co Ltd
17, BERNERS ST, LONDON, W.1
Put DASH in your Programmes

immediately when the warning sounded, in what
was called 'diffused lighting' (later called 'glimmer'
or 'pinprick' lighting). There was also street
lighting of such low intensity that it could be left on
during a raid. This gave a pale glow round the base
of the few lampposts on which it was installed.

A new Lighting (Restrictions) Order was
produced in January 1940 and stayed the
governing order, with little change, almost until
the end of the war. One drawback which would
become obvious during the incendiary raids on
cities was that blackout curtains in unoccupied
premises (usually because the residents were safely
installed in the shelter) allowed small fires inside to
grow into big fires unnoticed from the exterior as
the blackout curtains shielded the fire from outside
view.

In September 1944 'Dim Out' was introduced.
This allowed light to be seen from windows (other
than skylights) as long as the glass or window
curtain was not transparent. On 24 December that
year, the ban on the use of unshielded motor
headlamps was lifted, and in April 1945 even the
Dim Out lighting restrictions were abolished
everywhere except in an area within 5 miles of the
coast. Yet it was not until VE-Day that the lights
came on again, 'All over the World', in the words
of the song.

air-raid warnings

In the First World War air-raid warnings had been
devised to give people time to get to shelter. The
police in coastal areas would report sightings of
aircraft and their heading by telephone; these
reports would be collated and likely targets
contacted. The warnings themselves had then been
given by different methods, including maroons,
factory hooters, and policemen in cars and on
bicycles carrying placards saying 'Take Cover',
and blowing their whistles.

The police reporters had evolved into the
Observer Corps, who in their early days were still
special constables. In January 1936 the Home
Office sent a circular to Chief Constables in the
Observer Corps' South East zone, outlining a
warning system; nine months later this was
expanded to cover the whole of Britain, dividing it
up into a series of warning districts which could be
given 7–10 minutes' warning of aircraft approach
by telephone. At the same time tests were being
carried out on various ways of sounding the
warning. The siren was chosen as the best possible
method of delivery and by the end of 1937 it was
decided to develop a suitable siren. In addition, a
separate, distinctive warning for poison gas was to
be devised. Experiments tested the best kinds of
equipment which people wearing anti-gas suits and
gas masks could use to give gas warnings. From
this the gas rattle, a kind of large football rattle,
was chosen to give the warning, and a handbell to
give the all-clear.

In May 1938 the Home Office air-raid warning
system was put into place and *War Emergency*

Instructions and Information was published in September 1939: '*Warnings of air raids will be given in town and suburban areas by sirens or hooters. In some places the warning will be a series of short blasts and in other places a warbling or fluctuating signal which rises or falls every few seconds. The warning may also be given by police or air raid wardens blowing short blasts on whistles. Directly you hear any of these sounds you should take cover if you can. Stay in your place of shelter until you hear the "Raiders Passed" signal which will be given by sounding the sirens or hooters continuously for a period of two minutes on the same note. If poison gas has been used, you will be warned by means of hand rattles. If you hear hand rattles you must not leave your shelter until the poison gas has been cleared away. Hand bells will be used to tell you when there is no longer any danger from poison gas. Make sure that everyone in your house understands the meanings of these signals.*' Handbells were also to be sounded when it was safe to leave shelter if sirens had been put out of action by the raids.

The warning system was already well established by the time of the Munich Crisis. On 15 September 1938 the London system was in full operational order, and within a week most of the rest of the country had followed. Tests in October and in the new year showed that the system was working well.

The police had the responsibility for sounding the public sirens. Outside central London, the sirens were often supplemented with factory hooters; in many cases, however, these could only be sounded during the day, unless factory owners or managers kept their phones continually manned.

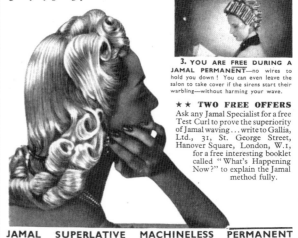

Above
This advertisement demonstrates one of the problems thrown up by the warning. Most women had their hair permed, and this meant sitting under the drier for half an hour or so. And of course that was when the warning went, and you had to go to the shelter. The answer was the machineless perm.

Right
An early air-raid warning system being tested in the early 1930s. The final system would prove less 'Heath Robinson'.

Ten days before the outbreak of war the system was put into full readiness, and factories were informed that hooters were no longer to be used except for air-raid warnings. On 1 September 1939, the public warning system was fully operational.

Throughout the early months of the war,

SHELTER AT HOME

The New Government

STEEL INDOOR 'TABLE' SHELTER

IS NOW AVAILABLE IN THIS DISTRICT : PARTICULARS FROM

numerous false alarms meant that every-one became very familiar with the sirens, which soon earned nicknames such as 'Wailing Willy' or 'Moaning Minnie', and the warning signal with its up and down note became popularly known in London as 'the wobbler'. It was found that the two-minute warning had a depressing effect, with people remarking that its drawn-out wail was worse for morale than the ensuing raids and in September 1940 it was decided that both all-clear and warning signals would be sounded for only one minute.

Events dictated the need for differentiated warnings. In south-east coastal towns, such as Dover, which experienced shelling, it became the custom to sound the siren twice in succession for shell fire, with the 'raiders passed' one hour after the fall of the last shell. Later, with the formation of the Fire Guard to tackle incendiaries, other ways to signal that these were being dropped were evolved; in some places this was done by repeated blasts on whistles, in other areas the signal was given by banging dustbin lids.

In a strange way, the sirens epitomised the raids: *'When they sound the last all-clear'* was a very popular song, looking forward as it did to the end of hostilities, and on VE-Day one of the features of many local celebrations was exactly that – they sounded the last 'All-Clear'.

air-raid shelters

In 1917 a Cabinet Committee had reported in favour of a shelter policy of 'dispersal', or encouraging the public to rely in general on the protection offered by their homes rather than to gather in crowds in any public place. This continued to be the government line between the wars.

A Home Office circular of 28 March 1938 stated that *'After careful consideration of all factors His Majesty's Government has reached the conclusion that the wisest policy is to aim at the dispersal of the population. Generally speaking, therefore, persons who, at the time of an air raid, are either in their own homes or in other buildings should remain there.'*

Tests had shown that only very deep and extremely stoutly built shelters were actually bombproof. Apart from the (not inconsiderable) problem of the cost of such shelters, it was also argued that people would have about seven minutes' warning of a raid (at best) and the distance most could travel in this time, in the blackout, would be just a few hundred yards. Having bombproof shelters within a few hundred yards of people's houses would be impossible in all but the most densely-populated areas, and even there, the

Left
Poster for the indoor steel table shelter, universally known as the 'Morrison'. The Anderson had done its job well, but it was cold, draughty and damp, and after a while many preferred to gamble on staying indoors – and the Morrison was the answer. (HMSO)

Right
Signs like this would be displayed in stations, so that people arriving on a train would know that a warning had been given in the area.

AIR RAID WARNING IN OPERATION

SOUTHERN RAILWAY

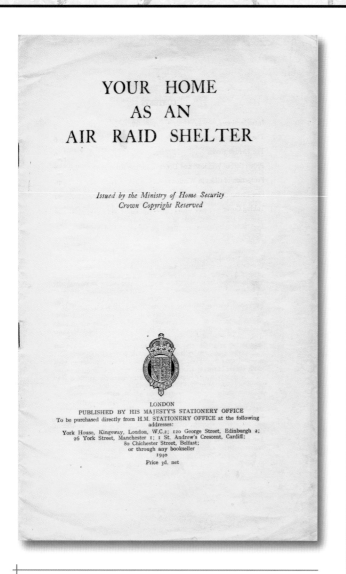

problem of getting large numbers of people down several fights of stairs in subdued light and an atmosphere approaching panic ruled out the possibility of their use. Indeed in March 1943 disaster was brought about under these circum-

stances in the rush to enter the shelter at Bethnal Green Underground station.

What could be provided was blast and splinter-proof shelters, capable of protecting people from all but a direct hit. Obviously such shelters *would* receive direct hits, and the government's thinking was that a system based on small, family-sized shelters would not only cut down response times to warnings, but that casualties caused by direct hits on them were likely to be more regular, but smaller than the rarer but more disastrous effect of a direct

CIGARETTES

REFUGE ROOM

hit on a large, densely packed shelter. The total number of deaths and injuries would probably be the same over a period of time, but the ARP and casualty services would be able to deal far more effectively with a steady trickle, and the effect on morale was also important – think of deaths on the road today, hugely more numerous than those of air crashes, but which of the two gets the headlines?

People were, therefore, encouraged to provide their own shelters. A Home Office circular of March 1938 stated: *With the advice and instruction*

Other types of shelter

AIR RAID SHELTER →

You couldn't always be sure to be at home when the warning siren sounded; sometimes you would be out on the street.

For this purpose the government had required local authorities to provide public shelters. Signs would be provided, painted on walls or hung from street lights. Here is a shelter direction sign on a Belisha beacon.

Basements in existing buildings might be strengthened for shelters, or specially built. These air-raid wardens, seen here in about 1940, are standing in front of a typical brick-built surface shelter.

Schools had to have their own shelters. At first they were used only by children, but after a public outcry they were open to all after school hours.

These might be built in the school basement, but often they were in the form of purpose-built shelters, usually underground.

(Once inside, lessons would continue.)

that local authorities will be giving on air raid precautions, it must be assumed that householders will generally do what they can to increase the natural protection of their own homes. The government's ARP policy is, therefore, based primarily on encouragement of construction by all householders who can afford to do so of refuge rooms, shelters, trenches or dug-outs in their own homes.'

the refuge room

The first type of shelter proposed by the Home Office was the 'refuge room'. This was primarily aimed at protection against poison gas. **The Protection of Your Home against Air Raids,** issued by the Home Office in 1938, stated that *'If air raids ever come to this country, every home should have a refuge specially prepared in which the whole household could take cover in greater safety.'*

A Ministry of Home Security booklet, **Air Raids – What You Must Know, What You Must Do** talked about choosing your refuge room: *'A room facing the garden is generally better than one facing the street, because the soft earth will allow a bomb to go in deep before exploding, and so will reduce the danger from bomb splinters. The barricading of window openings with brick, concrete, or earth walls is a useful safety measure. If this is not done and the glass is left in the windows, it should receive some protective treatment.'*

Another government leaflet, *Your Home as an Air Raid Shelter,* continued: *'Make certain that the walls enclosing the refuge are of solid brickwork or*

CHURCHMAN'S CIGARETTES

MAKING A DOOR GAS-PROOF

Above
Churchman's cigarette card showing how to use an old rug to make a door gas-proof.
Right
Another card from the Churchman's ARP set, this time showing some of the items to have in your refuge room, including a radio, record player and tinned food.

stonework and not of timber framing covered with stucco or weather-boarding, as these provide no protection. A small or narrow room is to be preferred, because, in the event of part of the house collapsing from a very near explosion, the roof or ceiling over it will be more capable of resisting the fall of debris, such as loose slates or tiles, than a roof of wide span. Of course, if you can get material and labour for propping up the ceiling over the refuge room, it is not so important to choose a small and narrow room.

As a general rule it is desirable to avoid rooms with large windows; bay windows in particular will require large amounts of material to block them in order to keep out blast and splinters.

In the typical suburban house, the kitchen or scullery will often, though not always, be found to be the most suitable, particularly if the door faces either the next house or a garden wall. A ground floor room should generally be chosen in preference to one on an upper floor as it provides greater over-head protection against falling shell splinters or machine-gun fire. Also bomb splinters may strike upwards through window openings and floors.'

Much care had to be taken to make the room gas-proof. **S. Evelyn Thomas's Handy Wartime Guide** gave directions: *'Seal up all cracks and openings through which gas can enter, e.g. chimneys, ventilators (including those below floor level), windows, skylights, hatches, and doors, as well as all less obvious entries, e.g. cracks in the walls and ceilings, spaces between floorboards (even if covered with carpet or linoleum), waste pipes and overflow pipes in wash-basins or cisterns (unless there is an S-bend containing water), and holes where pipes pass through the walls.*

Use wetted paper, old blankets, carpets, rags or sacks to seal up large openings (such as ventilators and chimneys), and cover fireplace openings with plywood, plaster board, or something similar. Seal up all small cracks and crevices with adhesive paper or with putty, or with a pulp made of sodden newspaper.'

The door had to be made into an air-lock. This was done by nailing a piece of wood padded with felt to the floor, so that the closed door pressed tightly against it, while strips of felt, or draught excluders, were nailed around the inside of the door.

Then a blanket was fixed outside the door (if the door opened inwards), or inside the door (if the door opened outwards), by nailing strips of wood over the blanket along the top of the door frame, down its whole length on the hinged side, and a third of its length on the other side. The remainder of the blanket was left free so that people could go into and out of the room.

The same guide listed the objects essential for your refuge room:

A Roll-call List of all who Should be Present.
Gas masks for every person.
Electric torch and spare battery.
Electric light (if possible), otherwise candles and matches.
Hammer, nails, and pickaxe.
Some clean rags and pieces of string.
Scissors, needles, cotton, and thread.
Tables, chairs, and large screen.
Portable wash-hand stand or basin.
Sanitary utensils, paper, disinfectant.

CHURCHMAN'S CIGARETTES

EQUIPPING YOUR REFUGE ROOM—A

Washing things: Towels, sponges, and soap.
Food in airtight tins or jars.
Flasks for hot tea, coffee, etc., or an electric kettle.
Mackintoshes, galoshes, gum boots.
Wireless set or gramophone.
First-aid box, containing bandages, lint, cotton
wool, smelling salts, sal volatile, safety pins, anti-
septic, surgical spirit, bleach ointment.
A good supply of water (in airtight containers)
for drinking, etc.
Plates, cups, knives, forks, tin-opener.
Books, cards, games, and toys.
A bucket or box of sand, a shovel and a rake to
deal with a possible incendiary bomb.
A simple hand-pump and length of hose.
A pair of non-inflammable dark glasses.
A mattress or mattresses.
Blankets for re-sealing windows if necessary, and
for warmth. Also eiderdowns, rugs, etc.
Important Documents. Keep important documents
(such as insurance policies, bank books, birth
certificates, identification cards and ration books)
in a handy suitcase or deed box, which you can
take with you into your shelter when you hear
the alarm.

In the event all this was far too complicated for many people, and the gas-proof refuge room was a rarity, although those with cellars often used them as shelters, but without the gas-proofing.

In the autumn of 1938, events in Europe spiralled to a head. Hitler was demanding that Czechoslovakia hand over parts of her territory to Germany; Europe stood on the brink of war and near-panic ensued. Gas masks were issued and

trenches were dug in public parks, and many people hastily followed suit in their own back gardens.

REVETTING TRENCH A.
& ENTRANCE B.

CORRO-IRON NAILED TO
SUPPORTS WITH 6" NAIL

SHOWING.
WALL PLATES,
CORR-IRON,
WOODEN TRENCH,
SUPPORTS.
(UPRIGHT & SPREADER)

B — ENTRANCE
FLOOR 6" LOWER.

WITH PROTECTION SPACE FOR 6 PEOPLE

trenches and dug-outs

'If you have a garden, you can dig a trench. Don't dig a deep trench, unless you know how to make one properly. Deep trenches are apt to fall in if the sides are not specially supported.

But a shallow trench will give you quite good cover. Dig down about 4½ feet, and with the earth you dig out fill boxes or sandbags and stack them up to a height of about 15 inches all round the edge of the trench above ground level. If you can get some corrugated iron or old boards, put them over the top of the trench with a few inches of earth on top to keep them in place' (from *Be Wise and Do the Job Now*, a Ministry of Information leaflet issued in October 1939). **S. Evelyn Thomas's Handy Wartime Guide** recommended that: *'A* *trench 10ft long by 4½ft wide by 6ft high should comfortably accommodate six persons for a period of three hours when the curtains are down. For each person over six, allow 18in extra length. If the trench is large enough, fix a wooden seat along one side.'*

For men who had been on the Western Front in the First World War, building a trench or dugout in the back garden was grimly familiar, while for those who had not had that experience the government published plans. They were indeed a good temporary measure, but in many cases they soon flooded or even collapsed with the onset of rain.

It was recommended that a concrete floor be put in, which incorporated a gulley to carry off the water, and that walls should, if possible, be reinforced, if possible with concrete again. *Your Home as an Air Raid Shelter* added that *'Several kinds of sectional shelters are also marketed that*

are designed to be put together in a garden trench and to hold up the earth at the sides and overhead. Most of them are made of concrete.'

Digging even a simple trench '10ft long by 4½ft wide by 6ft high' would take hours of hard work, and the subsequent concreting in of the base and the shoring up of the walls and roof would take skills many did not possess. It was only natural then that building firms would step into the breach.

private shelters

The Czechoslovakian problem came to an end with the Munich conference, where Britain and France caved in to Hitler's demands and gave him everything he had demanded. Neville Chamberlain, the British Prime Minister, returned promising 'Peace for our Time', yet the government pushed on with its ARP schemes. In October 1938 Sir John Anderson was appointed head of the ARP Department. He reiterated the policy of dispersal and promised to help householders by supplying a mass-produced shelter which they could erect themselves in their own homes, to be supplied free to poorer inhabitants of endangered areas. This meant people with incomes of less than £250 a year, and if they had more than two children, this was raised by £50 per

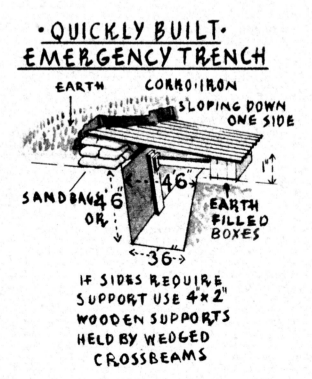

· QUICKLY BUILT·
EMERGENCY TRENCH

EARTH   CORRO·IRON
         SLOPING DOWN
         ONE SIDE

SANDBAGS 6"
OR
←--36-->
46"
EARTH FILLED BOXES

IF SIDES REQUIRE
SUPPORT USE 4"×2"
WOODEN SUPPORTS
HELD BY WEDGED
CROSSBEAMS

child. '*Householders who are not eligible to receive free shelters or strengthening materials, have to pay for their own shelters, but they can obtain the [Anderson] or strengthening materials through the local authority, and may pay by convenient instalments*' (from **S. Evelyn Thomas's Handy Wartime Guide**). While the shelter was available for sale to those whose income exceeded the stated amount, these would only be sold after the free ones had been issued. In the aftermath of the Czechoslovak panic many were not prepared to wait that long. S. Evelyn Thomas continued: '*Alternatively, other forms of shelter can be constructed out of sandbags, concrete blocks, bricks, or corrugated iron. Some of these can be purchased partly or completely ready for erection, while there are available numerous types of pre-cast concrete or iron fittings with which garden shelters can be easily and quickly built.*'

From the time of the Munich Crisis many types of private shelter were advertised: **The Complete First Aid Outfit Book and ARP** reported that '*It was only to be expected that the announcement of the Government's shelter policy should have been followed by numerous advertisements from firms offering to supply shelters at comparatively reasonable costs to householders not eligible under the scheme of free distribution of the "Anderson" garden shelter or the alternative concrete shelter. Broadly speaking these privately-designed shelters follow closely the official types, and are constructed as a rule either of steel or of concrete (though brick ones*

Possibly one of the easiest and most economical ways of constructing an efficient splinter-proof shelter is to use large precast concrete tubes, laid like a section of a sewer, either wholly or partly below ground. The illustration shows a small garden tube shelter, such as may be purchased complete, with a rockery over the top.

Left
Building firms advertised private air-raid shelters, many of which were small. You clearly could not stand upright in this one.

Above
Most of the better shelters were made from pre-formed concrete sections, which, like this one, could be extended to house the required number of people.

are not unknown). One rather unusual pattern, suitable for gardens of the suburban type, and capable of accommodating four or more persons, consists of 6ft long concrete tubes built of reinforced concrete 4 inches thick. These tubes are supplied in short lengths sealed together with dove-tailed joints, and they may be installed either completely or only partially underground. The advantages claimed for this shelter are that no seepage of water

into it is possible, and that even when only partially sunk into the ground it can form the basis of a very effective rock garden.

Other shelters follow the design of the semi-circular Nissen hut so familiar to soldiers in France during the World War of 1914–1918. These are made of strong corrugated iron sheets supported on a steel and timber framework, and they, too, can be sunk entirely or only partially below ground. Further types resemble the square garage so often seen in suburban districts, the main differences being that the shelter is smaller and much more stoutly constructed.'

Costs varied; the most expensive private shelter in the country was reported to have cost £24,000 (roughly £1 million today). This was 30 feet below ground and reached by its own lift. Others were far less luxurious and far cheaper, with the cheapest a little under £50 [£2,000] supplied and fitted. These were little more than a large buried pipe. In the country, where land was not the problem it could be for town-dwellers, people adapted the idea of a buried pipe, and made their own shelters by burying cars, old industrial boilers or other large tanks. Another rural solution was to burrow a shelter into a haystack.

anderson shelters

In November 1938 Sir John Anderson was appointed to take charge of Air Raid Precautions in Britain. He immediately commissioned the engineer William Patterson to design a small and cheap shelter to be erected inside the average

working-class home. Problems with the idea soon arose; most such homes did not have a spare room which could be dedicated to such a shelter. Focus shifted back to the trenches dug at the time of Munich, and the idea of an outdoor shelter, erected inside a hole in the ground, was chosen.

Within a fortnight, the first model was produced; it would cost about £5 to manufacture – less than the cost per head of trenching or providing concrete structures. The new shelter was examined by experts led by the engineer Dr David Anderson; their report was favourable, and production of the 'Galvanised Corrugated Steel Shelter' was announced to Parliament on 21 December. An estimated 10 million were to be supplied free to

poorer inhabitants of endangered areas.

The Anderson, as the shelter soon became universally known (after Dr David and not, as many people think, Sir John), was intended to accommodate four, or at a pinch six, people and was made of fourteen corrugated galvanised steel sheets, weighing about 8cwt. It was designed to be sunk in the ground and covered with earth or sandbags and crucially could be erected fairly quickly by unskilled labour. It was 6ft high, 4ft 6in wide, 6ft long and provided with an emergency exit. Different sized shelters could be made by varying the number of sections which made up the body of the shelter. The 'Standard', for six people, was made up of 3 pairs of curved sheets; this could be enlarged to a

'Double' to take ten people, or reduced to the 'Small' size, 4ft 5in long, to take four people.

Delivery of the new shelters began in February 1939 to householders in Islington, North London. The railway companies had contracted to deliver the shelters direct to where they were to be assembled. Thus many came home to find a pile of corrugated iron sheets and a bag of bolts lying in their back yard.

The first job was to decide on the placing of the shelter; it had to be at least 15ft away from the house, so that the latter would not collapse on top of it, and avoiding any drains. Then came the worst part, digging the hole, usually 7ft 6in long by 6ft wide and 4ft deep; the earth taken out of the hole would be used to cover the shelter once erected. For keen gardeners this was a tragic moment as their beloved lawn was sacrificed. For those unused to digging this task could take several days and be fraught with danger; there were many instances of a fork or pickaxe over-enthusiastically thrust through someone's foot. In several cases, it was a job which was never finished, and hundreds of Andersons lay rusting in piles.

Once the hole was dug, erection of the shelter started; four channel pieces were put together to hold the sides in place, then the corrugated panels assembled. On the standard-size shelter there were fourteen of these; four flat sheets at the front, four at the rear, and three curved sheets at each side.

When these had been put together, the hole around the outside had to be filled in, ramming the soil in hard, and the remaining soil from the hole placed over the top. For this reason the sheets at the back and front were longer than at the sides, creating a sort of retaining wall to hold the soil in place. Finally a blast wall to protect the entrance was to be built, either of bricks, or of orange boxes filled with soil or rubble.

After construction was complete, many people turfed over the top, or used the earth to grow

Left
A typical Anderson shelter, turfed over and prettified with some flower boxes.

Below
Putting up the Anderson. One of its main drawbacks for many people was that it had to be put together by the householder.

This is one of the many illustrations from the leaflet giving directions for its erection.

The completed Anderson shelter. Now the earth from the hole in which the shelter is erected has to be put over the top of it, with the extended front and back sheets acting as retaining walls.

vegetables or flowers. Garden magazines and seed suppliers made recommendations as to suitable shelter-covering plants, such as berberis, cydonia, nasturtiums and cotoneaster.

By April 1939 nearly 300,000 Andersons had been delivered, and by the outbreak of war, almost one and a half million free Andersons had been distributed, out of a projected total of two and a half million. In October 1939 a limited number of Andersons went on sale to the public, costing from £6 14s to £10 18s depending on size.

By summer 1939 the chief drawback of the Anderson – its susceptibility to flooding – had become clear. Sometimes this was due to a high water-table, and in these cases the government recommended that the shelter be sunk less deeply into the ground, 3ft, or, at a minimum, 2, and extra earth placed over it. By 1941 the depth had been cut again to a minimum of 1ft. For those already erected a cinder or concrete floor was suggested, with a sump in one corner, which had to be regularly baled out. In extreme cases the floor and walls were concreted over, up to ground level; however, as no waterproof membrane was used, this often worked only temporarily.

In such cases, or where for some other reason it was impossible to put up an Anderson, a 'brick-built domestic shelter' might be built above ground. These were like a small version of the common brick-built public street shelter. As the name suggests, they had brick walls and a reinforced concrete roof. The conditions which meant that an Anderson could not be erected would usually be common to a neighbourhood, so there were two - and four - family versions made, usually spanning

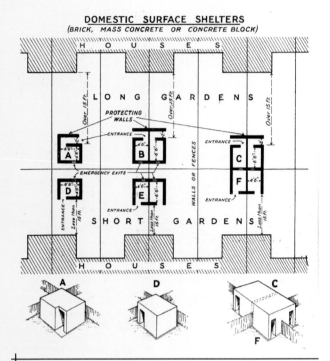

Above

For those whose garden was unsuitable for the Anderson, through flooding for example, there was the domestic brick shelter. These could be built individually, in pairs, or in fours, as this diagram shows.

two or four gardens. Each family would have their own discrete section, with party walls to save building costs, and escape hatches between sections.

Another cause of damp in the Anderson was the shelterers themselves; condensation formed on the inside walls and ran down. Official advice was to paint the inside of the ironwork with paint or shellac varnish and to throw dry sawdust on to the paint while it was still wet. Alternatively, the inside could be covered with linoleum, wall- or plaster-board, fixed on wooden battens.

In April 1940 production of Andersons was suspended due to a lack of steel. By that time over 2.3 million shelters had been supplied including 500,000 four-person and 100,000 ten-person versions. This was a large figure, but it fell short of requirements, and it was decided to utilise those shelters which had lain unerected in many gardens. In May everyone to whom an Anderson had been issued free had to have it erected and covered within ten days, or inform their local authority why they had failed to do so. If the householder was genuinely incapable of doing so, the local authority would arrange for putting it up; if not, the shelter would be removed and issued to someone else.

Shelters were often adapted. Floors were put in and covered with lino, carpet or matting, deck chairs or other chairs were installed, as were camp beds, lilos, and sleeping bags. First aid kits and battery-powered radios were common, as were oil lamps, candles and torches. Food and cooking equipment were also popular, as were wind-up gramophones, cards and board games. Heating was also needed; hot water bottles or heated bricks were suggested, as was the 'flower-pot stove'. **ARP Hints for Housewives** gave directions:

'You will need two large flower pots and a candle for this.
1. Fix the candle at one side of the hole in the bottom of one of the pots (don't place it over the hole), and stand the flower pot on something which will raise it from the ground; three empty cotton reels of the same size do very well.
2. Light the candle and put the second flower pot upside down on the top of the first.
3. If you want to keep a kettle hot, place a metal curtain ring on the top and stand the kettle on it. This candle stove does not use up enough oxygen to be dangerous, and as the top flower pot warms up, heat will be given off.'

The government had expected raiding to be heavy but brief, and the time spent in the shelters

Above
Stirrup-pump practice. Behind the people is a typical single brick-built surface shelter, supplied to those who could not, for whatever reason, have an Anderson. (HMSO)

quite short. What actually happened was that people would often spend hours in their shelter, usually at night; this necessitated sleeping provision. In January 1941, the Ministry of Home Security gave directions in newspapers for making bunks for an Anderson shelter. That summer the government began to supply proper bunks. Unfortunately the small, four-person Andersons were too small to erect bunks in.

morrisons

There were of, course, people who did not have a garden in which to erect a shelter, and yet others who because of age or disability were unable to go outside to a shelter and for them an indoor shelter was needed. The problem was handed over to Lord John Fleetwood Baker and the staff of the Research and Experiments Branch of the Ministry of Home Security, and by the end of 1940 they had designed such a shelter.

Called the Morrison, after the new Minister of Home Security, Herbert Morrison, it was a rectangular steel cage, 6ft 6in long, 4ft wide and 2ft 9in deep with a steel-plate roof. It had been designed to be erected inside the house and, when not in use, to double as a table.

The **Kent Messenger** of 14 February 1941 reported that: *'The new indoor private air-raid shelter, providing a bed for two adults and one child at night, and a table by day, will be available to the public by the end of March.*

A proportion of the shelters will be distributed free to people with incomes below £350. Others will be available for sale to people with higher incomes. The cost has yet to be decided, but it will probably be between £5 and £8.

The shelter resembles a large dining-room table of stout steel. Underneath are springs to support a mattress, and walls

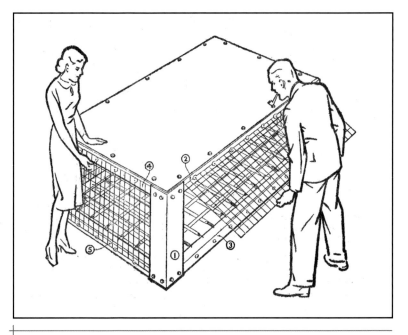

Above
Illustration from the government leaflet, *How to Put up Your Morrison Shelter*, showing the removable mesh side panels which enabled you to get in and out of it.

Below
Another illustration from the same leaflet, showing the shelter in use as a table.

Right
Shelters were not built for comfort, and the onset of winter proved a real problem for those using them. This poster gives some tips for keeping warm in the shelter. (HMSO)

IDEAS FOR WINTER NIGHTS

1 Make yourself this sleeping bag

Take any Army or similar thick blanket about 7 feet long and 6½ feet wide (pieces of old blankets could, of course, be joined together). Line with muslin or cotton material to within a short distance of the top. Sew straight across both blankets and lining horizontally at intervals of about a foot, thus making pockets which should be well stuffed with folded newspaper. The newspaper stuffing should be changed every month.

Fold the two sides of the blanket towards the centre and sew together to within about 2 feet of the top. Sew together at the bottom. Sew tapes on the open sides of the bag at the top so that they can be tied together when the person is inside.

Alternatively, the bag could be made of two blankets sewn together, but without the stuffing. In either case, the blankets should be ironed inside and out once a month. A sleeping bag should be aired every day.

When you are not sleeping on a thick mattress, you need as much covering under you, as on top of you. Therefore, besides your sleeping bag, and even more if you are not using a bag, have a good thick layer of newspapers or brown paper on your bunk, to lie on. Paper is draught-proof and does not pass warmth.

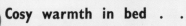

2 Cosy warmth in bed . . . . .

If you haven't hot water bottles for all the family, use hot bricks. They are very effective. Just heat the brick in the oven for 2 hours before coming to the shelter. Wrap it up well and it will give out warmth for hours.

3 Here's a simple flower-pot heater

Stand the candle in a 6-inch flower-pot so that the hole is not covered; put a second flower-pot over the top. The top pot soon warms up, giving off a lot of heat. Raise the lower pot off the ground.

4 Have a hot drink before going to sleep

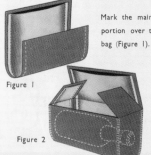

If you have not a thermos flask, you can make a "hay bottle", which will keep a drink hot.

Cut a square of any old woollen material, 8 inches longer than the bottle. Line with thin muslin or cotton material, sewing down the sides and leaving the top and bottom open, to be stuffed.

Cut two strips of woollen material, 8 inches to 10 inches long and 4 inches to 5 inches wide, rounded at one end. Line as before, for about two-thirds of the length, leaving a flap at the end.

Figure 1

Figure 2

Mark the main square into three. Fold the lower portion over the centre, making the lower half of a bag (Figure 1). Sew the two strips to each side of this case, thus filling in the sides (Figure 2). Stuff tightly the main part and the side pieces with hay or straw, and sew down the lining. Make a similar bag of American cloth, but not lined or stuffed. Put the bottle in the woollen bag, fold over, tuck in well; roll up and pin the top flap over. Put this in the American cloth bag and roll up again. Fasten securely.

5 A Balaclava helmet

A Balaclava helmet, such as every soldier knows, will keep draughts off your head. Start knitting now—for yourself and the family.

★ **DO NOT HAVE BRAZIERS OR OIL STOVES IN THE SHELTER — THEY GIVE OFF DANGEROUS FUMES** ★

ISSUED BY THE MINISTRY OF HOME SECURITY

PRINTED FOR H.M. STATIONERY OFFICE BY J.WEINER LTD, LONDON, W.C.I. 51-6593

of steel netting are fitted to prevent injury from flying debris.

Delivery will be made in parts, but the shelters can be put together by two people in just over an hour. No applications should be made for them now. Local authorities will notify residents in vulnerable areas when supplies are available.'

In the event the purchase price was £7 12s 6d. A two-tiered model was also produced for larger families. These were 4ft 3in high and cost £9 15s. The price of the Morrison was reduced to £7 in September 1941, a refund being made to people who had paid the higher sum. There was no hire purchase system, such as there had been for Andersons.

It often became the custom for the children to sleep in the Morrison, while Mum, and Dad, if he was not in the forces, would join them if the siren sounded. By the end of the war over 1 million Morrisons were in use.

And what about pets? From the very beginning, dogs and cats were not allowed in public air raid shelters, the main fear being that they might be driven mad by the noise, and become a danger to the human occupants. An RSPCA

LOOK before you sleep

ALL WINDOWS AND INNER DOORS OPEN?

WATER IN BUCKETS?

SAND IN BUCKETS?

GAS MASK, CLOTHES AND TORCH HANDY?

GOOD NIGHT!

Above

Government poster advising on how to be prepared for nightly air raids. (HMSO)

pamphlet, **Animals and Air Raids**, suggested that *'Some dogs and cats are terrified by noise. It is difficult to suggest a satisfactory remedy apart from sedatives. Some dogs will submit to the following: Place under the ear flaps, not inside the ears, a wad of cotton wool and then tie the cover over the head with the strings under the chin. Few cats will tolerate anything of the kind.'*

There was no reason why you could not take your pets into your own domestic shelter. Bob Martin's advised that: *'Dogs and cats react to the emotions of their owners, and it is therefore important that they be handled without fuss or undue agitation. Keep your dog with you during a raid. Install his sleeping basket in your refuge room or shelter, and allow him to sleep there as often as possible so that he will settle down quickly in an emergency. Experience of raids has proved that dogs do not easily panic. A tray of loose earth, dried sawdust or sand should be placed in a corner of the refuge room for the convenience of the dog. Also provide him with a bowl of fresh drinking water. . . . It is advisable that a sedative be given to your dog immediately an air raid is imminent. In the case of excessively nervous dogs it is advisable that a muzzle be kept at hand as an additional safeguard. However harmless or safe a dog may be in normal circumstances, he may do injury to you or others in an extremity of fear. Such an event is unlikely if a sedative is promptly administered. Owners must keep their dogs under control during air raids. The Police have full power to destroy any which are at large and may become dangerous. . . . Cats and dogs require the same precautions and treatment.'*

Bob Martin's did, however, recognise that some owners might not want their dog with them in a somewhat cramped Anderson. *'In some circumstances kennels may be preferred as shelters. A kennel can be protected against flying splinters and blast of explosion by placing it in a hole deep enough to allow it to rest with its roof not more than a foot above the general level of the ground. The hole should be wide enough to allow a space of two feet in width all round the kennel. Make a rampart around the edge with sandbags, or the dug out earth, so that the top of the mound comes above the level of the kennel roof. Do not dig the hole in an excessively damp spot. This must be particularly noted if you live in a clayey district. Protect the kennel from dampness by placing it on four bricks, one at each corner, and lining the bottom of the depression with bricks or ashes.'*

And what if you did not have your own shelter? The RSPCA pamphlet recommended that: *'If you live in a flat, have no private shelter and cannot send your animals into the country, remember they have the same measure of protection as yourself from explosive or fire, except that you can go into a public shelter and they cannot. Then, and only then, consider if it would not be wise to have your animals destroyed. The Society, whilst being against wholesale slaughter, will do this for you if you take your animals to their Inspectors or Clinics. Petrol is short. We cannot collect animals. The responsibility is yours, but do not leave the decision until raids occur.'*

arp at home

There were several precautions which you were encouraged to take with raids in mind. The government was expecting large numbers of casualties in the first few days and had stockpiled cardboard and plywood coffins with this eventuality in mind. Identification of the expected thousands of bodies would in itself pose a problem, and the government leaflet *War Emergency Instructions and Information* included the following: *'You should carry about with you your full name and address clearly written. This should be on an envelope, card or luggage label, not on some odd piece of paper easily lost. In the case of children a label should be sewn on to their clothes, in such a way that it cannot easily come off.'* Identity bracelets and discs were popular, and many of the better gas-mask cases incorporated identity labels.

Being prepared for air raids was also important. **S. Evelyn Thomas's Handy Wartime Guide** advised: *'So that every member of your household will know precisely how to act and what to be responsible for during a raid, start regular rehearsals forthwith. Give each person a job: one to shut the windows, one to see to the cat, one to turn off the gas, and so on. You cannot do everything yourself, but if you do not plan NOW, nothing will be done when it is wanted.'*

Another government leaflet, *Before, During and After the Raid*, gave more advice: *'Make plans now to go and stay with friends living near, but not too near, in case your house is destroyed. They should also arrange now to come to you if their house is knocked out. It's comforting to feel that everything is fixed up, just in case.'*

Housewife magazine in October 1940 extended this idea: *'Mrs. Lane, Stroud, has found a different way of "doing her bit." I have turned out every conceivable available place in my house to enable my relations and friends to store trunks, cases, clothing and valuables, in case of a raid on their own house. Each person has their allotted place in safety, and each is able to come and get whatever she wants, whenever she wishes. They are most grateful.'*

Even if your house was not destroyed, a near-miss could leave you with all your windows blown out. **1001 Household Hints** advised: *'When windows are entirely out, cut calico to required space, allowing for turning, then tack into position and paint with boiled linseed oil.'* Or *'For small panes and cracked windows, use stout white paper painted with boiled linseed oil. This makes them entirely weatherproof and permits daylight to penetrate.'*

The booklet, **Air Raids – What You Must Know and What You Must Do** advised: *'One of the best protections for window panes is a light-coloured cloth, such as cheese cloth, stuck to the inside of the window with flour paste (¼oz of borax should be used to 1 pint of flour paste, to prevent mildew). Curtain net stuck on in the same way gives good protection; so does a screen of wire netting fixed on the inside of the window, provided the net has not a bigger mesh than ¼in. If strips of*

sticky cloth tape are used, they should be criss-crossed so that no space of clear glass is more than 4in. each way. Most of the lacquers and varnishes sold for strengthening glass need to be often renewed. Strips of ordinary paper give almost no protection.'

Even in wartime, windows had to be washed; how did you do this without washing off your anti-blast protection? **1001 Household Hints** had the answer: *'When cleaning windows covered with splinter net dissolve ¼lb. size in half-gallon of water. Sponge down. This not only cleans the window but also refastens the loose corners – caused by frost and sweat during the winter.'*

Dealing with incendiary attacks was something the householder was expected to do themselves, or in concert with their neighbours. The small 1kg electron incendiary bomb became one of the Luftwaffe's most effective weapons – a single bomber was able to carry several hundred of them, thereby starting fires over a large area and completely overwhelming the fire services. For this reason, the stirrup pump was developed. Neighbours might club together to buy one, and if you owned one you were encouraged to display a sign in your window or on your gate 'Stirrup pump here'.

War Emergency Instructions and Information suggested: *'Clear the top floor of all inflammable materials, lumber, etc. See that you can get easily to any attic or roof spaces.*

Water is the best means of putting out a fire started by an incendiary bomb. See that water is available about the house. Have some ready in buckets, but do not draw off water if you can help it during an air raid. Be careful not to throw a bucket of water directly over a burning incendiary bomb.

Above
The stirrup pump was the basic tool for dealing with incendiary bombs. As you can see, the price was not exorbitant, and many householders invested in one.

The bomb would explode and throw burning fragments in all directions.

You may be able to smother a small bomb with sand or dry earth.'

After the disastrous fire-bomb attack on the City of London in late December 1940, the government hurried to organise people to tackle the incendiary bomb threat. A leaflet issued by the Ministry of Home Security in 1941 stated: *'Every group of houses should have its fire party: every party keeping watch over its own group of houses, their gardens, and the roadway; the members making their own arrangements to watch in turn during alerts. If you are the head of the household, call your family together and make up your minds which of you will volunteer for membership of the fire party, and will take training. One at least should serve. If two or three can do so, all the better. It lessens the burden on others, and helps to make up for empty houses and for households where all the members are elderly or infirm, or are night workers. Women, as well as men, are members of the Civil Defence Force. Women should consider whether they can become members of fire parties. Many thousands will no doubt do so. We are all of us in this fight for liberty and decency.*

See that your house, shop or office building

(i) is easy to enter quickly if a fire breaks out;

(ii) has a rake, to drag a bomb off the roof or away from anything inflammable;

(iii) has a supply of sand and water handy, and where they are easily seen;

(iv) has a ladder available or near by;

(v) has its attic or top floor cleared of inflammable material.

Your warden or the fire brigade will tell you how to set about getting stirrup pump and sandbags, and anything else you want to know.

Get a stirrup hand pump if you can. Large numbers are being issued to local authorities for this purpose. Get two or three sandbags, three parts filled, which are very useful for smothering bombs.

This is urgent work, for the defence of your home or your business, and the community in which you live. Act at once. See your warden. Form your "fire party" immediately.'

And what did you do if your house was damaged in a raid? The book **War Time Household Repairs** gave directions: *'If your house is damaged during a raid, the matter should be reported at once to the local authority. A form will be given to you to fill up and, when it is properly completed, you will be entitled to some compensation; but unless you are*

Below

The Redhill scoop, hoe and container. The idea was to use the hoe to manoeuvre the incendiary into the scoop, then transfer it into the sand–filled container where it could burn itself out harmlessly.

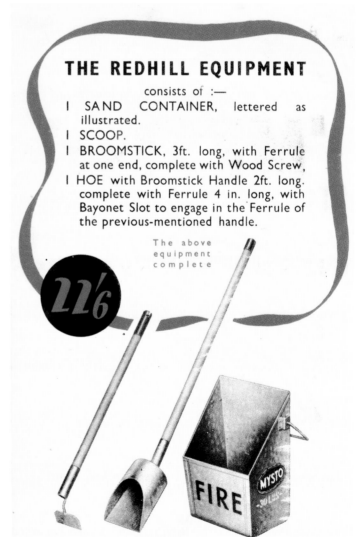

THE REDHILL EQUIPMENT

consists of :—

1 SAND CONTAINER, lettered as illustrated.

1 SCOOP.

1 BROOMSTICK, 3ft. long, with Ferrule at one end, complete with Wood Screw.

1 HOE with Broomstick Handle 2ft. long. complete with Ferrule 4 in. long, with Bayonet Slot to engage in the Ferrule of the previous-mentioned handle.

The above equipment complete

22/6

FIRE

MYSTO

in financial difficulties no payment will be made until after the War has ceased. If you do not know where to apply for the necessary form any of the local A.R.P. Wardens will tell you the address or the post office can help.

In all cases of structural damage the official surveyor will inspect the house as soon as possible to decide what must be done. Thus you will have the benefit of sound advice as to whether it is safe or not to go on living in your home.

Most of the houses which suffer as a result of raids are made uncomfortable rather than dangerous and, if you are by nature a handy person, you will want to set about making the place once more habitable. Temporary or urgent repairs may be done immediately, but others of a permanent nature should be started on only with the permission of the surveyor's department. This, however, is a matter which can be usually fixed up in a few moments over the telephone and need cause no serious delay.

In any kind of temporary repair the great thing is to use makeshift materials that already exist in the home and to buy as little new material as possible.' As the war progressed, wardens' posts often kept materials for temporary repairs.

So your area has been bombed, you've escaped with a few broken windows and some ceiling plaster down, but disaster – the water, gas and electricity have been cut off. Utility companies had their own emergency repair parties with helmets bearing the letters RP/G for gas or RP/W for water, and so on. But for a while you might be without water or power. The water boards issued their customers with advisory leaflets, such as this from the South Staffordshire Waterworks Company, dated May 1941:

'SANSPRAY'
FIRE BOMB EXTINGUISHER
The fire-watcher's friend!

A tubular sand container, 5 ft. long, with metal scoop. Does everything that can be done with buckets, scoops and rakes, *and does it better.* Can be hung anywhere to save floor space. Equally suitable for factory or cottage.

S1

5/9
EACH
RETAIL

Generous Trade
Terms on Application.

J. Howarth & Co., Daisyfield Works, Padiham, Lancs.

Above
Another of the many proprietary anti-incendiary bomb devices available, though few were as effective as the stirrup pump.

Right
Early incendiaries were fairly light, and many would bounce or roll off roofs, to fall harmlessly into the garden. Later variations had a heavy nose, so that they would punch through roofs and floors. (HMSO)

'To minimise inconvenience, until the water mains are repaired, householders should keep in store sufficient water for drinking and cooking purposes to last for at least 24 hours. This water should be put in suitable clean receptacles such as buckets, basins, bottles or jars NOW before a raid takes place. If the receptacles are covered, the water will keep clean and pure for some time and need only be renewed about once in three weeks.

On no account should baths be filled with water at night and emptied to waste next morning as this would result in a general shortage of water throughout the district with serious consequences in cases of fires and also to the supplies to factories engaged on war work.

Householders should make themselves familiar with the stop tap controlling their water supply, whether inside or outside their building, so as to be able to turn it off promptly in case of need to prevent flooding or waste.

During a raid do not draw any water except in case of dire necessity and then as little as possible.' After the raid: 'Efforts will be made within 24 hours to convey water in tanks to districts deprived of their piped supply, or consumers will be directed to the nearest points where a supply of water is available. Householders are reminded that water may be drawn from their hot water systems so long as there is water in their tanks, provided they put out the fire heating their boiler and boil such water before drinking. Instructions may be given by loud-speaker vans of the Ministry of Information or through Wardens or by other means that it is

THE NEW INCENDIARY BOMB IS HEAVIER than the older bomb and penetrates deeper

Search all floors including basement

necessary to sterilise all water in certain districts before using for drinking or cooking purposes. This will happen where there is danger of water becoming contaminated owing to damaged sewers. Consumers should then comply with the following instructions: Either boil all water or, if boiling is not possible, first add a heaped teaspoonful of Chloride of Lime to one pint of water, stir, and allow to settle. Then add one teaspoonful of this solution to each pint of water used and after stirring allow it to stand for not less than five minutes and then add one crystal of photographic hypo to remove the taste of chlorine. As an alternative to Chloride of Lime MILTON may be used – ten drops to a pint or one teaspoonful to a gallon, adding hypo after five minutes. NOTE. Supplies of Chloride of Lime should be obtained now, before an air raid occurs, from any chemist.

When the risk of contamination is over notice will be given by loudspeaker vans or otherwise.'

So you had water, but the power was still off; the British remedy for all ills – the cup of tea, is unavailable! For this awful event there was what was called 'emergency cooking'. The WVS and Girl Guides, among others, gave demonstrations of cooking over an open fire.

Alternatively you could build an 'emergency cooking stove'. The Women's Voluntary Services issued a leaflet giving instructions: *'Build a Field Kitchen in your own backyard now! Everyone should be able to cook for themselves and their families under emergency conditions. The morale of the Civil Population in wartime is just as important as ammunition and aeroplanes and a proper meal is one of the best stimulants for moral courage. It is*

just as important a job to keep family life going as to fight with the Forces or work in a factory.

In times of stress hot cooked food is more appetising and more easily digested than cold food from a tin. Plan now to be able to produce this at any time.

Reports are coming in from many Centres where members of the W. V. S. Housewives' Service are arranging demonstrations and learning to build field kitchens.

The following is a description (see opposite) *of building the simplest form of cooker with a chimney to stop the smoke getting into the food. The exact type of cooker you build will depend entirely on the materials you have at hand. Build this now while you can gather your materials, and while you have plenty of water. It will not last indefinitely as the mud dries out and crumbles away, but once the materials are there you can easily rebuild it when you need it, and you will learn more each time.'*

Woman magazine of November 1941 gave advice, and recipes, for just such an event: *'You've heard of cooking meals over a candle flame – let's hope you'll never be reduced to that! But it is possible that some day you may find you have to cook a meal without the ordinary means of doing so. Here are some meals* (see page 59) *that can be cooked over an open fire, or in a haybox, or can be prepared without any cooking at all. If you have to cook on an open fire, try a one-pot meal. I suggest as a menu: Meat, vegetables, barley or rice in the saucepan, steamed sponge pudding in steamer.'*

THE EMERGENCY COOKING STOVE

The shape and size of your cooker will be governed by the materials you can collect.

You must have: *Bricks* – broken or whole, but anyhow to include some half bricks. *Hot-plate* – preferably flat sheets of metal, or failing that corrugated iron, or anything else you can find. One piece will have to have a hole punched for the chimney. *Chimney* – piece of piping at least four inches in diameter and about 2ft. long or more or piece of old metal or earthenware chimney. *Earth* – you will want a heap of earth about 4ft. high for cementing the bricks together. If it is stony it will need sifting. *Plenty of water* – in buckets. *Spade, trowel, or small piece of wood or metal* – a builder's trowel for preference.

You should be able to obtain permission to collect most of these materials by asking at the Police Station or Town Hall.

• You must first prepare your, earth or "pug" as it is called. This should be in a small heap and the best way to get it thoroughly wet is to clear a hole in the centre and fill this with water, then with your spade lift the dry earth once, give it a good turnover and repeat the process until it is all thoroughly dampened and looks like prepared cement.

• You have got to build your walls to suit the size of your hotplates so first wet the ground where you are going to build and then lay the hotplates down and draw a line around them. Then add the piece of metal with the hole in it for the chimney and draw a line round this.

• Now collect two piles of bricks and pug and put them within easy reach of each side of your site and have a bucket of water standing by as you must wet each brick before you build it in. Place lines of pug on the ground down the lines you have drawn and across the back, leaving the front open. Set the first row of bricks into this, putting a little of the pug between each brick. Now cover the bricks with about an inch of pug before you lay the next row of bricks.

• You must build three courses, or rows of bricks, one on top of the other taking care that the bricks lie quite level and in as straight lines as possible. Take a look at any brick wall to see how they should be laid. It will be found easier to start at the middle of the back and work down each side.

• On the top of the third course of bricks put another good layer of pug, and lay the metal plate on it, also the metal plate with the hole in it for the chimney at the back end. If corrugated iron is used as a hot-plate, it may be found necessary to stamp it out and support it with two or three bars of iron which should be set into the pug.

• Now lay more pug on the edges of the metal plates and seal them in. You must also lay a line of pug across the cooker dividing the metal plate for the chimney from the hot-plates, and lay a course of bricks in this and also round the chimney end of the hotplate forming a square round the chimney.

• Now set in your chimney; fit the piece of piping for the chimney over the hole in the metal plate. It does not matter if it does not fit exactly. Set four bricks in pug round the pipe to hold it steady and cover these bricks and the piece of piping with plenty of pug. Now fill up the whole square where the chimney is with rubble and pug, building well up the base of the chimney.

• Your cooker is now complete and the fire should be laid with paper or sacking and long pieces of wood. At first smoke will come out of the cracks in the pug, but you can easily smear these in and build up more pug over the outside of the bricks.

• This is the simplest form of cooker with a hot-plate for boiling only, but there are many varieties. You can set in fire bars two bricks high and have your hot-plates, two or three bricks above the firebars, or, if you are building on earth, you can dig a pit for the ashes. Both these variations are to ensure more draught for the fire.

You can easily build in an oven by using an oil drum or old water tank and fixing this into the chimney part so that the heat circulates round it.

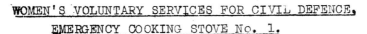

WOMEN'S VOLUNTARY SERVICES FOR CIVIL DEFENCE.
EMERGENCY COOKING STOVE No. 1.

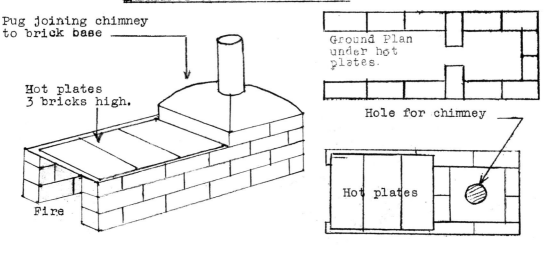

Pug joining chimney to brick base

Hot plates 3 bricks high.

Fire

Ground Plan under hot plates.

Hole for chimney

Hot plates

CORNED BEEF HASH

¾lb corned beef	1oz dripping
1 dessertspoon flour	salt and pepper
1 pint stock or water	toast
1 dessertspoon gravy powder	
cooked vegetables or rice	

Melt the fat and mix the flour and gravy powder in it. Cook for two or three minutes, then add the stock and bring to the boil, stirring well. Mince the meat and add this.

Simmer gently for about ten minutes until thoroughly hot. Remember that the meat is already cooked. Serve with rusks or fingers of toast and plenty of vegetables or rice.

Cooking time: 15 minutes. Serves 4 people

CURRIED VEGETABLES

1oz dripping
1 dessertspoon curry powder
1 dessertspoon flour
3oz carrot, turnip, swedes, potatoes
1 pint of stock or 1 pint of water with 1 teaspoon of meat extract
salt

Melt the fat. Mix in the flour and curry powder and cook over a low light for five minutes. Add the stock and bring to the boil. Put in vegetables, prepared and cut into one-inch cubes. Simmer for thirty minutes with a lid on the saucepan. Then quickly remove the pan from the light, wrap it in newspaper and pack into the hay box. It will continue cooking slowly and be ready in about two hours, but will keep hot for considerably longer if left in the box.

Cooking time: 2 hours. Serves 4 people

RICE PUDDING

1 pint milk	salt
2 dessertspoons sugar	2oz rice

Bring the milk to the boil, sprinkle in the rice and the other ingredients. Boil for ten minutes. Then put a lid on the pan, wrap the pan in newspaper and pack it into the hay box. Arrange that the curry and the pudding are ready to go into the box at the same time.

Cooking time: 2 hours. Serves 4 people

Left

A member of the WVS demonstrating the construction of an emergency stove.

SARDINE SALAD

1 cabbage heart or other raw green vegetable	1 lettuce
	1 beetroot
1 swede or turnip, carrots	salt, pepper
1 tin of sardines or herrings	mustard
Chopped parsley or carrot tops	cheese
2 tablespoons vinegar	rusks
4 tablespoons oil	margarine

Shred the green vegetable, grate the carrots, swede and beetroot. Flake the fish roughly. Mix all these together with the dressing made by mixing the oil, vinegar, pepper, salt and mustard. Serve at once. Sprinkle over it the chopped parsley and grated cheese.

Serve with rusks or wheatmeal bread and margarine. This, with a milk drink, will make a nourishing and substantial meal.

Preparation time: 10 minutes. Serves 4 people

EMERGENCY BREAD

1lb. self-raising flour
1 teaspoon salt
½ pint milk and water

Mix the flour and salt and make a fairly soft dough with the milk and water. Turn on to a floured board and flatten to about half inch in thickness. Divide into twelve scones and bake in a hot oven for twenty minutes or until they feel firm when pressed at the sides.

Cooking time: 10 minutes. Makes 12 large scones

The Ministry of Food asks every housewife

TO READ

Most newspapers and magazines are running special wartime cookery features. Read them regularly. It is a good plan to cut out the items that interest you and keep them handy in a scrap book.

TO LISTEN

Broadcasts have been arranged to give all the latest practical information about buying, preparing and cooking food. Look out for them. They tell what foods are in season and how they can be used.

TO WATCH

Simple demonstrations in cookery and meal planning are being arranged up and down the country. Ask for particulars from your local Food Office or Education Authority. Go along and take your friends.

your food in wartime

In the First World War the German submarine fleet had attempted to win the war by starving Britain of the imports of raw materials and food vital for her survival. In spite of shortages and food queues, the government had resisted the calls for rationing, only introducing it in February 1918, the final year of the war.

As Britain began to prepare for another war, it was clear that our reliance on imported goods would once again be our Achilles heel and, as the European situation grew bleaker, the government set up the 'Food (Defence Plans) Department' in

1936. Its remit was to prepare plans for the supply of food in the event of war, including rationing. Such a scheme, involving over 40 million people, would involve a massive amount of planning, with blank ration books being printed in secret as early as 1938.

In war the government would have to be in complete control of the supply of essential food-stuffs, and the Department began to build up huge stockpiles. As with other preparations, the Munich Crisis of September 1938 put an increased emphasis on the question of food. People asked whether they should lay in their own emergency stock of food in case of war, though some argued that this would cause shortages. In February 1939, the Board of Trade announced that it had '*no objections to the accumulation by householders in peace time of small reserves of suitable foodstuffs equivalent to about one week's normal requirements*', and that these would actually prove a useful backup to the government's stockpiles.

Confusingly, that month the government issued a pamphlet, **War Emergency Instructions and Information**: '*Stocks of foodstuffs in the country are sufficient. In order to ensure that stocks are distributed fairly and to the best advantage the Government are bringing into operation the plans for the organisation of food supplies which have already been prepared in collaboration with the food trades. Steps have been taken to prevent any sudden rise in the price, or the holding up of supplies. For the time being you should continue to obtain supplies from your usual shops. You should limit your purchases to the quantities which you normally require.*'

IMPORTANT

The Food "Defence Plans" Department of the Government advises everyone to store sufficient food for a week or more as a precaution against emergencies.

Heinz products offer you the greatest protection—for these foods keep perfectly and you can live on them indefinitely. Each of the following varieties is a meal in itself, ready prepared, perfect in flavour and rich in food value—the best you can buy for the money. Why not live well and inexpensively in strenuous times.

Baked Beans with pork and tomato sauce	pound tins—2 doz. in case,	10/-
Spaghetti in tomato sauce with cheese	pound tins—2 doz.	,,	13/-
Cooked Macaroni in cream sauce with cheese	pound tins—2 doz.	,,	15/-
20 Varieties of Soup	2 doz.	,,	14/-

Strained Foods, for babies and invalids—12 kinds. They are equal in every respect to the freshest of vegetables—cooked in a way that retains all their natural elements. They are of high vitamin content and are recommended by the medical profession everywhere. This is the surest way of protecting the babies and invalid members of the family.

Most families are carrying two or three tins of these different varieties in the larder. Your grocer is prepared to sell you these in case lots.

H. J. HEINZ Co. Ltd.

HARLESDEN **57** LONDON

Baked Beans	- 3d, 5d, 10½d per tin	Macaroni	- 4d, 7½d per tin
Spaghetti	- 3½d, 6½d, 1/1½ per tin	Soups	- 5d, 7d, 1/2 per tin
	Strained Foods	- 6d per tin	

57

Above
The government recommended that every household equip itself with an emergency food supply. Manufacturers were quick to cash in.

Right
A typical Ministry of Food recipe, from 1945.

In July 1939, a series of Civil Defence leaflets were delivered to every household in the country, including no 4, *Your Food in War-Time*. This expanded on the theme of an individual store of food: '*For those who have the means, a suitable amount of foodstuffs to lay by would be the quantity that they ordinarily use in one week. The following are suggested as articles of food suitable for house-holder's storage:*

Meat and fish in cans or glass jars; flour; suet; canned or dried milk; sugar; tea; cocoa; plain biscuits.

When you have laid in your store, you should draw on it regularly for day to day use, replacing what you use by new purchases, so that the stock in your cupboard is constantly being changed.

Any such reserves should be bought before an emergency arises. To try to buy extra quantities when an emergency is upon us, would be unfair to others.'

The leaflet also set out the basics of the rationing scheme: 'Certain foods, soon after the outbreak of a war, would be brought under a rationing scheme similar to that which was introduced during the latter part of the Great War. In the first instance, rationing would be applied to five foodstuffs – butcher's meat, bacon and ham, sugar, butter and margarine, and cooking fats. Later, it might be necessary to add other articles.

The object of this scheme is to make certain that foodstuffs are distributed fairly and equally and that everyone is sure of his or her proper share.

Before rationing begins application forms would be sent through the post to every householder, who would be asked to give particulars of everyone living in his home. These forms, when filled in, would be returned to the local food office set up by the local Food Control Committee, which would issue the Ration Books, one for each person.

You would then register at a retail shop of your own choice for each rationed food. This registration is necessary to enable the local committee to know the quantities of rationed foods which each shop would require. There is no need to register with a shop in peace time. It is not advisable to do so.

The Ration Books would have coupons, a certain number for each week. The Ministry would decide how much food each coupon represented, and you would be entitled to buy that amount. In the case of meat, the amount would be expressed in money. Thus, you could choose between buying a larger amount of a cheaper cut, or a smaller amount of a more expensive cut. In the case of other foods, the amount would be by weight.

For children under six years of age, there would

A Better Batter

... AND EASIER TO MAKE!

The same rich nourishment, the same golden crispness you'd get in a batter made with shell eggs; but less bother, because you use dried eggs, *and put them in dry*. Dried eggs, as you know, are fresh new-laid eggs with only the shell and water removed, and they are a body-building food, like meat. Why not make the most of them?

ISSUED BY THE MINISTRY OF FOOD · LONDON · W·1

Sausage Toad : 1 level tablespoon Dried Egg dry, 4 oz. flour, pinch of salt, ½ pint milk and water mixed, a knob of fat, 1 lb. sausages. Mix dry ingredients, add sufficient liquid to make a thick batter. Beat well. Add the rest of the liquid and beat again. Melt the fat in a tin, put in sausages and return to oven. When fat is smoking hot pour in batter, and bake in a very hot oven for 30 minutes. Serves 4.

be a Child's Ration Book, but the only difference would be that a child would be allowed half the amount of butcher's meat allowed for a grown-up person. On the other hand, the allowance for a heavy worker will give him a larger quantity of meat. For catering and other institutions, special arrangements will be made.'

With the outbreak of war the Department became the Ministry of Food; it immediately took control of all food imports, while retail prices of the most important foodstuffs were controlled, meaning that a maximum price was set. This had to be displayed in all suppliers' premises. Early controlled foods included eggs, butter, condensed milk, flour, sugar, tinned salmon, potatoes and dried fruits. Local councils were ordered to set up Food Control Committees, whose first task was to license every butcher, baker, grocer, milkman, greengrocer, café and restaurant in their area.

Friday 29 September 1939 was National Registration day; all households were issued with a form, or schedule, in advance of that date. Instructions with it included: *The return on the schedule herewith will be used not only for National Registration but also for Food Rationing purposes. It is to your interest, therefore, as well as your public duty, to fill up the return carefully, fully and accurately. Help the Enumerator to collect the schedule promptly by arranging for him to receive it when he calls. When the Enumerator collects the schedule, he must write and deliver an Identity Card for every person included in the return.'*

In the last week in October ration books started to be sent out. As had been stated in the July Civil Defence pamphlet, for the general public there were two types of book, a buff-coloured one (the General book) for all those over the age of six, and a green one (the Child's book) for those aged six or under. There were other books for those whose jobs required them to move about, such as travelling salesmen, and another for merchant seamen.

These first ration books were dispatched through the post – a mammoth task. The **Mid-Devon Times** reported that: ' *"Of the 29,000 ration books dealt with by the staff of Newton Abbot Rural Food Control Office all but 24, whose identities cannot at the moment be established, were sent out by Jan 6th,"* declared the Deputy Food Executive Officer (Mr W. S. Hearder).*

Mr Hearder added that the work of writing out the new ration books had been done almost wholly by voluntary helpers, considerable help having been given by students of Stover and Ingsdon Schools and by senior pupils of the Southwark Central School. A tremendous amount of extra work had been entailed, added Mr Hearder, by the fact that many people had failed to give their national registration numbers, or had filled in their cards of application incorrectly. In some cases, said Mr Hearder, practically nothing was put on the cards and in others Christian names had been put where surnames were required and vice versa. Some people had applied for six or seven books in one name, but despite all these difficulties all the books, except twenty-four, had been addressed and dispatched in good time.'

There was no food rationing as yet, although this was clearly only a matter of time. People were instructed to register with shops supplying the items, butcher's meat, bacon and ham, sugar,

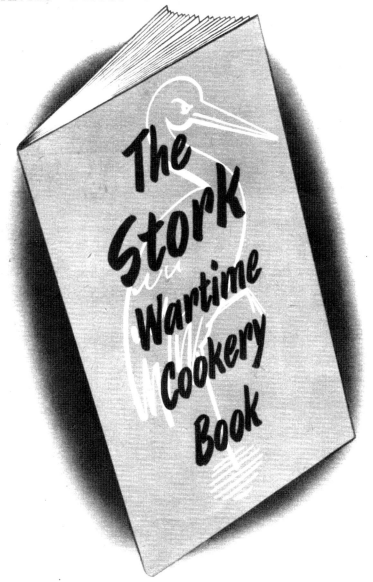

Free

A COMPLETE GUIDE TO NOURISHING MEALS FROM PRESENT-DAY SUPPLIES

The Stork Wartime Cookery Book

butter and margarine, and cooking fats, mentioned in the pamphlet. You could register with a different shop for each item, or a single shop for the lot, or a combination. On 1 November the Minister of Food, W. S. Morrison, announced that butter and bacon (including ham) were to be rationed, but that this would not start before mid-December – the exact date would be announced later. *'Provided that imports continue at the present rate, as there is good reason for assuming that they will, the ration for both bacon and butter will be 4oz a week for every individual consumer, i.e. 1lb of bacon and 1lb of butter for a family of four persons.'* He then spoke of sugar, supplies of which were sufficient to avoid rationing for some time if people restricted themselves to one pound a week.

Left
Housewives were inundated with wartime recipe books and leaflets using non-rationed and non-shortage items, as with this one from Stork margarine.

Meals bought in catering establishments would be subject to rationing, but not small items. So a bacon sandwich constituted a meal and therefore needed coupons, whereas a buttered roll was not a meal, and did not.

On 29 November, Morrison announced that rationing would commence on 9 January 1940, at the levels previously stated. Then, at the last minute, on 28 December it was announced that sugar would also be included, at 12 ounces per person.

From this point on rationing became an ever-changing fact of life. New items were added to the list, while the amounts supplied were changed from time to time, usually downwards. In response to this, alternatives were sought: bacon is a good example. There was macon (smoked mutton), becon (smoked beef) and vencon (smoked venison). *The trade tried various ways of making macon and in due course a group of politicians and tradesmen tried out the novelty at a party in London. They sampled it fried, grilled and boiled, and the general verdict was that the first two methods were better than the third. The Minister of Agriculture, Sir Reginald Dorman-Smith, praised the product, although not extravagantly. Other guests found it remarkably uninteresting; perhaps it had not been cured with the right smoke or rubbed with the right spices. "Macon Is Not So Hot," said a farming journal. "It tasted mainly of salt, and as a substitute for crisp, appetising bacon it was nowhere." These sentiments were those of the country at large. Few people bought macon twice and a good many never bought it once'* (from **The Phoney War on the Home Front**). In the event, these substitutes disappeared with the arrival of meat rationing.

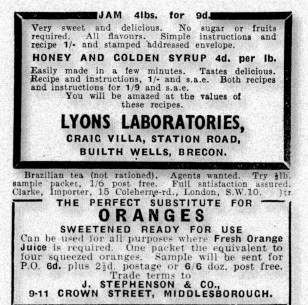

Above
'Substitutes' sprang up for rationed or shortage articles; unfortunately many were just ways of parting you from your money.

Rationing spawned a rash of substitutes for foods that became scarce during the winter of 1940–41. Some of these were legitimate, others were little more than a confidence trick; milk substitutes, consisting of flour, salt, and baking powder and sold for the high price of 5 shillings a pound, or onion substitutes which were merely 'water and a smell'. In October 1941 the Ministry of Food made an order forbidding the manufacture or sale of any substitute food except under licence. This never completely stamped out the practice; small-scale local operations continued, as Ministry officials had far too much to do to chase such small law-breakers. As usual with such scams, people on the whole soon cottoned on.

The Ministry of Food and women's magazines responded to rationing with suggestions for alternatives, or recipes which either used fewer of the rationed items or none at all.

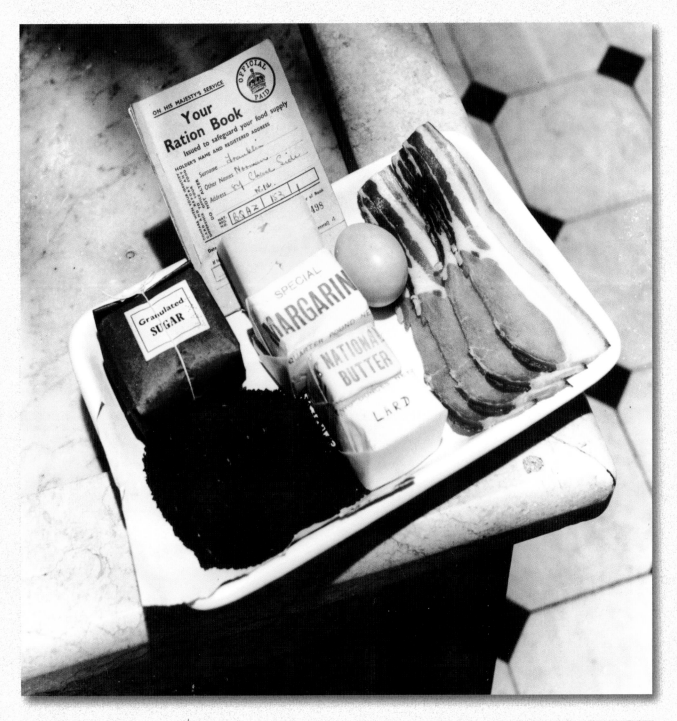

rationing

In this section we will look at the different items to be rationed, and some of the tips, alternatives and recipes which appeared. Unless otherwise stated, all amounts are per person, per week.

bacon

Bacon and ham were two of the first items to be rationed, on 8 January 1940, at the rate of 4oz. By the end of the month, however, this was doubled to 8oz, but in June it went back to 4oz, where it mainly stayed. Not only among the first, they would also be among the last, not going off ration until June 1954.

One tip was to save your bacon rinds. Then fry them until crisp, grind them, and add to rissoles, soups, gravy or fish cakes as flavouring.

Savoury Bacon Olives

These, you were assured, would 'make a little bacon go a very long way'.

Ingredients:

6oz bacon rashers

3oz sausage meat

1½oz breadcrumbs

¾ level teaspoonful mixed herbs

1½ level teaspoonfuls chopped parsley

salt and pepper

2 or 3 dessertspoonfuls milk

1 slice bread

some mashed potatoes

Remove the rind from the bacon rashers and spread them out with a knife to make them as thin as possible. If they are very narrow this will also widen them. Then cut each rasher into halves.

Mix the sausage meat with the breadcrumbs, herbs and parsley, season with pepper and salt, then add sufficient milk to moisten.

Divide the stuffing into equal portions, allowing one portion for each half rasher, and form them into small rolls. Roll up a portion in each piece of bacon.

Run a skewer through the rolls, place them on a tin and bake them till they are tender.

Cut a slice of bread, not too thick, into one-inch strips, then cut it into squares and again into triangles. When the stuffed bacon rolls are cooked, take them up and keep them warm for a few minutes whilst you toast the sippets [morsels], toasting them in the tin with the bacon fat.

Have some potatoes ready boiled and mashed, then heap them along the centre of the dish. Arrange the rolls on the top, and the sippets round them, and serve the bacon olives hot.

"Sorry, Sir—no macon. We're using bacon as a substitute now"

The recipe book **Cooking in Wartime**, by Elizabeth Craig, gave instructions for cooking one of the substitutes, macon, or mutton ham, as she also refers to it.

Boiled

Place macon in a saucepan. Cover with boiling water, and bring to a simmering point. Simmer slowly till tender, allowing ½ hour to each pound of mutton ham. Add to cooking water a sliced, peeled medium-sized turnip, a sliced, scraped carrot, a peeled, medium-sized onion, stuck with cloves, and a bay leaf. When tender, leave to cool in water in which it is cooked, then drain, and roll in dried breadcrumbs.

Baked

Boil as described, but instead of covering with crumbs, carefully peel off the rind, and rub fat thickly with light brown sugar. Prick with cloves to taste. Place on a rack in a baking tin. Pour a bottle of cider over the ham. Bake for ½ hour in a slow oven, basting every ten minutes with the cider in baking tin. Serve hot or cold.

Very few people mourned when just two months later, with the introduction of general meat rationing, the various bacon-alternatives disappeared.

butter

Butter was first rationed on 8 January 1940 at 4oz. As with bacon, this was found to be too severe, and was doubled to 8oz on 25 March, but by 3 June it was halved once again to 4oz.

On 22 July margarine was included in the ration scheme, with a total of the two set at 6oz. This could be taken in any proportion. By 2 September, however, this was tightened up, with butter forming at most 4oz of the 6oz, and on the 30th dropping to a maximum of 2oz. In March 1941 the butter portion doubled, from 2oz to 4oz, falling back to 2oz again in June. In November that year the total went up to 7oz, although butter remained at 2oz, where it would stay, although the total bounced between six and seven ounces. Butter eventually came off ration in May 1954.

With the butter ration so tight, people could not afford to waste any, especially on the wrapper; this, you were assured, could be achieved by placing the butter in cold water before unwrapping it. Spreading became an art; the rule was 'scrape it

Far Left
Advert from December 1939. Soon sauces and other flavourings would be in great demand to give the stodgy and somewhat boring wartime fare a little boost.

Above Left
Bacon rationing brought with it attempts at substitutes, such as Macon (smoked mutton). As this Sillince cartoon shows, these too were soon in short supply.

pepper and salt and heat through in the oven.'

1001 Household Hints recommended that you: *'Wash half a pint of lentils and boil gently with sufficient water to cover them. Then stir in three ounces of grated cheese, two ounces of margarine, one cupful of breadcrumbs, some grated nutmeg, and pepper and salt to taste. Stir the mixture well and let it simmer for ten minutes. Place in jars and when cold pour melted margarine on the top. Spread on bread, instead of butter.'*

on, then scrape it off'. This could be made easier by heating a bowl with boiling water, and, when hot, placing it over the butter dish, making the butter nice and soft and easy to spread.

Making the butter go further was a good trick. The Ministry of Food recommended mixing the butter with an equal amount of mashed potato, while *'You can increase the butter ration if you warm a little milk and beat it into the butter.'*

Alternatives to butter for spreading on bread included *'Melt slightly ½lb margarine and mix in a small jar of cream, beat thoroughly, then leave to set. You can hardly tell the difference between this and butter.'* And *'Use beef dripping in place of butter when you make toast. Season with*

Left
Brown & Polson advert from July 1942, 'to make your butter ration go further'. Of interest is the use of the words Utility Dress, utility clothing having been brought in at the end of 1941.

Above
How to make your own mini-butter churn, from **Housewife** magazine, December 1944.

Alternatives for pastry-making included beef or mutton dripping beaten to a cream with a squeeze of lemon juice added, or sixpennyworth of marrow bones, cracked open and the marrow removed and put in the oven to melt. *This will produce a lovely lot of fat, which makes delicious pastry and cakes when cold.*

A good butter substitute can be made by skimming 1lb. of kidney beef suet. Shred very finely and pound it well, moistening it with a little pure olive oil until it becomes one piece of the consistency of butter. It is then ready for use and should be used in exactly the same way as butter for pastry making. This is also very nourishing on hot toast.

You could try churning your own butter. By 1944, Fortnum & Mason were selling a miniature churn for 9s 11d, which could also be used to mix dried milk or dried eggs.

sugar

Sugar was first rationed on 8 January 1940 at 12oz; it was cut to 8oz on 27 May, then as a Christmas treat, raised back to 12oz for the holiday week. In June 1941 it was raised to 16oz for 4 weeks, falling once again to 8oz. It remained at 8oz, except for two brief periods: November/December 1941, 12oz, and July 1942, 16oz. Between November 1943 and April 1944 the sugar ration could be taken in the form of preserves. Sugar finally went off ration in September 1953.

In **Housewife** magazine of October 1940 Ambrose Heath gave recipes for cakes and puddings without sugar. These included:

Potato and Carrot Cake

4oz flour, 4oz grated raw potato, 4oz grated raw carrot, 8oz mixed fruit (sultanas, raisins, currants and peel if you like), 2oz fat, 2 teaspoonsful baking powder, 1 teaspoonful bicarbonate of soda.

Rub the fat into the flour, mix in the potato and carrot and then the mixed fruit, and finally the baking powder and the bicarbonate of soda. There should be enough moisture in the carrot and potato to mix the cake. Grease a deep cake-tin, put in the mixture, and bake for about forty minutes.

Chocolate Rice Pudding

All you have to do is to grate and melt some chocolate (how much depends on how chocolatey you want the pudding to taste), add it to your milk, and make the rice pudding in the usual way. Mothers who find their children won't eat rice pudding plain, should note this simple expedient!

Advice was that you could use far less sugar in your cake mixture if you sifted the salt in with the flour. Fruit could be stewed using half the sugar if you made up for it with a pinch of bicarbonate of soda. Start cooking the fruit with the soda and, when half done, add the sugar. For rhubarb, soak the lengths in water for about half an hour.

Alternatively you could scald it before stewing, when only half the sugar would be required. Prunes could be cooked without sugar if a few sultanas were added while they were cooking.

Other tips were halving the sugar in tea by pouring the boiling tea directly on to the sugar, while in making mint sauce sugar could be saved by chopping the mint finely, then mixing it well with a ½ teaspoonful of sugar – leave for 1 hour then add vinegar.

SULTANAS

are cheap

FROM 6d. lb.

According to quality

No need to cut down on sugar foods — You can get *extra* sugar from sultanas. And now delicious sultanas are plentiful — even more so than pre-war. And they are cheap — even cheaper than pre-war. Children love sweet dishes and the fruit sugar in sultanas is an *immediate* source of energy. Let sultanas save your sugar ration — use them generously in cakes, puddings, pastries, and in the excellent homely dishes for which the English housewife is famed. Sultanas give you extra *natural* sugar at a remarkably low price — they're now in the shops — buy more, use more.

SULTANA BREAD
1 lb. Self Raising Flour, ½ te... salt, 5 oz. sultanas, 2 oz. m... 1 oz. sugar, ½ pint milk a... mixed. Sift flour and salt in... Rub in fat. Add other di... dients and mix in milk...
greased bread tin for abou...

CURRIED MINCED BEE
1 lb. Minced Beef, 1 oz... 1 tablespoon flour, 1 tablesp... powder, 1 onion sliced, 2 oz... ½ pint stock, 1 teaspoon lem... salt, 4 oz. cooked rice. Heat... in stewpan. Fry onion unt... add meat, put in flour an... powder, stir and cook... minute, add lemon, sul... stock and stir until ingredi... Cover and simmer for 30...

BREAD & BUTTER PU...
5 or 6 thin slices of bread sp... margarine, about 1 pint m... sultanas. Cut off the c... divide each slice of bread... arrange in layers in greased... Sprinkle each layer lavi... sultanas, beat egg, mix w... and pour gently over th... Let it stand for 1 hour... bake in moderately cool... 45-50 minutes.

SULTANAS FOR BREA...
Take a handful of sultanas... them in cold water for... hour. Strain, and add... your breakfast cereal. As... ative, sultanas alone wi... Take care to wash them fir...

FIGS *If you prefer figs to S... tanas, try them chopp... up in the recipes given above. Figs... one of the richest sugar foods. They... almost as plentiful as sultanas just n... and very economically priced.*

& plentiful

Above
Advert for sultanas from April 1940, promoting them as a substitute for sugar. Soon they too would be in shortage, and in January 1942 they would go on the points rationing scheme.

Right
Meat was an even greater part of the national diet in the 1940s than it is today, so meat rationing hit hard. Any substitute was welcome.

meat

Meat was rationed on 11 March 1940 at 1s 10d (for under-sixes, 11d). Sausages and offal such as liver, kidneys and tripe, were not rationed. In September, the adult meat ration was raised to 2s 2d, falling back again in December. On 6 January 1941 it fell to 1sd 6d – this now included offal – but two days later it fell once again, to 1s 2d (though all offal, except ox-skirt, was once more off ration). It reached its lowest point, a mere shilling, in March that year before rising to 1s 2d in July. From February to May 1942 and April to July 1943, two pennyworth of it had to be taken in corned beef. Alternatives were at a premium; fish rocketed to over four times its pre-war price, and the government was forced to bring it under price control; by 1943 horsemeat, or horseflesh as it was known, was commonly available, while in January 1945, whale meat, almost universally hated, and an Australian fish, snoek (pronounced snook), widely considered to be inedible, were on sale. In June 1954, meat, along with bacon, became the last items to be taken off ration.

No coupons required

Remember now that meat rationing has commenced what good nourishment you can get from Foster Clark's Soups. You can taste the prime beef in Foster Clark's meat soups, succulent and rich as a cook's stock-pot. And in their delicious vegetable soups you can taste the fresh vegetables, cooked to a turn, with every atom of nourishment retained.

NO INCREASE IN PRICE
2½d square makes **5** plates
1d square makes **2** plates

FOSTER CLARK'S SOUPS

You need soup more than ever

All wartime influences are compelling you to reduce your consumption of meat. So it is more important than ever to remember that soup feeds you. Soup warms you. Soup nourishes you. Soup fills you with a glow and keeps out the cold. Foster Clark's Soups help you to make your money go further, they are invaluable for adding nourishment and flavour to stews and hashes.

Off-ration meat was immediately seized upon as an excellent way to supplement people's rations. As such it was soon in shortage, and a major part of the under-the-counter trade. The Ministry's recipe book, **Food Facts for the Kitchen Front,** talked about offal: *Few people realise how many kinds of offal there are. Many of them are delicacies, all of them can be made into nourishing and palatable dishes. Here is a list of offal:*

Ox tongue, Ox heart, Ox liver, Ox tail, Ox kidney, Ox skirts, Ox cheek, Ox sweetbreads, Ox tripe.

Calves' liver, Calves' tongues, Calves' sweetbreads, Calves' head (scalded), Calves' hearts, Calves' feet, Calves' kidneys.

Sheep's liver, Sheep's hearts, Sheep's sweetbreads, Sheep's tongues, Sheep's kidneys, Sheep's heads.

Pigs' liver, Pigs' tongue, Pigs' hearts, Pigs' kidneys.

Chitterlings.'

The 1942 Ministry of Food leaflet, *Wartime Food for Growing Children*, extolled the use of offal: *'Don't forget that meat not on the ration is as good a builder as rationed meat. Sheep and calves' heads, brains, trotters and heels, hearts and tails – they are builders all. Yes, even haggis and faggots, to say nothing of the comedians' joy, tripe.*

Good heavens, I had almost forgotten rabbits! Before the war we turned up our noses at rabbits in our house, but it's a different story now. And tinned builders, remember, are as good as fresh builders, whether it's meat or fish or beans.'

There were many recipes for cooking offal, including stewed tripe with celery, curried tripe,

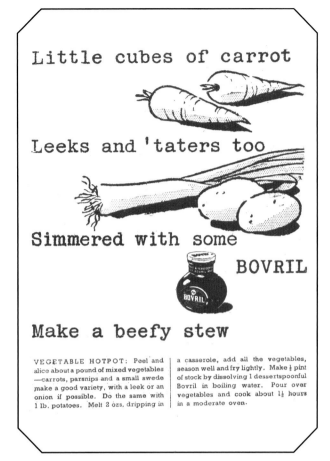

Little cubes of carrot

Leeks and 'taters too

Simmered with some

BOVRIL

Make a beefy stew

VEGETABLE HOTPOT: Peel and slice about a pound of mixed vegetables —carrots, parsnips and a small swede make a good variety, with a leek or an onion if possible. Do the same with 1 lb. potatoes. Melt 2 ozs. dripping in a casserole, add all the vegetables, season well and fry lightly. Make ½ pint of stock by dissolving 1 dessertspoonful Bovril in boiling water. Pour over vegetables and cook about 1½ hours in a moderate oven.

Above
Making a non-meat meal taste meaty was every housewife's goal, in this case with Bovril.

stuffed tripe, liver dumplings, cow heel with parsley sauce, stewed ox cheek, pigs' and sheep's trotters, brawn, sheep's head roll, baked stuffed sheep's heart, sheep's head broth, boiled cows', sheep's or pigs' head, faggots, and even brains on toast.

From February 1942 the requirement to take part of the meat ration in the form of corned beef spawned a fresh wave of recipes, like this one from the **Home Companion**.

Farmhouse Pie

Required: 4oz corned beef

1lb mixed vegetables

pepper and salt

gravy powder or meat cube

mashed potatoes

a little dripping

Method: Wash and prepare the vegetables and chop finely. Cook in a very little salted water, in a covered saucepan, until tender, about 7 minutes. Drain well and reserve the liquid. Flake the corned beef and mix with the vegetables. Turn into a greased pie-dish and moisten with the vegetable water thickened with a little gravy powder or meat cube, and season to taste. Cover with a thick layer of mashed potato, rough up the top with a fork, and dot with pieces of dripping. Bake in a moderate oven for 30 minutes.

The amount of meat in sausages became a sore point. One correspondent of **Picture Post** in March 1940 (when meat was first rationed) wrote: '*When is a sausage not a sausage? When it's a bread pudding! Recently we have had two brands of sausage. The first brand seemed to be made almost entirely of bread and grease, very nasty grease too, which stuck in our throats and almost choked us. The second was made of bread alone, with a generous dash of pepper. Is it too much to expect that the national sausage, being of almost no value, would cost less, instead of more, than the unrationed? They were called pork sausages, but any self-respecting pig would blush at being made a party to such profiteering.*' The magazine replied that the '*Minister of Food has announced that "The question of controlling the price and meat content*

of sausages is one of some complexity," and hopes to find a solution soon.'

You could also make the small meat ration go further; one tip was to add either a cupful of whole rice or a breakfastcupful of breadcrumbs when stewing mince, which, you were assured, would make it go twice as far. However, for some people, the whole thing became just too much trouble. Eva White, quoted in **The Home Front**, wrote: '*The meat situation became so impossible that we decided to become vegetarians. To do this we had to get certificates signed by a doctor and a minister. We were entitled to twelve to sixteen ounces of cheese a week each, as well as dried bananas, fruit*

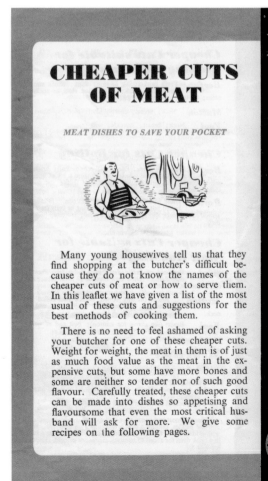

Left

Meat was rationed by value, so using the cheaper cuts made the ration stretch. This leaflet from the Ministry of Food shows how to do just that.

Right

Throwing away the water that vegetables had been boiled in was almost a crime in the Ministry of Food's eyes. It could be used as the basis for a soup or a stew, and given meat flavouring – this time by Oxo.

Mixed Grill a la Woolton

(Serves 4 people and avoids rationed meats)

4 lambs' kidneys

4 tomatoes

4 small sausages

2 large or 4 small mushrooms

2 lambs' sweetbreads

2 small slices calves' liver

½lb new potatoes

Seasoning.

Method: Skin and core the kidneys. Blanch the sweetbreads. Thread each portion of kidneys, sweetbread and liver on a skewer, sprinkle with melted fat and cook under a red-hot grill for from 7 to 10 minutes. Sprinkle the tomatoes, mushrooms and sausages with a little melted fat, and cook on the flat grill tin. Serve with chips or straw potatoes.

*(from **A Kitchen Goes to War**, pub. 1940)*

bars and nuts. I was very popular at Christmas when I was able to take a small bag of almonds to each of our neighbours. When I was asked to give a small prize for a Lexicon Drive at the local church I offered two pounds of mixed shelled nuts and this was the most popular prize on the table.'

Don't throw the VITAMIN vegetable water away!

SOUP the OXO way!

Add OXO to your vegetable water and you have a delicious soup — almost a meal in itself. This extra nourishment and goodness makes a welcome addition to war time meals. See how the family will enjoy its rich beefy flavour.

Still 1d. each— 6d. packet of 6

OXO MAKES IT BEEFY

tea

On 8 July 1940 the national drink, tea, went on ration at 2oz; as a special Christmas gift from the government that was doubled to 4oz for the holiday week that year. As part of the welfare scheme for children the under-fives' tea ration was withdrawn in January 1942. At the other end of the scale an extra tea allowance for 70-year-olds and over was introduced in December 1944. The ration was increased to 2½ oz a week in July 1945, and abolished altogether in October 1952.

It was now vital to make the most of the tea ration. **Practical Hints in War Time** gave instructions for making tea: *When tea is made in the following way, more of the flavour is brought out of the leaves with the result that a saving of actual tea is made. Warm the pot while the kettle is being heated up; put the dry tea in the pot and, when steam comes out of the kettle, hold the pot over the steaming spout for one minute. Then pour the boiling water into the pot immediately.'*

Housewife magazine in October 1940 sought tips from its readers; these included saving left-over tea in a thermos flask and grinding the tea leaves with a pestle and mortar. This, it was stated, would save half the usual amount of tea if used directly it was ground, while the addition of a pinch of baking soda in the teapot when making tea could save almost a teaspoonful of tea every time. Finally, if you opened both ends of the tea packet you could get almost an extra spoonful from the folds at the bottom.

Suggested alternatives from various sources included the leaves of the common marjoram or wood sage, lime or elderberry blossom and rose hips.

Coffee was of course a more common alternative to tea, although this too was in short supply. There were tips for this too: each teaspoonful would go half as far again if you warmed the coffee before pouring on the boiling water, while *'if the quality of the coffee is not as good as one could wish for, put a very small amount of salt in it'*.

Again there were alternatives, in this case acorns; large, plump ones being best. Remove the shells and roast carefully, either using a coffee roaster or an iron frying pan with a lid, constantly shaking it – the outer skin would then easily be knocked off. Grind them in an ordinary grinder. They could then be used either as a 'coffee' by themselves or added, as with chicory, to real coffee.

cooking fat

On 22 July 1940 the last of the five items named in the July 1939 Civil Defence leaflet, cooking fat, was rationed at 2oz, although you could take this in margarine if preferred. In November 1941 this was increased to 3oz, but dropped back to 2oz two months later, where it mostly remained until it went off ration in May 1954.

Fatty meat could be a source of cooking fat. **Home Companion**, in June 1943, suggested that you: *'trim the fat off before you cook it, and when you have a goodly amount saved up, pop all the bits in a deep pan, cover with water and stew very gently. Set aside to cool, then spoon off the thick layer that has formed – you've got the very thing there for your fish and chip fries!'*, while **Housewife**, October 1940, suggested: *'Cut the*

Making the FAT RATION go further

1 The use of *potato* in dishes reduces the quantity of fat required and, provided potato is used in moderation, the result is satisfactory.

Use potato in :—

(*a*) Pastry.	See War Cookery Leaflet No. 3.
(*b*) Scones.	See War Cookery Leaflet No. 3.
(*c*) Puddings.	See War Cookery Leaflet No. 13.
(*d*) Cakes.	See below.

fat off cutlets, breast of lamb, etc. Put it into a tin and run it down into dripping in a hot oven. Use the fat that runs out for pastry and cakes. The remaining pieces of fat are now brown and chippy. Sprinkle some rice flour or ground rice over this and chop it up as small as possible. Then use as suet.'

Left
Mazawattee tea advert from 1939; note the 'hermetically sealed' 'gas-proof' tin.

Above
Ministry of Food leaflet, *Making the Fat Ration go Further*. People were advised to render down fatty meat or bacon, while the publishers of **Goats** magazine recommended frying bacon in goat's milk!

Or you could cut out fat altogether by using water instead of fat when roasting the Sunday joint, which, you were told, would make the joint more tender. *'The natural juices of the meat mix more easily with water, making gravy more nourishing and digestible.'*

All these things went on ration in just under seven months, but after the rationing of cooking fat, no new items were added for the next eight months.

preserves

On 17 March 1941 jam, marmalade, treacle and syrup went on ration at a total of 8oz a month. A full month's ration was issued for March, although there were only two weeks of the month left. This was doubled to 1lb a month at the end of July. On 20 October mincemeat was included, and fruit curd and honey were added on 15 May 1942, while on 26 July, treacle and syrup were transferred to the points system. From 25 June 1943 the preserve ration could be taken as an equivalent weight of sugar if preferred.

The basic problem which necessitated preserve rationing was the sugar content, although with some preserves, such as marmalade and lemon curd, the fruits involved were in extreme shortage. Experiments showed that fruit acids were partially neutralised by sodium bicarbonate, thus requiring less sugar to make them palatable; half a teaspoonful per pound of raw fruit was recommended. Further savings of sugar could be made by making two separate batches of jam, one, for immediate use,

HARTLEY'S REPLACE FAMOUS MARMALADE *with* **ALL-ORANGE WARTIME SPECIAL**

The Ministry of Food decrees that we must not manufacture any more of our world-famous Aintree Marmalade this year. But we are all ready with a really first-rate wartime marmalade in the best Hartley home-made tradition. Half the oranges in this new marmalade are the finest that come from Seville, the other half being sweet. These, blended with sugar, ensure the very best product that can be made to-day.

So remember to look out for the green label—and remember, too, that delicious as the new marmalade is, we're looking forward to seeing Aintree Marmalade back on our breakfast table just as much as you are!

Above
Advert for Hartley's wartime marmalade. Shortages of fruit and sugar made jams and preserves short, and in 1941, they too went 'on the ration'.

made using only ¾lb sugar to 1lb of fruit, and one, with the normal 1lb fruit to 1lb sugar, for storing.

Oranges soon became a rarity, and with them marmalade. One tip for eking out any marmalade you had was to dissolve an orange jelly, and while still hot, to add a 1lb jar of marmalade to it. This would give you nearly three times the amount you started with.

This is a recipe for *'Mock Lemon Curd'* from the Ministry of Food Leaflet no. 6: *Carried Meals, Snacks and Sandwiches*

Mock Lemon Curd For 4

2oz custard powder or cornflour

1½ gills water

1 pinch bicarb. soda

Lemon substitute to flavour

2 tablets saccharin

½oz margarine

Blend the cornflour with a little water, boil up the rest of the liquid, and pour over the blended cornflour. Return to the pan. Boil and cook for 2–3 minutes. Crush the saccharin tablets and stir in until dissolved. Add the flavourings and margarine and bicarb. Beat well and use when cold.

And when you had made the jam, you weren't quite finished; to get everything possible you were told to boil some water in the pan, then strain carefully; this would give you a *'really delicious fruit drink, much appreciated by the kiddies'*. Home Chat, August 1944.

There were tips for using less jam in making a tart or pie; only half the quantity of jam would be needed if a layer of cooked rice was spread on the bottom with the jam on top. Alternatively the jam would go further in pies if it was heated and mixed with a little of the syrup from tinned fruit.

Once made the jam could not be allowed to go mouldy. One tip was to cut rounds of tissue paper the size of the jam-jars, soak the tissue rounds separately in vinegar, and then place on top of the jam, under the lid. Should this or other precautions fail, mouldy jam was not to be wasted; skim the top, put the rest into a pan and boil up again.

As with any shortage item, alternatives were suggested. One of these was a sandwich filling with national or wholemeal bread, made by finely grating six medium carrots, then adding two teaspoonfuls of cocoa and a nut of margarine, and mixing well together.

Below

Brown & Polson advert from November 1943. Like many wartime words, the use here of 'plenty' was relative, and refers to autumn being the jam-making season.

'B & P' COOKERY CORNER

PLENTY OF JAM NOW !
Victoria Puddings with Jam Sauce

3 oz. fat, 1 oz. sugar, 1 level tablespoon dried egg, 2 tablespoons plum jam, 6 oz. flour, 1 teaspoon household milk, water.

Beat the fat, sugar and dried egg together till soft and creamy; add the jam and beat again. Add the flour and household milk sifted together, and enough water to make a fairly soft consistency.
Half-fill some greased dariol tins; put into a steamer, cover with greased paper and steam about 45 minutes.

Serve with JAM SAUCE: ½ pint water, 2 tablespoons plum jam, ¼ oz. sugar, 1 level tablespoon Brown & Polson Cornflour.

Put the water, jam and sugar into a saucepan and boil for 3 minutes; strain and return to the pan. Add the cornflour mixed smoothly with a little cold water, stir till boiling and boil for 1 minute. Add a little pink colouring, if liked.

⸱⸱ For advice on cookery problems write to Mrs. Jean Scott, Cookery Service Dept., 20, Stratford Place, London, W.1.

BROWN & POLSON
CORNFLOUR
HAS HELPED HOUSEWIVES FOR A HUNDRED YEARS
Issued by Brown & Polson, Ltd.

cheese

On 5 May 1941 cheese was rationed at the miniscule rate of 1oz. This was doubled to 2oz on 30 June, and raised to 3oz on 25 August 1941. At the same time a supplementary cheese ration of 8oz was introduced for agricultural workers, miners and other heavy workers, this extra ration rising on 10 December to 12oz. Like milk, the supply of cheese, and hence the ration, varied seasonally; over the next year the general ration rose to 4oz in June, then to 8oz in July, falling to 6oz in January, 4oz in February and 3oz in May. Over the same period the special ration rose to 16oz before dropping to 12oz. Cheese eventually went off ration in May 1954.

When the first ration was announced at 1oz, shopkeepers protested; it was impossible to measure this amount accurately, especially for dozens, or even hundreds, of customers. The Ministry gave way and allowed them to issue a month's ration at a time. Registered vegetarians, including Orthodox Jews and Moslems, were given extra cheese instead of meat. To register you had to have a certificate signed by a doctor and a minister of religion.

With such a small general ration it was important to make the most of your cheese. One tip when cooking with cheese was to add a dash of curry powder to the cheese; this meant that you would need only half the amount of cheese. And you certainly couldn't afford to let the cheese go mouldy; as with jam, vinegar was the answer – cheese would keep fresh if wrapped in muslin wrung out in vinegar, while in hot weather it would not become greasy on the surface if wrapped in a clean damp cloth and kept in the cool.

You could, of course, make your own cheese if you had enough milk. **Housewife** magazine, in December 1944, gave the following instructions for making cheese from household powdered milk: *'First mix a cup of dried milk (4 tablespoonsful powder to 1 cup of water) and cover with cheesecloth and place in a warm spot to sour. Do not disturb during the souring. When ready it should be quite solid.*

Next mix a quart of milk (1 cup powdered milk to 4 of freshly boiled, tepid water). Stir in the first cup. Cover and stand aside to set as before. When you have a firm smooth curd, put it in a double boiler, or basin over hot water, and heat slowly, stirring up from bottom with a wooden spoon. At slightly over body heat remove from fire and boiler. Pour into cheesecloth square and hang to drain, approximately three hours.'

milk

In July 1940, the National Milk Scheme started. Under the scheme children below the age of five and expectant and nursing mothers were supplied with a pint of milk a day, either free, or at 2d a pint, depending on their means. What milk was left over was shared by suppliers among the remainder of their customers, averaging about three pints a week each. You had to register with a milk supplier, normally the milkman who made deliveries in your road. There would have been little choice in this – in order to save manpower, roads were divided up by the various dairies so each had its 'own' streets. Commercial production of ice cream and cream were prohibited.

As usual, alternatives were sought, in this case condensed milk, and as usual these alternatives in turn went into short supply; from 1 September 1940 the distribution of condensed milk became controlled with supplies to retailers limited, being based on past sales.

distribution schemes

Distribution schemes were a form of rationing where existing stocks would be shared out among consumers on a local or national basis. This was not always done equally, as some people were considered 'priority cases'. These would be children or the sick, who were given a set amount, and once this was done the rest would be divided among everyone else.

Left
Soft cheese advert from March 1940, promoting soft cheese as an alternative to butter. But cheese, too, would be rationed just over a year later.

Above
Ministry of Food publicity shot showing a woman using the new powdered egg from the USA. (HMSO)

please leave
extra MILK
for me

THE ESSENTIAL FOOD
FOR
GROWING CHILDREN

MILK

 ISSUED BY THE MINISTRY OF FOOD

PRINTED FOR H.M. STATIONERY OFFICE BY THOS. FORMAN & SONS LTD., NOTTINGHAM. 51-2632

In mid-April 1941, the general supply of milk was cut by one-seventh under the Milk Restriction Scheme, although this did not apply to the priority cases, now joined by 'invalids' who, on production of a doctor's certificate, were entitled to up to fourteen pints a week. On 1 October, this scheme gave way to the Milk Distribution Scheme, under which children under one year old received fourteen pints a week; expectant mothers and the under-sixes continued to receive seven pints (nursing mothers were now excluded), children between six and eighteen years old, half a pint and invalids seven or fourteen pints. Again, whatever was left over was shared out, although now on a national rather than a local basis, supplemented by condensed milk.

From November 1941 National Household Milk (dried milk) was introduced. This was imported from America, dried, to save shipping space. It came in tins, containing the equivalent of seven pints of milk, in two types; partly skimmed (half cream with vitamin D added) printed in red on the tin, and full cream (also with vitamin D added), printed in blue. Wartime tins were headed 'Ministry of Food', while post-war versions were titled 'Welfare Foods'. That month evaporated milk from America began to be used to supplement liquid milk supplies at the rate of one tin per customer per month, continuing until February 1942.

From March 1942 condensed milk was put on points (it was available points free on production of a medical certificate, for premature and sick infants under six months of age), as general milk supplies were raised, first to two-and-a-half pints a week, then to three. In May all restrictions on the supply of liquid milk were suspended, and the supply of National Household Milk discontinued, while people who lived in remote areas and who could not obtain supplies of liquid milk were permitted to obtain condensed milk points-free. Then, at the end of August, milk restrictions were reintroduced, at the rate of three pints a week for non-priority cases. This would continue to be the pattern of milk supply, becoming increasingly tight throughout the winter, then easing substantially to mid-summer.

Left

Ministry of Food poster promoting extra milk for children. The Ministry under Lord Woolton was determined that rationing would ensure that children got everything they needed to grow fit and healthy.

Above

Ministry of Food advert for the new powdered eggs and milk, shipped from the USA, showing how bringing them over in powdered form saved much-needed shipping space.

Every drop of milk was precious; you were encouraged to rinse out used milk bottles with a little water. This could then be used to make up the required amount for sauces, cakes and puddings. Allowing milk to go sour was a sin, but as ever there were tips for this; in hot weather milk could be kept from turning sour by a small piece of horseradish put into it in the morning, or by stirring a quarter of a teaspoonful of bicarbonate of soda into a pint of milk.

Should you still have sour milk in spite of these precautions, all was not lost. You could make 'an acceptable drink' for a hot day. [The word 'acceptable' here sounds very suspicious.] Put half sour milk and half water together, then shake well. Alternatively you could take a pint of sour milk, add sufficient sugar to sweeten, beat with an egg and whisk for five minutes, then add a few drops of flavouring essence, such as vanilla, strawberry or ginger.

Sour milk could also be used to make scones, cakes, Yorkshire pudding and milk [cream] cheese. For the latter, pour the sour milk into a muslin bag, tie it up and leave to drip overnight. Next day, turn the curd into a basin, beat well with a wooden spoon, season with salt and pepper. Finely chopped onion or chives could be added according to taste. A flavouring of sage also gives a happy variation. Make into a neat pat and put it on to a square of muslin, big enough to fold over and completely cover the cheese. Leave standing in a cold place until required.

A variation was to strain the milk in the muslin bag as for cream cheese, then add a little mustard, pepper, salt and Worcester sauce according to taste and spread on slices of toast. Grill until brown.

Home Chat magazine in August 1944 suggested you: *'Cut stale bread into thin slices and sandwich them with a layer of cream cheese made from the sour milk. Make a batter with two ounces of flour, one dried egg, and a little household milk. Dip the sandwiches into the batter and fry a golden brown in hot fat. Drain on paper and dust with pepper and salt.'*

Or you could make 'White Custard'. To do this you had to whisk the sour milk well; it must be a complete clot. Add sugar and vanilla, whisk again. Then serve. Alternatively you could add a dessert-spoonful of raspberry jam instead of the vanilla.

Even burnt milk was not to be wasted; this could be mixed with a little cocoa and cornflour to make a chocolate blancmange in which the burnt taste would not be noticed.

And if you had no milk, a solution of 1 table-spoonful of oatmeal to a pint of water, boiled and left to cool, was recommended as a substitute for milk when making plain cakes and scones. Cold coffee could be used in place of milk when making gingerbread, spiced fruit cake, and steamed ginger or chocolate puddings.

eggs

At the end of May 1941 Lord Woolton announced that eggs and fish were to be rationed. In the event, neither happened, but at the end of June a distribution scheme was introduced; under this people would receive one egg a week if available, but it was often only one every two weeks. (In 1942 each registered customer received 29 eggs, in 1943, 30).

In November 1941 a priority scheme, similar to that for milk, was introduced. The priority cases were nursing mothers (for six months after the birth), expectant mothers, invalids and child's ration book holders. These would receive four eggs for every one for the general public. Egg shortages had already led many people to keep poultry in their back garden; they were asked not to register for the distribution scheme, but they were not barred from doing so.

On 24 June 1942 American powdered eggs were made available to domestic consumers. Each customer registered under the egg scheme was allocated one packet of dried eggs, equivalent to twelve eggs, costing 1s 9d; this had to last until October. Poultry-keepers were now barred from receiving shell-eggs, but not dried eggs, from suppliers. Indeed, if you produced more than a few eggs, you had to become the supplier for your family and neighbours who registered with you. Poultry feed was rationed, individual allowances being tied to the number of registrations.

As usual, tips abounded. Dropping a pin in the water when boiling eggs stops the cracked ones oozing out. You could make an egg go three or four times as far by mixing as for scrambling and adding cold cooked rice, bread soaked in milk and cold mashed potatoes or oatmeal.

The arrival of dried egg called for new cooking methods and tips; when making omelettes and scrambled eggs the addition of a pinch of baking powder was said to make them far lighter.

Above
'For the monthly egg' – this caption for a home-knitted egg-cosy from **Stitchcraft** magazine – says it all!

Right
Ministry of Food advert from 1944 encouraging the use of dried eggs.

NO EGG SHORTAGE

—a dozen a month for everybody!

SOME TIPS ON MAKING DELICIOUS EGG DISHES

" Take a dozen eggs," said Mrs. Beeton. Well, the present allowance of dried eggs means a dozen eggs a *week* for the average family, more than most people used before the war !

Remember that dried eggs are new-laid shell eggs with only the shell and the water taken away.

Make an omelette by allowing 3 or 4 eggs for two people. " Reconstitute " the eggs, add seasoning, beat well, and cook in smoking hot fat until all the egg is set. Cook it *quickly*, and don't overcook.

When making cakes and puddings, add the eggs *dry* to the other ingredients and add the water afterwards. Eggs are a grand nourishing food for children and dried eggs have the full nutritional value of shell eggs.

Don't mix dried eggs with water till you are ready to use them.

A packet of 12 Dried Eggs costs only 1/3d.

Issued by the Ministry of Food, London, W.1

GOODALL, BACKHOUSE & CO., LTD., LEEDS

Ideal Home magazine, in December 1943, recommended: *'Reconstitute dried egg (one table-spoonful per person) preferably with milk instead of water, then scramble lightly. Put in bowl, add 1 tablespoonful flour, a little finely chopped chives or spring onion, 1 teaspoonful milk, pepper, salt and juice of a tomato, and mix well together. If not firm enough add a little more flour. Shape into croquettes, dip each in flour, then in a little milk, and then in breadcrumbs, as for fried fish. Fry quickly in hot fat.'*

Eggs are an ingredient for many recipes, so alternatives were keenly sought; for fish cakes use tapioca that has been put in water sufficiently long to make it a jelly instead of eggs to bind the ingredients. For recipes which require several eggs use one egg and make up with cornflour,

while you could use grated carrot instead of eggs in batter pudding.

The light, eggless cake was a wartime quest; tips here included using your oven slightly hotter than usual, or using gelatine as a substitute for eggs, while a teaspoonful of sugar dissolved in a little milk would make an effective substitute for glazing cakes, buns, and scones.

onions

Onions became a real scarcity with the fall of France and the Channel Isles in the summer of 1940, when, famously, they were given as raffle prizes. For a while they were virtually impossible to get hold of, but home production soon began to fill the gap. By the following summer's harvest domestic production was high enough to permit the introduction of an onion distribution scheme in September 1941, when consumers were asked to register with a retailer. At the end of October there was a distribution of 1lb per head, reserved for seven days, after which what remained were sold on a first-come first-served basis. Those who grew their own onions were asked not to take up this allowance, although there was no compulsion. Each September for the next two years a similar distribution took place, but by 1944, home production was so high that the scheme was dropped.

Far Left
Advert from November 1942, for Goodall's products; note the egg substitute powder which 'contains no eggs' and the batter mix which requires no 'eggs, flour or butter'.

Left
No eggs, less sugar and no points required – the wartime housewife's dream!

To make onions go further, you were told to add one or two onions to a pot roast. When the roast was cooked, the fat was poured into a jar to produce onion-flavoured dripping, for flavouring. Onion skins were also used for flavouring, dried in the oven and when brittle, powdered in your hands and stored in airtight jars. A teaspoonful of grated onion, added to a stew when it was ready and simmered for one minute, would give as much flavour as a whole onion cooked with the stew. In the absence of any onions, you could use a small tin of onion soup, made thicker with flour and a small amount of margarine.

When you could get them, **1001 Household**

I was front-page news a year ago . . . more precious than gold to those lucky enough to get a pound of me. That was because you relied on having me brought to you from abroad. Yet, if women and older children, as well as men, are sensible enough to Dig for Victory now, you can have me ALL THE YEAR ROUND for only the cost of a packet of seeds . . .

YOU SEE, I AM ONE OF THOSE CROPS YOU CAN STORE

DIG FOR VICTORY NOW!

★ ★ ★ *If you haven't a garden, ask your Local Council for an allotment. Send NOW for Free pictorial leaflets "HOW TO DIG" and "HOW TO CROP" to Dept. A.103, Ministry of Agriculture, Hotel Lindum, St. Annes-on-Sea, Lancs.*

ISSUED BY THE MINISTRY OF AGRICULTURE

Hints suggested '*Onions are lovely baked whole in the oven with a kidney inside. A kidney can also be baked inside a large raw potato. Season well, place in a hollow between the two halves of the potato, and cook slowly. All the blood from the kidney soaks into the potato and tastes delicious.*'

oranges

In May 1941, the distribution of oranges was limited to areas which had suffered heavy bombing. At the end of September priority was given to holders of the child's ration book for seven days, with a maximum of 1lb per customer noted in the back of the book; in December this was shortened to five days. In October 1942, the priority allowance was raised to 2lb for each holder of the child's book, while holders of the blue, junior book were now entitled to 1lb. In July 1943 expectant mothers became a priority. The first general allocation was not until February 1944, when even lemons were available in some districts.

In **William Carries On** (1942), William Brown needs a lemon: *"'Lemons?' said Mrs. Brown as if she could hardly believe her ears. "Lemons? I hardly remember what they look like."*
"There's a picture of 'em in the 'cyclopaedia," said William helpfully.
"I don't think I even want to remember what they look like," said Mrs. Brown bitterly. "No, I've not seen one for weeks."
"If you wanted to get hold of one," said William, "how would you start?"
"I shouldn't," said Mrs. Brown. "I've given it up. After all, it's no use breaking one's heart over a lemon."

During 1940, onions, an integral part of much 1940s cooking, became really scarce, as most were imported from the continent, now German-occupied. But by 1941, the Dig for Victory scheme had stepped in to fill the gap.

Oranges were extremely rare, and when they could be found were sold singly, 'for children only'. (HMSO)

"But suppose you had to have one," said William, "what would you do?"
"I shouldn't do anything," said Mrs. Brown. "What with onions and eggs, and icing sugar and cream I've just given it up. There's nothing one can do."

points rationing

On 11 March 1941 the 'Lend-Lease' Bill was passed in the USA. Goods from America began to flood into Britain, including food. Dried milk and eggs, tinned fruit, meat and fish, and things new to the British public: Spam, Mor and Soya flour. These could not be rationed – there wasn't enough for everyone to be guaranteed a share, and supplies were erratic. A new form of rationing had to be used. The system used for clothes rationing provided the solution. Everyone would receive a certain number of 'points' each month in a separate pink ration book, commonly called the 'pink 'un', which they

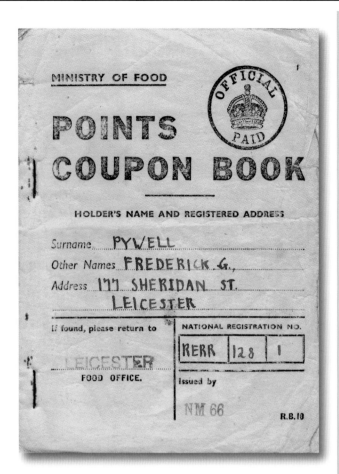

height in April 1942, this went up to twenty-four, but normally the allowance was twenty.

The introduction of the scheme was to take place on what was dubbed by the Ministry of Food 'Points Day'. This was planned for 17 November 1941, but was delayed until 1 December by a problem which was to plague the scheme: the shortage of points goods actually available in the shops. The Ministry did not want Points Day to be a damp squib, so the launch was delayed in order to build up stocks, during which time the Ministry stopped the sale of canned meats, beans and fish, the first points items. This gave it the added bonus that when the scheme began it included items which had not been available for some time.

The scheme was surprisingly popular. Rationing had turned the housewife into someone who picked up the allotted rations; the points scheme reintroduced an element of choice in shopping. You could buy several small items, or save up for a special treat.

The list of points items continued to grow; in January 1942 rice, sago, tapioca, dried fruit and canned peas went on points, joined one month later by canned fruit and tomatoes, in April by breakfast cereals and condensed milk, in August, biscuits, treacle and syrup and in December, oat flakes. Points rationing came to an end in May 1950.

could use in any shop, on a range of shortage items, each having its own points value. One of the great advantages to the scheme was that the government could quickly vary the points required for various items as supplies/stocks fluctuated, and items could go 'on points', or become 'points free'. Further, the allocation of points could also fluctuate: the original points allocation was sixteen a month, at its

Left
Breakfast cereals were 'on points' – 3 coupons a packet in the case of Shredded Wheat in December 1944.

Right
Chocolate is scarce, says this advert for Caley's chocolates from December 1941. Within a year they would be on ration, and a box like this almost unprocurable.

Share your **CALEY CHOCOLATES** this Christmas

Chocolate is scarce . . . but Caley's make the best of it !

Treacle Honeycomb

3 cups treacle or golden syrup

¼ cup water

1 tablespoonful vinegar

1 cup granulated sugar

1 teaspoonful baking soda

1 teaspoonful lemon essence

Method: Put the treacle or golden syrup, sugar, water and vinegar into a large pan and boil until a little turns brittle when dropped into cold water. Stir in the soda. This will make the mixture foam and rise in the pan so it is important to use a large saucepan. Add the lemon essence. Pour mixture into greased tins so as to form thin layers.

Old-Fashioned Ginger Tablet

4 tablespoonfuls sugar

2 tablespoonfuls heated golden syrup in a breakfast cup and sufficient milk to fill the cup

2oz margarine

1 dessertspoonful ground ginger, or a little more or less according to taste

Method: Put the milk, golden syrup, and margarine in a saucepan. Mix the ground ginger with the sugar and add. Bring gently to the boil and boil for 12 minutes. Remove from the fire and beat mixture until it gets sugary. Pour into a well-greased tin.

Milk Chocolate

2 dessertspoonfuls golden syrup

2 heaped teaspoonfuls cocoa

2 dessertspoonfuls milk

Method: Warm the syrup until it runs like water. Mix the cocoa and the dried milk well together, then pour on the syrup. Beat together thoroughly. Spread mixture on a greased tin. When quite cold, remove from tin and cut into squares.

sweets

Not exactly food, sweet rationing was introduced on 26 July 1942 at a rate of 2oz. A separate ration book, called the 'Personal Points' book, actually more accurately a card, was used for this. In August the ration was doubled to 16oz a month, dropping in October to 12oz a month. From July 1943, the personal points coupons were contained in the food ration book. In February 1951 rationing was lifted, although this proved short term. Sweet rationing was eventually abolished in February 1953.

In October 1943 **Home Companion** commented: *This rationing of sweets is fine. It ensures that we all get our share. Just the same, particularly where there are children, or you're giving them a party, it's good to have some simple and economical recipes for extras.'* It went on to give recipes for home-made sweets (see box).

The government recommended carrots as an alternative to sweets, while many women used their ration as 'treats' for shopkeepers, hoping for a little 'under the counter' food in response. Chocolate makers produced 'ration' bars of just the right size, Mars Bars advised consumers to cut them into slices to make them go further, while Barratts produced the 'Ration bag' containing three ounces of mixed sweets and a small toy – later this would be renamed the 'Jamboree bag'. Children tended to go for sweets from the jar, and hundreds and thousands were popular as they could be eked out, as were 'pips'. One alternative was off-ration cough sweets.

non-rationed food

Of course not all food was rationed. Some of it, like bananas, was almost impossible to get, some, like potatoes, was reasonably plentiful, and the government encouraged their use.

bread

THIN SLICES MAKE HoVIS go further!
BEST BAKERS BAKE IT
Macclesfield

Bread, 'the staff of life', had been a central part of the nation's diet since time immemorial. Whether it be for breakfast toast, sandwiches for lunch or afternoon tea, or bread and butter with dinner, bread was a part of almost any meal; in 1945 bread made up 20% by weight of all food eaten in Britain! The rationing of butter in January 1940 hit this hard, but conversely, the rationing of other foods served to encourage the consumption of bread. Yet home production of wheat could not in any way match the demand for bread.

A Ministry of Information booklet, **Civilian Supplies in Wartime,** described the problem: *'Before the war white bread, which was eaten by almost everybody, was made from flour from which all the bran and most of the wheat germ (which contains most of the Vitamin B and iron present in wheat) had been extracted. The deterioration of the shipping situation during 1940 made it desirable to increase as far as possible the percentage of flour extracted in milling and, at the same time, the nutritional value of the loaf, and in March 1941 the National Wheatmeal Loaf was put on the market, made of flour of 85% extraction instead of the normal 73%. In spite of much propaganda the loaf was not widely popular and many bakers did not find it worthwhile to make it.'* At the same time bread prices were brought under government control.

Woman magazine of October 1941 advised: *'To save crumbling the bread when cutting a new loaf, dip the bread knife into boiling water before slicing the loaf.'*

Only 14% of bread sales were for brown bread; in response, the Ministry of Food started experiments in the fortification of white bread by the addition of vitamin B1. However, the worsening of the shipping situation demanded drastic measures; on 11 March 1942 Lord Woolton announced that all flour production must henceforth be of the 'national wheatmeal' variety, known as 'national flour'. Advice was that when using national flour you should use a little more liquid than usual for mixing, allow a little longer for baking, steaming or boiling, extra pan greasing was required and a little more seasoning.

Production of white bread was prohibited from 6 April, except under special licence, and only those with a doctor's certificate could purchase it. This was not always as difficult as it sounds. The film **Waterloo Road** (1944) clearly shows how easy it was to find a doctor who, for suitable remuneration, would issue one. Yet most people, grudgingly or otherwise, accepted the new bread as yet another of the trials of total war, and the changeover released 600,000 tons of shipping for other purposes.

Civilian Supplies in Wartime continued, *'For a period it was necessary to conserve shipping space still further by the addition of a small proportion of home-grown rye, oats, and barley to the loaf, but these admixtures are now no longer necessary. The loaf is now [December 1945] composed of flour of 80% extraction which, however, still retains the greater part of the vitamin and mineral content of the wheat.'*

'To waste bread in these days is nothing short of a crime,' declared **Practical Hints in War Time**, *'yet its composition now is such that it soon becomes stale and unappetising. To make old bread new again, sprinkle it with a little cold water; then put it in a cloth that has been dipped in water and well wrung out, and place it in a hot oven for about ten minutes. At the end of the time, take off the cloth and put the bread back in the oven for five minutes. The bread will now be crisp and equal to new.'*

Another tip for stale bread, from the **Home Companion** of June 1943, advised: *'Cut it into wafer slices, and when you've next got the oven on, pop them on a baking sheet and leave them in at the bottom. Leave till the toast is brittle and a crispy*

Ask for NATIONAL WHEATMEAL BREAD *it saves shipping!*

brown, when you can take it out, cool and store away in tins. Melba toast is delicious spread with your breakfast marmalade.' **1001 Household Hints** suggested *'Crusts left over when making sandwiches should be toasted in the oven with a little salt sprinkled over them. They make a delicious accompaniment to soup or mince.'* It was pointed out that oatmeal could be used in place of part of the flour in biscuits, cakes, and scones. It was also suggested that you mix oatmeal into your week's supply of flour, at the rate of three parts flour to one of oatmeal, although this mixture would not keep so well as plain flour.

There were ways to keep bread fresh; one suggestion was to put one or two small potatoes, washed and dried but not peeled, in the bread basket to keep it moist and fresh. But stale bread could also be ground into breadcrumbs, for use in cooking, or, as an alternative when frying fish or cutlets, you could use coarse oatmeal instead of breadcrumbs. Bread itself could be an alternative to pastry, as in this recipe for 'Cold Fruit Pudding' from **Woman & Home**, of July 1942.

Cold Fruit Pudding

Ingredients:
1lb rhubarb or other seasonal fruit
¼ pt water
Sugar to taste
Bread – as required
Custard

• Wipe the sticks of rhubarb with a damp cloth, trim off the green leaves, then slice the fruit into small pieces and weigh. Stew it with the water until tender, adding sugar to taste.

• Cut slices of bread one-third of an inch thick, then trim them into convenient-sized pieces for lining the dish. Either a basin or soufflé dish may be used. You will require one which holds 1¼ pints.

• Fit portions of bread round the side of the dish, then line the base, using the trimmings to fill up the gaps. It is better to remove the crust when lining the sides, as the bread is more pliable without the crust. The crusts may he used up if required to fill up odd spaces, or some may be cut into small pieces and put into the centre with the hot fruit.

• When the fruit is cooked, pour off some of the juice, then pour the boiling fruit into the prepared dish. Cover the fruit with bread, then stand the pudding on a dish, with a plate or saucer on the top, and leave it for twenty-four hours, with a weight on top to keep it pressed.

• When the pudding is ready, turn it out on to a dish, pour some custard over it, and serve the remainder in a sauce boat. Serve the left-over juice from the fruit with the pudding.

During the blitz, when long hours were spent in the shelter, sandwiches became a way of life. Many people had traditionally gone home for lunch, but with the war this became impossible; lunch breaks became shorter and travelling far more difficult. For some this meant subsidised meals in the works canteen or the British restaurant, for many others it meant sandwiches. Sandwich spread recipes abounded to make this more interesting. **Mother & Home** magazine, of February 1942, recommended these made-without-butter sandwiches:

Cold mashed potato spread on wheatmeal bread and sprinkled with a suggestion of chopped bacon.
Peanut butter spread on brown bread with a flaking of kipper.
Cheese spread with grated raw carrot.
Fish paste or dripping on hot toast.
Cheese spread and chutney.

Cheese, of course, was tightly rationed. **The Home Companion** of May 1943 gave this recipe for a spread made out of odds and ends of left-over cheese. *'First grate your cheese finely, and when you've got four ounces done, add to it half an ounce of margarine, a dash of nutmeg and a small teaspoonful of Worcester sauce. Mix well with a fork, then pot.'* **101 Ways to Save Money in Wartime** gave another, recommending *'Cooked sieved butter beans mixed with a little melted margarine and finely grated cheese to flavour. Season rather liberally with salt, pepper and made mustard, and use as required.'*

The booklet gave recipes for other spreads, including pea spread, made from canned peas, mashed and mixed with any kind of flavouring – sardines, Marmite, cheese or chutney. Another unusual filling was parsnip paste, made with 1lb of boiled parsnips, mashed with 2oz of margarine, with salt, pepper and Bovril or Marmite added. Then there was home-made fish paste, made from cooked minced haricot or butter beans, flavoured with anchovy essence. One last surprise filling was 'Cole Slaw': *'Mix finely shredded crisp white cabbage with a good curry sauce.'*

Precious
CRUSTS

No scrap of bread is too small to save— it means saving valuable shipping space. Of course your best and most direct way of helping, is to take less bread into the house. Most households find they can do nicely with three-quarters of the bread they used to buy and yet can give every member of the family all the bread he or she individually needs.

The secret is in eating up every scrap of bread that comes in. Don't forget the end of the loaf. It's the bit that's apt to get left over. You always intended to do something with it. But how often was it thrown out, after all! Half a slice of stale bread saved by everyone in this country every day, means a convoy of 30 ships a year freed to take munitions or men to our fighting fronts. If you explain this to your family you'll find them eager enough to help you save on bread !

Save Bread : Save Ships
4 things you can do

1 **Cut down your purchase (or making) of bread.** Most households find they can do nicely with three-quarters of the bread they used to buy.

2 Put the loaf on the dresser or side table. Cut only as required.

3 Use every crumb.

4 Don't eat bread whilst potatoes are on the table.

Some ways of using up STALE BREAD

CRISPY PIE-CRUSTS. Cut bread into dice ⅓ in. thick. Cover a savoury pie with them, setting the dice closely together. Pour over them a little thin custard (salted) taking care that every piece of bread is moistened. Bake in a brisk oven.

SOAKED BREAD. This is the foundation of a countless number of puddings and cakes. No bread is too stale for it, and there is no need to remove any crust. Break into small pieces, put into bowl, cover completely with cold water and soak thoroughly. If the bread is to be used for a savoury, use vegetable boilings instead of water. Then squeeze the bread hard, put back in the bowl and beat with a fork until quite free from lumps and pieces of crust. The beating is most important and makes all the difference between a dull heavy pudding and a smooth, spongy texture.

MINCED SLICES. Mix 8 ozs. mince with 4 ozs. cooked mashed potatoes and 4 ozs. fine crumbs. Season to taste. Roll out on a floured board into an oblong ½ in. thick. Cut into slices and fry in a very little hot fat or grill for 5 to 7 minutes. Serve with leek sauce.

MAKING RUSKS. Cut bread into neat figures, or fancy shapes, about ½ in. thick. Bake in a warm oven until crisp and golden brown. Pack in an air-tight tin. This is a valuable emergency store which will keep good for months.

TURN WASTE INTO DELICACIES!

ISSUED BY THE MINISTRY OF FOOD

Above
Even stale bread and crusts were too precious to be wasted – you could be prosecuted for feeding them to the ducks!

potatoes

Potatoes were one of the few things which we could grow easily, and in bulk, in Britain. As such they became central to our diet. The Ministry of Food's leaflet *Wartime Food for Growing Children* from 1942 included: *'Don't forget the old potato. It's a grand food, an energy food and to some extent a builder – yes, and a protective food as well, for if you eat plenty of potatoes you make sure of one vitamin at least. And potatoes, by the way, don't need shipping space.'* Eating potatoes instead of an imported product was continually touted as a way of saving shipping space: *'Eat them in place of bread and other cereals.'* The problem was to make potatoes interesting; to this end the Ministry introduced 'Potato Pete', a cartoon character who had his own recipe book, and even a song.

Recipes abounded, with new ways of cooking potatoes, such as Potato tart from **Housewife** magazine, August 1943: *'This is made with raw potato, and new potatoes would be particularly suitable. Make some pastry, and roll out two rounds of the same size, about a quarter of an inch thick. Cover one of these, leaving a margin round the edge, with round slices of raw potatoes about the size of a half-crown, piling these up until you have a heap about an inch high, and seasoning each layer of potato slices very lightly with salt and pepper. Put the other round of pastry on top, and close the edges all round, first wetting them slightly and then pinching them together. Bake the tart slowly for an hour, then take off the top, and pour in some reconstituted dried egg powder, to which you have added a little milk or, better, cream off the top of the milk. For a tart large enough for four, a level tablespoonful of the powder mixed with three tablespoonfuls of milk should be enough. Put on the top again, and bake just long enough for the egg mixture to set, about ten minutes or so, and then serve hot. It may be found easier to do this if you use a pastry-lined plate, as the top will be more conveniently removable.'*

Below
Advert for Potato Pete's recipe book, containing lots of ideas for ways of cooking potatoes.

"STEP LIVELY WITH ME" says Potato Pete

You get the *extra energy* you need in wartime from potatoes. They guard you against illness too. Don't just serve potatoes once a day, cook them often and buy less bread. Give the family such tasty dishes as Floddies for supper or Potato Pancake for dinner. There are so many easy dishes to make — and they're all energy-givers.

POTATO PANCAKE

Cooking time : 20 minutes. *Ingredients :* 1 lb. mashed potatoes, ½ lb. cooked carrot, milk, salt and pepper. *Method :* Whip the mashed potato to a loose creamy consistency with a little milk. Season well with salt and pepper, add diced cooked carrot. Pan-fry slowly in very little fat until crisp and brown.

FREE—ask at any of the Food Advice Centres or Bureaux for a free copy of the Potato Pete Recipe Booklet, or write direct to the Ministry of Food, London, W.1.

Potato Pete's recipe book

Potatoes keep you FIGHTING fit

"Potato Pete"

by SONNY MILLER and HUGH CHARLES

IRWIN DASH MUSIC CO. LTD
17 BERNERS ST. LONDON W.1

They could be used in sweet dishes, such as
'Potato Cakes and Jelly'

Half pint Chivers Jelly (made up in the usual way)
4oz cooked potatoes   2oz fat   a little milk

Rub potatoes, flour and fat together. Mix into a stiff paste with a little milk. Roll out thinly, cut with pastry cutter and bake in hot oven. When cold spread each with a little jam (if desired) and cover with chopped jelly. (Chivers Jelly, June 1941)

Every part needed to be used. *'To peel potatoes is wasteful. We should cook them in their skins. The whole of the potato is good food.'* If, however, you did peel them, the peelings could be used in 'Peelings de luxe' (from **101 Ways to Save Money in Wartime**): *'Clean potato peelings, fried crisply in a little dripping, sprinkled with chopped parsley and a little salt and served very hot, make an economical breakfast dish.'*

Potatoes could be used to bulk out shortage foods; the **Home Companion** of 6 March 1943 suggested: *'Next time you buy a tin of salmon, double it by flaking it into mashed potatoes. The two together whisk up into a lovely creamy consistency which you can shape into cakes, flour, and fry up into a tasty savoury dish. Sausage meat can double up too, if you plump it out with spuds.'*

They were not just used as a straight substitute for other food items, but even as a substitute ingredient, as in 'Potato Pastry', used in savoury dishes.

4oz flour   half-teaspoonful baking powder
pinch of salt   2oz dripping
½lb cooked and sieved potatoes

Sieve together flour, baking powder, and salt. Then rub in dripping and potatoes, and form into a stiff paste with a little water. Turn on to a floured board, knead slightly and roll about a quarter of an inch thick.

Turnovers (made with potato pastry) from **Food Facts**, April 1943

Make your pastry in the usual way, but with one-third cold mashed potato – as dry as possible – and two-thirds flour instead of all flour. The fillings will depend on what you have handy. Pop the turnovers in the oven with any other baking you do.

There was even a recipe for a cake mixture using mashed potato (Ministry of Food leaflet: *Making the Fat Ration go Further*)

6oz flour   1½oz sugar
2oz fat   1 teaspoon baking powder
2oz mashed potato   Household milk to mix
1 dried egg, reconstituted

Method: Rub fat into flour, add baking powder, sugar and potatoes. Mix to a stiff consistency with the egg and milk. Turn into a greased tin and bake for 1 hour.

green vegetables

As with potatoes, green vegetables could be successfully grown in this country, either commercially, or in your 'Dig for Victory' garden or allotment. For the latter, the Ministry of Agriculture recommended runner beans, winter greens, leeks, brussels sprouts, parsley, lettuce, carrots, beetroot, turnips, summer cabbage, onions, radishes, peas, summer spinach, and potatoes. Other home crops included broccoli, kale, spring cabbage, red cabbage, and artichokes.

Fruit was short, so vegetables were needed to provide vitamins, particularly A and C. To this end the Ministry of Food encouraged the 'correct' way of cooking vegetables to maximise the vitamin intake.

Cooking Vegetables Correctly

If vegetables are cooked carelessly much of their food value is lost. Their Vitamin C, the fresh fruit vitamin, is easily destroyed by bad cooking. Throwing away the cooking-water also wastes valuable mineral salts and vitamins. So when you cook vegetables follow these rules:

1. Use as fresh as possible. If you grow your own vegetables do not gather them until you actually need them.

2. Wash the vegetables thoroughly, but avoid soaking where possible and never soak for long. Half an hour in cold salted water is enough for even the most tight-hearted cabbage.

3. Scrub root vegetables and scrape them, or if tough-skinned peel thinly. Remove the dark outer leaves of cabbage and use these shredded in soups or stews. Do not throw them away because they contain more of the vitamins and mineral salts than the more tender inner leaves.

4. Slice root vegetables and shred the green ones, break cauliflower into sprigs. They cook more quickly this way.

5. Never drown your vegetables. You need only just enough water to keep the pan from burning – usually a teacupful will do. As less water is used less salt is needed.

6. Cook with the lid on the pan. If you have no lid a plate can be used. This point is important because the vegetables are to be steam boiled and if the steam is allowed to escape the pan will go dry and burn.

7. Boil briskly for 10–15 minutes giving the pan an occasional shake. Old root vegetables may require longer.

8. Drain off any liquid and use for making soups and gravies or thicken with flour (1oz to ½pint) and use as a sauce.

9. Serve the vegetables at once. Keeping hot or re-heating will destroy the vitamin C. Before serving, if you can spare it, add a teaspoonful of margarine to the vegetables and toss well. Old fashioned wasteful methods of cooking vegetables are a danger to health, especially when there is a shortage of fruit. Moreover, correctly cooked vegetables are much nicer to eat than badly cooked ones.

Because of the shortage of fruit, plenty of vegetables, particularly green and red, should be eaten to provide Vitamin A and C in the diet. It is suggested that each day's menu should include:

(a) One serving of potatoes.

(b) Servings of two vegetables, if possible, besides potatoes, one preferably of the green and leafy variety.

(c) A raw vegetable salad (a foundation of raw, shredded cabbage or brussels sprouts or watercress is better nutritionally than lettuce, which has less Vitamin C).

(Ministry of Health Leaflet)

Unlike today, vegetables were very seasonal; salads were for the summer only, so the Ministry worked hard to offer alternatives in the form of raw vegetables. *'Raw vegetables are excellent as sandwich fillings, as alternatives to rationed jam and cheese. Also as salad, served with hot or cold dishes.'*

The **Home Companion** of October 1943 pointed out that *'Sprouts, by the way, are delicious eaten raw sometimes, believe it or not. Grate them finely and mix in a salad with shredded carrots – if you know what's good for you, because this is the sort of supper dish that's certainly going to get you putting a better complexion on life! You know what they say about "a salad a day".'*

Vegetable pie was the classic dish: *'Prepare 1lb of mixed vegetables such as carrots, swedes, celery, sprouts, potatoes. You will also need 1 breakfast cupful of cooked haricot or butter beans. Cut the vegetables into small pieces and arrange them in layers, together with the beans, one layer to each vegetable, in a pie-dish, seasoning each layer with salt and pepper. Pour in a teacupful of stock or vegetable water. Prepare an extra 1lb of potatoes and cut them into neat slices. Arrange the potato slices, overlapping each other, on top of the other vegetables to form a crust. Put on the top a few small pats of dripping. Bake in a moderately hot oven until the top is golden brown, and the vegetables inside are cooked (about three-quarters of an hour)'* (Ministry of Food).

OUR FOOD TODAY

Nº 3

VEGETABLES & SALADS

Left
Ministry of Food leaflet showing ways to serve green vegetables; like potatoes they were plentiful, if somewhat boring.

Above
The Ministry of Food had to work hard to sell a nation used to consuming largely meat and puddings the idea of eating healthier, and more plentiful, fresh vegetables and salads.

Most such recipes were less specific about the vegetables to be used – *'take 1lb of seasonal vegetables'*. The substitution of potato pastry for the sliced potato on top gave you the most famous wartime dish – The Woolton Pie. For those who needed meat, gravy and soup makers suggested adding their product to vegetable pies and stews to give them a meaty taste.

oatmeal

One other home product touted by the Ministry of Food was oatmeal. Traditionally used for porridge and biscuits, the Ministry recommended its use for thickening soups and stews: *'To two pints of soup or stew add 1½ – 2oz of oatmeal. This should be added to the soup or stew about 30 minutes before serving.'* It could also be used in sweets: *'Toast medium or fine oatmeal on a tin in the oven, or beneath the grill, till golden. This makes it tasty and digestible for sprinkling over fruit, stewed or fresh, individual sweets in the same way as chopped nuts.'* Oatmeal could also be used for oat cakes, oatmeal bread, oatmeal stuffing, mealy pudding and Brose: *'Prepare and slice a turnip and a few carrots, or any other vegetables you have. Put in a pan with a meaty bone, cover with water and boil until tender. Put one handful of oatmeal into a bowl (a separate bowl is required for each person) add a pinch of pepper and salt and a small piece of margarine. Now add a ladleful of stock while still boiling, and stir. The amount of stock may be varied to suit the individual taste. The vegetables can be eaten as a second course and the remainder of the stock used for soup the following day.'*

101 Ways to Save Money in Wartime suggested 'Fried Peas': *'Drain the liquid off a tin of peas. Roll them in oatmeal, salted. Fry lightly. Thicken the liquid with pea flour. Flavour with half a meat cube. Pile the fried peas in the middle of the dish, pour around the gravy and surround with mashed potatoes.'*

wild food

Country people had always made use of the wild food thrown up by nature, and even most 'townies' were aware of the glory of blackberry time. However, in wartime, as with all other food, the 'Hedgerow Harvest', as the Ministry of Food called it, had to be utilised to the full, and this meant acquainting town-dwellers with the full range of food which might be gathered from nearby heath or woodland. The Ministry's leaflets pointed out the various elements of the harvest, and gave advice for their use. Some of these were hardly new to the table, such as blackberries and mushrooms; some, like nettles and seaweed, were a strange novelty, too much so for many. Quite a few of the recipes were for extra flavouring, in the form of sauce, ketchup, or jelly, which in a time of (by necessity) plain food, was always welcome.

Mushrooms were hardly new, but many a town-dweller put off picking the delicious wild mushroom by tales of poisoning. **1001 Household Hints** directed: *'To distinguish between mushrooms and poisonous fungi, sprinkle a little salt on the spongy underpart. If this turns yellow they are poisonous. If black, they're wholesome.'*

With a good crop, you might make 'Mushroom

Food for the picking

Blackberrying is a traditional custom that most of us have enjoyed at one time or another. There are other Hedgerow Harvests too, that provide good things for the larder. So why not take the children and go a-harvesting? Be sure, however, that in their excitement they do not damage bushes or hedges, or walk through growing crops, or gather mushrooms, for instance, in fields without getting the farmer's permission.

Elderberries are delicious stewed with half-and-half apple; or made into jam with an equal quantity of blackberries. Wash and strip them from the stems before using.

Sloes look like tiny damsons. They are too sour to use as stewed fruit, but make a delightful preserve with marrow.

Crab Apples. For a drink or flavouring, Crab Apple juice is a good substitute for lemon juice. Put the apples to sweat, choose only the sound ones, take off stalks, beat the fruit to a mash and press the juice through a thick cloth. Leave for a day or two until bubbles appear. Put into clean dry bottles and cork well, securing the cork with wire. Store in a cool place. The juice will be ready in about a month's time.

Rowan-berries (Mountain Ash) make a preserve with a pleasant tang, admirable to serve with cold meats. You can make the preserve of the berries alone, or with a couple of apples to each pound of berries.

Hips and Haws should not be picked until perfectly ripe. Hips—the berries of the wild rose, make a vitamin-rich jam. Haws—the berries of the may-tree, make a brown jelly that is very like guava jelly.

Nuts. Cobnuts, walnuts, chestnuts and filberts are good keepers. Choose very sound,

well-coloured nuts. Remove them from their husks, spread them out and leave to dry overnight. Pack cobnuts and filberts tightly into jars or crocks and cover with an inch layer of crushed block salt. Pack walnuts and chestnuts in a similar manner but cover with an inch layer of sand instead of salt. If the containers have lids, put them on top as an extra precaution against shrivelling. Packed in this way, your nuts should keep till Christmas. Beechnuts make good eating, too. Store them as you would cobnuts. Use as almonds.

Mushrooms are very easy to dry and make an excellent flavouring for winter soups and dishes. Small button mushrooms are best for drying. Gather them in the early morning; before the mushroom fly has had time to attack them. Simply spread them out to dry in the air.

Blackberry and Apple Jam. Here is a favourite recipe :— *4 lbs. firm blackberries, 1½ lbs. sour apples, 4½ lbs. sugar, 1 breakfastcupful water.*

Core and slice the apples. Put in the preserving pan with the water and cook till quite soft. Add the blackberries and bring to the simmer. Simmer for 5 minutes, then add the sugar (warmed) and boil rapidly until setting point is reached. (Make first test after 10 minutes.) Put into hot jars and seal.

Hedgerow Harvest Leaflet containing many useful recipes for using wild produce will be sent to all who ask. Please send postcards only, addressed to The Ministry of Food, Room 627G, London, W.1.

ISSUED BY THE **MF** MINISTRY OF FOOD
(S46)

Ketchup' (from a Ministry of Food leaflet, October 1944): *'Any edible mushrooms can be used, but fully developed ones are best. Break mushrooms into pieces, put them in a bowl and sprinkle with salt about 2oz to each lb mushrooms. Leave for three or four days and stir at least once daily. Place the bowl in a slow oven and cook mushrooms gently for about 1 hour, then strain off liquor. To each quart liquor add about 1 teaspoonful each of whole allspice, dried root ginger, and peppercorns, and a few cloves, a little cinnamon and spice. A small onion and herbs can be used if preferred. If ground spices have to be used, add about one quarter these quantities if desired, during the original cooking. Simmer the spiced liquor till reduced to about half original quantity. Strain and bottle the sauce, while it is still hot, into warm bottles and seal at once.'*

Many of the nuts eaten before the war came from abroad, and they soon disappeared. In Britain there were still walnuts, hazelnuts and chestnuts, and people were also advised to look for the beech nut, or beech mast, in the early autumn. These were not to be eaten raw, but baked in the oven and then eaten with a little salt, like peanuts.

Elderberries had long been used for wine, but they could also be used for jam, syrup, vinegar, or dried and used instead of currants in suet puddings or tarts. Then there was Elderberry Pie: *'1lb elderberries (use ripe, black elderberries stripped from stalks) 1 tablespoon golden syrup, warm water, 2 or 3 cloves, ½lb pastry.*

Nearly fill pie dish with berries, add cloves. Sweeten with syrup. Pour over 2 or more tablespoons water according to size of pie. Cover with pastry. Bake in brisk oven till crust is browned. Then lower heat and allow fruit to simmer for a further 10 to 15 minutes.'

HOW TO MAKE USE OF THE

HEDGEROW HARVEST

The fields and hedgerows are now heavy with wild fruit. Here are some suggestions for jams and other preserves which will be particularly useful in the months to come.

Wild rose hips were an excellent source of vitamins A and C, which were difficult to get with the shortage of citrus fruit. These could be made into tea, a sweet sauce for puddings, or jam, which could be used in the same way as ordinary jam, or, as the Ministry leaflet pointed out, was *'very nice mixed with cereals for breakfast, and as a daily addition to the famous Swiss breakfast dish, called Muesli (Raw Apple Porridge).'*

They could also be made into a soup: *'Boil 6oz. of dried hips (soaked beforehand in water) with 3 pints of water, 3 cloves and some cinnamon, until soft (about 15 minutes). Rub through a hair sieve. Fry 1oz. of fat with 1oz. of flour and add the hip purée slowly. Boil the soup for 5 mins. and season with 3oz. of sugar, salt and lemon flavour. Add some milk, chopped chives or parsley, before serving.'*

The rowan, or mountain ash, berry could be made into a jelly. **Practical Hints in War Time** gave directions: *'Collect a quantity of ripe berries, wash them, then just cover them with water and boil until they are soft. Strain through coarse muslin. To each pint of juice, put 8oz. of sugar and boil up again. When a little of the juice sets, if poured on to a cold saucer, stop the boiling and pour into jars. Cover and store as for ordinary jams. This jelly goes admirably with cold mutton or can be eaten with relish when spread on bread and butter.'*

Even the humble nettle could be utilised; in spring when the leaves are young and tender they could be cooked like spinach or turnip tops and used as a substitute for greens, though the more adventurous, or perhaps downright stupid, were warned not to try to eat them raw in salads.

Crab apple juice, the Ministry said, made a good substitute for lemon juice: *'Put the apples in a heap to sweat and then pick out the stalks and throw away any fruit that shows signs of rottenness. Beat the apples to a mash and press the juice through a jelly bag or thick cloth. Put into clean dry bottles and cork well. It will be ready to use in about a month's time.'*

Soaked in fresh water overnight, then boiled in a little water until it formed a pulp, seaweed became the basis of a jelly. Before it set, sugar and flavouring were added, and colouring, such as beetroot juice. (The manufacture of 'table jelly' was banned in 1943.)

feeding domestic animals in wartime

Rationing brought another problem: how to feed your pets. Once again, there was lots of advice, although not on this occasion from the Ministry of Food. In its leaflet **Your Dog and Cat in Wartime**

Above
With jams and preserves rationed, and fruit in shortage, any suggestions were welcome, and many were prepared to try something new, and free!

Right
Sadly for dogs, they received no meat ration, and even bones were wanted for salvage!

BONES
WANTED

Bones make glue for aeroplanes and other essential war equipment

Don't throw bones away. Use them for stock and then

PUT THEM OUT FOR COLLECTION

PRINTED FOR H.M. STATIONERY OFFICE BY LOWE & BRYDONE PRINTERS LTD., LONDON, N.W.10. 51-7975.

Bob Martin's advised: *'Comparatively few dogs have been accustomed to most of the foods which are rationed, and various other nutritious materials which are useless for human consumption are quite suitable for dogs. Several breeders during the last war kept their kennels of dogs healthy on a diet which consisted mainly of potato peelings and meat offal. In practice you will find that only one or two items of your dog's regular diet will become unobtainable and substitutes can be easily found. For instance, boiled offal or horseflesh can be substituted for raw beef, and should meat become impossible to obtain Soya Bean flour or other protein food can be used. It is always wise to bear in mind the essential requirements of an adequate diet and a check should be made at intervals to see that a dog is receiving the ingredients necessary to maintain good health.*

A dog's diet should consist of the following:

1. Proteins for body building, such as: Fish trimmings, horseflesh, beans, butchers' waste, etc.

2. Fats for storing energy, such as: Bacon rind, skimmed fats from stocks and soups, gristle, etc.

3. Carbohydrates to provide immediate energy, such as: Stale bread and crusts, bakers' scraps, dog biscuits, middlings, greens (not potatoes), etc.

4. Minerals to aid digestion, such as: Stewed rabbit and chicken bones which have been dried and crushed to powder mixed in small quantities with food; a sprinkling of salt may be added occasionally.

5. Subsidiaries for ensuring adequate supply of vitamins, such as: Green vegetables, boiled nettles, dandelions, swede and carrot tops, raw carrot, apples, pears, MartinMilk and dried or skimmed milk.

Do not be discouraged if a dog does not take to his new food immediately. An animal is always suspicious of strange foods. See that your dog is given a plentiful supply of fresh drinking water.'

The RSPCA issued a leaflet, *Feeding Dogs and Cats in Wartime*, which advised that: *'This country has not reached a stage when the wholesale destruction of household pets is necessary, but every effort should be made to use for dogs and cats only such foods as are: (1) plentiful; (2) grown here; or (3) not suitable for human beings. In any case the Waste of Food Order, 1940, does not forbid the feeding of animals with food which could be consumed by a human being. Many people have been concerned at inaccurate statements that have been made on this point, but all animal owners can help to victory by keeping to the three principles mentioned above. Many people have been concerned at inaccurate statements made on this point. . . . Potatoes are plentiful and if you put in extra tubers when digging for victory you will not have it on your conscience that shipping space is being taken for food for your animals. Potatoes boiled in their jackets are not ordinarily recommended for dogs and cats, but the harmful effect is avoided if they are mixed with gravies made from bones. The bones can then be used for waste collection as their boiling does not interfere with their value for war purposes.*

There are also patent powder and gravy extracts on the market or you can purchase stewing meat with your coupons and give the gravy from such meat to your animal – it would be a sacrifice that every owner would be prepared to make.

As an alternative to potatoes: (1) dog biscuits and gravy; (2) boiled rice and gravy; (3) brown bread crisped in the oven; (4) canned (bottled) dog foods; (5) horseflesh; (6) carcase residues such as sheep's stomach, lungs and windpipe.

In this country, 15,000,000 tins of cooked meat foods for dogs and cats were manufactured yearly, before the war. To save metal these foods are now being put up in glass bottles at the rate of 300,000 a week.

It is often forgotten that cats, as well as dogs, should have access to clean water, even if plenty of milk is available. Like human beings, cats and dogs may object to the reduction or total absence of meat, but a gradual change to the new diet can usually be accomplished without undue difficulty.

The Ministry of Food will not permit the use of Cod Liver Oil as food for household pets.

The following suggested wartime diet is for dogs of about 20–25lb weight. Larger or smaller dogs should have proportionate amounts of food. The ration should not be given all at once and it is better to feed dogs in the morning and again in the evening.

(1) 6–10oz. of stale bread, rusked or toasted, or oatmeal made into thick porridge. Mix with 2 or 3oz. of meat scraps from the table, horseflesh or carcase residues from the butcher. The meat should be cut into strips, then boiled or stewed in a little water and added to the cereal after cooking.

(2) 5–6oz. of stale bread (as mentioned above) or a cereal food. Mix with 3–4oz. of chopped cabbage, cauliflower, brussels sprouts, turnip or other green leaves, mashed and boiled for about 15 or 20 minutes. Moisten the mixture with soup or gravy made from bones or scraps from the table, etc. The vegetables or water used for stewing should be added. Cats will usually eat the food recommended in the above

Left

In the absence of meat, table scraps and dog biscuits became the regular diet of many dogs.

Below

Feeding your dog could be a real problem, especially those that had been spoiled before the war, but the RSPCA and other animal groups came to the rescue with suggestions.

diets, provided there is included some meat gravy, sardine oil or other liquids made from fish trimmings.'

Meat designated as unfit for human consumption was sold through animal organisations. The Worthing Animals Dispensary, for instance, organised a system of rationing, selling horseflesh at 9d a lb and dried liver at 4d a lb. Yet some animal owners tried to cheat. In the **Worthing Herald** of 15 June 1941, it was reported that: *'If animal owners persist in grumbling about the amount of food that can be obtained for their animals, if they voice these complaints by writing persistent letters to the Government, and if they trail around from shop to shop to get more than their supply of meat – then pets may have to be destroyed in order to help with the war effort.'*

This view has been expressed by Mr D. G. Crouch, dispenser at the Worthing Animals Dispensary Clinic. Mr. Crouch states that many Worthing people will persist with complaints that they cannot get all the food for their animals that they think they should get. We as humans are rationed, says Mr. Crouch, so your pet must be grateful for less now that we are at war. It is no good saying my dog can't eat this, or won't eat that. The available food is perfectly fit for animal consumption. At the beginning of the war many people said they couldn't eat margarine, but they do.

At present, says Mr. Crouch, the Government has no intention of making an order for exterminating pets, but animal owners should be prepared for such a campaign which they themselves are helping to bring about.

Mr. Crouch is indignant with Worthing people who form a queue in the morning at one shop for

MEMO

Just a reminder

TO TRY AGAIN FOR

SPRATT'S

BISCUIT DOG FOODS

THE SURE WAY OF

SPRATT'S

'BUILDING-UP A DOG'

– may be lucky next time

dog's meat, and another queue in the afternoon at a different shop.

This situation means that people occupied during the daytime have difficulty in obtaining any food at all for their animals because all the meat has been sold.

People will persist in writing to the Government, said Mr. Crouch and saying that meat for animals should be price controlled. We in Worthing have up to the present time sold our meat at 1s. a lb. and we hope to keep it at that figure, but it can only be done if people play fair and ration their dogs as they themselves are rationed.

Because many people have been using the meat bought for their animals for their own consumption all dog meat will in future be sprayed with a blue or green naphthalene dye which is harmless.

Do not sacrifice your pet by grumbling, says Mr. Crouch. Teach him to eat what you give him.'

Alternatively you could make your own biscuits, using recipes such as this one from **Stitchcraft**, of December 1941:

'Mickey's Dog Biscuits

Quantities given make 1lb. *(67 biscuits if cut out with an egg cup; this size is best for a small dog).*

Required:

½lb. plain flour ½ pint hot water 2 Oxo cubes

½lb. oatmeal (fine, medium or coarse)

Cut up Oxo cubes, dissolve in hot water, then mix flour and oatmeal together in a large basin and with Oxo make into a paste that can be rolled thinly (about ¼ inch or less) on a floured board. Cut in small rounds with an egg cup. Roll and cut out trimmings. Put on lightly greased tins (you will need two really large ones), and bake in a good oven (Regulo 5 or 6) for about 40 minutes, when they should be light brown and hard. The more thinly they are rolled the easier it is to get them hard, and they take less time to bake.'

The advice for cats was mainly that they could be left to their own devices, supplemented by kitchen scraps and left-overs. However, in December 1941 one MP asked the Minister of Food about the possibility of a small daily ration of milk for cats, as these animals were a national necessity, keeping down rats and mice. The Minister replied that there was a shortage of liquid milk at that time, and

In Wartime as in Peace, no better food for Cage Birds than Hyde's is procurable. In spite of the scarcity of *plain Genuine Canary Seed* Hyde's still include a proportion in their Canary and Budgie Mixtures, and will do so as long as their stock lasts.

Hyde's BIRD SEEDS

(Established 1877)

Sold in 1/- packets by all dealers

Left
Like everything else, dog biscuits went into shortage, but you could always make your own, and recipes were published.

Above
Even bird seed was in shortage, and special wartime mixtures were sold, such as this.

that any allowance of milk for consumption by cats generally could only be provided by reducing the ration for humans.

Budgies had an especially bad time as supplies of seed, most of which were imported pre-war, became desperately short – breeders reported the price soaring from 15 shillings to £100 a hundred-weight. Speaking of canaries, budgies and parrots, the official magazine of the RSPCA, the **Animal World** of October 1941 reported that *'Now that imported seeds are scarce, the feeding of such pets* is an anxious problem. Nearly all our British weed seeds are suitable for such birds, though the mixtures preferable are largely to be determined by experiment. Budgerigars are more fastidious than canaries, but certainly both kinds will, on the whole – for it must be admitted there are disappointing exceptions – adapt themselves to an unaccustomed diet, especially when the seeds are supplemented by other items.

It has been suggested that acorns, chopped finely, might with advantage be mixed with seed. This suggestion, if practicable, would certainly seem of value. At this time of the year acorns are becoming plentiful and there does not seem to be any inherent objection to their use. True, they have a bitter flavour, but wood pigeons devour them greedily.

Foods found of value have been stale bread crusts, both brown and white, toasted and thoroughly dried, along with grated carrots and then mixed into a crumbly state by adding milk. For green food, lettuce and dandelion are recommended. ' In spite of such advice, thousands of budgies died from malnutrition.

And what of the other animals now being kept in many gardens? The **Girls' Own Paper** in September 1942 advised on their care: '*It is time to think what we can do for our animals and birds and bees in the coming winter. We must provide warm dry quarters for them. Hens like a dry floor for scratching, and hens that use a wired outdoor run will lay more eggs, and be much healthier, if the ground is well covered with cinders or clinker. Hens hate a muddy playground! But I expect food will be the worst winter problem.*

If you have been wise enough to grow vegetables

specially for feeding, you will get along quite well. For the hens you can use Jerusalem artichokes, beet, carrots, potatoes, swedes and turnips: these all store easily. Leeks and onions, and all sorts of winter greens are good too, and so are peas and

Above
Spratt's, the makers of dog biscuits, branched out into biscuits for rabbits, but as the advert implies, most rabbits were not kept purely as pets.

beans if they have been dried and then minced. As a rule all household scraps are good for hens, except tea leaves and rhubarb leaves, so gardeners should be able to keep them well fed.

Rabbits eat almost anything too, except the green parts of potatoes, broad beans and rhubarb. Don't give your rabbits too much lettuce: use other winter greens to vary the diet. Hay is useful too, and also such roots as parsnips, beet (sugar beet especially), carrots, and kohl rabi.'

The RSPCA even gave advice for the feeding of

wild birds, because *'a well-stocked bird-table during the winter months apart from its humanitarian point of view will ensure that the feathered inhabitants of our gardens live on to continue their beneficial work of destroying the insect pests during spring and summer.'*

The **Animal World** of November 1941 divided wild birds into two categories: those that mainly eat insects and those whose normal food is seeds. *'Amongst the former may be mentioned the Mistle Thrush, Song Thrush, Blackbird, Robin, Hedge Sparrow, Great-Tit, Coal-Tit, March-Tit and Blue-Tit and Wren. Amongst the latter may be mentioned the Greenfinch, Bullfinch, Goldfinch, Chaffinch and Sparrow. The Starling may safely be said to be omnivorous.'*

The paper suggested that the best food for insect eaters was *'the dyed horse-flesh sold for feeding dogs'* – this should be finely minced – as should *'Soft bacon rind free from fat (which is too useful for cooking purposes to be fed to birds) . . . this will be appreciated by blackbirds and thrushes. The cellular residue which remains when fat has been rendered down may also be placed on the bird-table; the various species of Tit are very partial to this. Most of the insect eating birds, especially tits and robins, delight in picking bones; mutton chop bones are rapidly cleared of every vestige of meat and gristle during hard weather. Both the mistle thrush and song thrush will eat shellfish and would no doubt appreciate fresh water mussels which are quite easily procured along the banks of most of our larger rivers including the Thames as far as London.*

All insect eating birds will greedily devour berries and fruits, the soft fleshy varieties being selected first. The partiality of the thrushes to rowan berries and the migrating starling to those of the elder is well known. Many of the Chinese species of berberis which produce the beautiful luscious translucent coral-red berries during the autumn months are heavily raided by blackbirds and thrushes. The same remarks also apply to the yew berry.

Generally speaking the berries of the holly, hawthorn, privet and ivy are the wild birds' iron rations and usually remain untouched until severe frost sets in and other supplies are cut off. The various species of tit may be truly said to be omnivorous, for nothing edible seems to come amiss to them. In addition to the flesh food already mentioned, they will eat boiled sweet or horse-chestnuts.'

Also suitable for the bird table were the grated hedge-nut kernels and acorns, while the kernels of beech-mast finely chopped would make a substitute for coconut and Brazil nuts. Pine and larch cones could be gathered and the seeds removed from between the woody scales. And, as an added incentive, *the cones themselves make a very excellent substitute for firewood'.*

All the weed-seeds suitable for canaries and budgerigars could be given to birds such as the greenfinch, chaffinch, bullfinch and sparrow. *'In addition, many species of decorative garden plants such as sunflowers, cosmos, china asters, scabious, evening primrose, etc., furnish considerable quantities of large wholesome seeds for our purpose. The delightful little hedge-sparrow seems to have a special fondness for the seeds of the antirrhinum and common field-poppy. Finches will also eat the seeds of the vegetable marrow when they are quite ripe.'*

STILL MORE
WASTE
PAPER
WANTED FOR
SALVAGE
Thanks
KEEP IT UP!
Gilroy
Printed for H.M. Stationery Office by Greycaines, Watford and London.
M.O.S. S&R. 194

around the house

Despite the more immediate problems posed by the Luftwaffe, the battles of the Home Front were fought by housewives on a daily basis. Feeding and clothing the family, and keeping the house clean, warm, and tidy have always been the day-to-day lot of the housewife, but in wartime that job was made increasingly difficult by rationing and shortages.

The list of those items either directly rationed or included in the points scheme grew ever longer; with admirable resourcefulness substitutes were found, and methods to eke out scarce items were passed round by word of mouth, by official leaflets and in the many women's magazines. Yet these tended to be only temporary solutions; the more successful substitutes soon became shortage items

BOY'S OWN PAPER

NOVEMBER 1944

9d

Bevin Boys

Previous Left
Salvage collecting became part of everyday life as Britain struggled to make up for its lack of natural resources.

Previous Right
A Board of Trade poster showing boys how they can do jobs around the house 'And So Help to Win the War'.

Left
'Bevin Boys', named after the Minister of Labour, Ernest Bevin, were conscripted to work down the mines to make up for a shortage of mine workers.

Right
Fuel, especially coal, was in desperately short supply as factories needed ever more power to feed the war machine.

themselves, and new substitutes had to be found. Similarly, the supply of materials used to make or repair clothes, such as old 'woollies' unstitched and re-knitted, was not infinite, and they too began to run out.

Nowhere was this battle of resources more marked than on the home front, often last in line when it came to supplies of goods, and nowhere was ingenuity more evident. This next section looks at some of the more important shortages around the house, concentrating on the solutions, many practical, some ingenious, and a few hare-brained, which appeared at the time.

fuel-coal

Coal was one product that the country was not short of in 1939. Britain produced a surplus of coal, which it exported. In the rush to conscript healthy young men into the forces, many whose civilian work was crucial to the country, such as farm workers, were taken, leaving these industries short of skilled men at a time when expansion was vital. It was, however, clear to anyone that Britain's industries would need power, and mining was made a reserved occupation. With the fall of France in 1940, Britain's position in terms of coal was further strengthened as France had been a major importer of British coal; mining ceased to be a reserved occupation for anyone under the age of thirty; younger miners left and within a year Britain's glut of coal had become a shortage.

The government worked hard to reduce unnecessary use of coal and its derivatives, gas and electricity. In October 1941 the Mines Department issued the leaflet *Economise in Fuel*, which included the following fuel-saving suggestions: *'At all times of the day restrict the use of fires and radiators, and, in the case of electricity, it is very important to curtail the use of current between 8 a.m. and 1 p.m. on all weekdays, especially when the weather is cold or foggy; hot baths should be taken at night and not in the morning.*

If possible share your cooker with your neighbour or neighbours. Gas or electricity can be saved and rations made to go farther if families arrange to club together for the cooking of the main meal. Why not talk over this modified form of community feeding with your neighbours?'

One month later, the Electrical Association for Women advised its members that: *'In view of the fact that the Government has stressed the need for the utmost economy in the use of all fuels, make your contribution to the war effort by adjusting your electrical habits, and remember that to economise voluntarily is better than having a compulsory scheme thrust upon you.'* This threat of

Have breakfast in the kitchen..

!.. and save having the sitting-room fire going until tea time.

SAVE FUEL* FOR THE FACTORIES

* COAL   COKE
GAS : ELECTRICITY
FUEL OIL · PARAFFIN

rationing if voluntary savings could not be made was regularly repeated. The leaflet continued, *'It will not be necessary to economise in the number of baths if the amount of water used is considerably reduced. On no account should either washing-up or hand-washing be done under a running tap.*

Avoid using bright shiny pans, since they reflect heat away from them. The pans which have darkened through use absorb heat more readily and brown the contents of the pan more quickly. Glass absorbs heat readily and is excellent for time and heat saving, since food may be cooked and served in the same container.

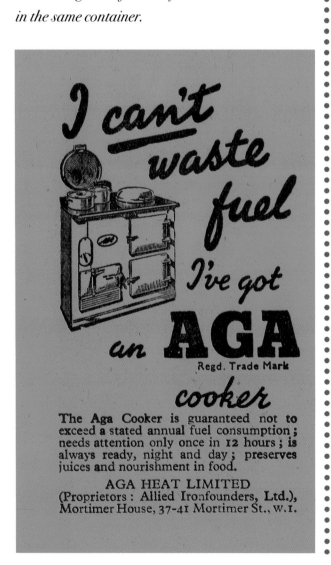

I can't waste fuel I've got an **AGA** cooker

Regd. Trade Mark

The Aga Cooker is guaranteed not to exceed a stated annual fuel consumption; needs attention only once in 12 hours; is always ready, night and day; preserves juices and nourishment in food.

AGA HEAT LIMITED
(Proprietors: Allied Ironfounders, Ltd.), Mortimer House, 37-41 Mortimer St., w.1.

Bread-tins pack into an oven with the greatest ease; all kinds of food may be cooked in them – they can be covered with grease-proof paper.'

Calls for rationing became more strident, and in April 1942 Hugh Dalton announced that a fuel rationing scheme was to be introduced in June. Food and clothing rationing were now an accepted part of everyday life, and the idea of fuel rationing was welcomed by many as an extension of the 'fair shares for all' principle. The Conservative Party, never really happy with rationing, revolted. As people moved up the class scale, so the houses they lived in became bigger, and consequently harder to heat; these homes would also be equipped with modern labour-saving devices, usually powered by gas or electricity. Yet under rationing all would receive roughly the same, the only difference being up to 30% extra for those living in the north, due to the harsher northern climate. This only added insult to injury for the Conservative MPs whose heartland was the south. Their revolt succeeded; the idea of rationing was dropped. Instead, a new Ministry of Fuel, Light and Power was created, one of whose main tasks would be to persuade the public to use less fuel; its propaganda machine swung into action. 'The Battle of Fuel is on!' the newspaper advertisements declared, and diagrams were published enabling the public to work out their family's 'fuel target'.

Left
Saving fuel for the factories by using an Aga, December 1943.
Right
In 1942, to cut down on domestic fuel consumption, a form of rationing was introduced. Fuel targets were set for each house, based on a fairly complicated formula, which included the number of rooms, with regional variations.

NUMBER OF ROOMS	NORTHERN	MIDLANDS	SOUTHERN
	HOUSE ALLOWANCE IN FUEL UNITS		
1	80	60	50
2	90	70	60
3	110	90	70
4	120	100	80
5	140	110	90
6	150	120	100
7 OR MORE	170	140	110

IN ADDITION, YOUR PERSONAL FUEL ALLOWANCE is 15 fuel units per year, which equals 7½ cwts. of coal or a corresponding amount of other fuels. This applies to adults and children alike.

NORTHERN AREA COMPRISES: Lancashire (including the County Borough of Manchester), Cheshire (only Stalybridge and Hyde division), Derbyshire (only the High Peak division), Yorkshire and all Counties to the north of these. The whole of Scotland forms part of the Northern Zone.

MIDLAND AREA COMPRISES: Cardiganshire, Breconshire, Herefordshire, Worcestershire, Warwickshire, Northamptonshire, Bedfordshire, Cambridge and Suffolk, and all Counties to the north of these up to and including Cheshire (other than the Stalybridge and Hyde division), Derbyshire (other than the High Peak division), Nottinghamshire and Lincolnshire.

SOUTHERN AREA COMPRISES: Pembrokeshire, Monmouthshire, Carmarthen, Glamorgan, Gloucestershire, Oxfordshire, Buckinghamshire, Hertfordshire and Essex, Middlesex, Berkshire, Kent, Surrey, Sussex, Hampshire, Wiltshire, Dorset, Somerset, Devon, Cornwall, and the whole of the County of London.

1 Fuel Unit Equals
½ Cwt. of Coal or Coke or 500 Cubic Feet of Gas or 50 Units of Electricity or 1 Gallon of Paraffin

By October 1942, the new Minister of Fuel, Major Lloyd George, reported that coal production was actually 15% below that of 1938. This translated to a shortfall of 11 million tons a year between the vastly increased need for power and actual production.

The Second Great War, edited by Sir John Hammerton, declared that *'throughout the year [1943] the Home Front was dominated by the problem of coal production. Coal lay at the bottom of the country's* *life, it was the basis of its capacity to make war. Yet insufficient coal was being produced, and nothing that was tried seemed able to lift the figure to what was needed to supply the domestic hearths, the fighting forces, and the demands of our overseas allies and friends.'* In spite of an increasing work-force, production was still a worry, and at the end of July 1943, the Minister of Labour, Ernest Bevin, announced that conscripted men might in future be sent down the mines instead of into the forces: they were known as the 'Bevin Boys'.

Left
The government issued 'fuel communiqués' giving targets and advice for cutting down on fuel consumption, such as this one from March 1943.
Below
Government leaflet advising the public to save fuel by lagging pipes and tanks.

FUEL *Communiqué*

THE BATTLE FOR FUEL

REDUCE THE 'PEAK'

The Peak is between 8 A.M and 1 P.M

1. LOOK ATTENTIVELY AT THE CURVE ABOVE, THEN READ ON.

2. It shows the consumption of electric power in Great Britain hour by hour. The actual amount used would be of value to the enemy so this is kept out of the picture.

3. Note that between 8 a.m. and 1 p.m. there is a peak or climax. This is when the war factories are using most electricity.

4. This peak throws a strain on the generating stations and makes them burn more coal.

5. By reducing your own consumption of electricity between 8 a.m. and 1 p.m. you can help to flatten out that peak and save the country's coal.

START TODAY

to use as little electricity as possible between 8 a.m. and 1 p.m.

REMEMBER: Two bars of an electric fire use 12 lbs. of coal in 4 hours. Use only one bar. *One million consumers using only one bar instead of two can save 2,500 tons of coal in a few hours.*

KEEP YOUR EYE ON YOUR FUEL TARGET

Issued by the Ministry of Fuel and Power

save fuel

INFORMATION LEAFLET

"LAG" and RELAX!

THE INSULATION OF HOT WATER TANKS AND PIPES

It is ESSENTIAL that we all safeguard our own stocks of coal and coke during the winter, particularly as this is the time of year when a sufficient supply of hot water is a necessity.

You put a tea-cosy over your tea-pot to keep the heat in and the cold out. "Lag" your hot-water tank and pipes and you will be applying the same principle.

BUT there's one great difference : ONCE you have "lagged" your hot water system you don't have to keep on doing it ; you can forget about it.

THREE ADVANTAGES OF "LAGGING"

1 By "lagging" a 25 gallon hot-water tank a TON OR MORE of COAL or COKE will be SAVED in a year.

2 Water in "lagged" tanks and pipes remains hot for a considerable number of hours AFTER the boiler fire has gone out.

3 Clothes can be aired over a "lagged" tank with no danger of their becoming discoloured by excessive heat.

Tips for saving fuel abounded; to eke out your precious coal **101 Ways to Save Money in Wartime** advised that: *'A half teaspoonful of saltpetre dissolved in 1 pint of water and poured over a scuttle of coals gives a brighter fire. The coal so treated will burn longer and consequently use less,'* or *'A good handful of common washing soda, dissolved in half a bucket of warm water, if thrown over a cwt. of coal and allowed to dry, will result in 25 per cent more burning power.'* The government suggested that you: *'Dissolve a tablespoonful of common salt in half a pint of water and sprinkle this over a small scuttleful of coal. The coal will not burn away so quickly and will give a solid red glow.'*

With coal in short supply you had to use whatever you could get. **Practical Hints in War Time** noted that: *'The coal we buy in these days seems to have more dust in it than formerly. Nevertheless, it must not be wasted. Some, of course, can be put on a bright fire or burnt in a stove with a good draught, but the quantity that can be used profitably in these ways is limited. It is a good plan to make briquettes with the rest. If you have clay as the subsoil of your garden, dig as much out as you have coal dust, mix the two together with a shovel, adding only sufficient water to bind. In other cases, buy some cement and use two-parts of coal dust and one of cement, again adding no more water than is needed for binding the mass. Then get a cylindrical tin, about the size that would hold 2oz. of tobacco and keep on ramming it full with the mixture, turning it out on end each time, on a board. When these briquettes are dry, they will burn with a nice glow. You can use them next day, but they are much more satisfactory if kept at least two months. Note that small sizes are more handy than large ones and remember that it is not advisable to poke them while they are burning.'* The government advised *'Small coal or slack, sawdust, and clay may be mixed together until they are about as thick as mortar. The mixture should then be moulded into convenient brick-like shapes, afterwards leaving it to dry; or the slack can be mixed with sawdust slightly moistened with paraffin and shaped into balls as big as an orange. You cannot light the fire with such bricks or balls, but they will keep a fire going a long time, and will give out strong heat if placed at the back of a grate with coal in front.'*

Cutting down the actual amount of coal in a fire was another method; **Woman's Weekly** in December 1944 (a very cold month) suggested that: *'A good way of helping to save coal is to make up a few fire-clay balls, and put them in the back of the grate, below the coal. The balls act in the same way as fire-brick, but, being small, they are more convenient to handle. Buy some fireclay at the oil-shop, and mix it up with a very little water to a stiff paste. Roll into balls about the size of a tennis ball, leave to harden, and then put in the fire. Lumps of ordinary chalk or pumice-stone about the size of a potato placed at the back of a fire will give you an excellent coal economy. The heat given out is amazing, and the chalk or pumice being non-combustible will last for weeks.'* **101 Ways to Save Money in Wartime** suggested that you *'Buy a firebrick about 2 inches thick. When the fire is burning brightly, lay the brick on top. The brick intercepts the heat that escapes up the chimney, becomes hot, and throws the heat out into the room,'* while **Housewife** magazine in October 1940 suggested *'3 or 4 good-sized*

lumps of pumice stone with the coal when the fire is laid; when the fire burns up, the pumice glows, giving out a good heat and thus saving coal. The pieces of pumice stone, of course, last indefinitely.'

Nothing should be wasted. The Ministry of Fuel and Power told the public in February 1943: *'Don't forget to sieve the cinders. If all the cinders in Great Britain in open fires in one year were sieved, 2,000,000 tons of coal would be saved.'*

And when there was no coal? An advert for Bowmans' furniture in February 1944 advised how wood might be used instead of coal: *'When you put split logs on the fire, put the bark side in towards the chimney and the split side out towards the room. This will prevent sparks flying out and burning* holes in the carpet or hearth rug.' **1001 Household Hints** directed: *'Take two parts of coal dust to one of sawdust. Dissolve a little glue in boiling water, and mix into the coal dust and sawdust. Form into shapes, and leave to dry thoroughly before using. These bricks throw off a great heat and are sure coal savers.'* **Housewife** magazine of October 1940 suggested wrapping *'grass cuttings from the lawn in newspaper, making it into small bundles and pack them neatly into boxes or cartons. When the bath water is required, these are stood by the stove and after the fire is once going the bundles are put in. They burn with a fierce white heat, are clean to handle and make no clinker. The cuttings of a medium-sized lawn provide about eight baths.'*

electricity

'Put that light out!' had been the cry of the enraged air-raid warden, now it was taken up by the Ministry. **Home Companion** in January 1943 told its readers that: *'Firelight is a kindly mellow light which draws us all closer together. And isn't that "homey" fireside circle a lovely memory for one who has to leave it? Firelight flickering over the room, lingering over loved and familiar things, throwing into soft shadow the faces of his dear ones,' and 'Can I get there by candlelight?' – not to the Babylon of the nursery rhyme this time – but into bed! If you could and only would think of the "bull" you'd score on the fuel target every time! Candles abound in the shops just now, and if you let one light you to bed you won't be tempted to read when you get there, or spend ages titivating in the cold before you get there!'*

Practical Hints in War Time suggested that: *'If you want to make a candle last a quarter to a half as long again as it ordinarily does, varnish the cylindrical side but not the tip. You can do a pound of candles in ten minutes and the trouble is well worth while. Stand each one upright on end while it is drying and do not use until perfectly hard,' and 'In many halls and passages which used to be brilliantly lit the moment darkness fell, we now find a dimly lighted night light. The change-over has been made to accord with the black-out rules and, also, for the sake of economy. But night lights are not so very economical, if burnt continuously. Try the following and you will have a light – true, it is only a glimmer – that really saves. Take a candle that has already burnt sufficient to level down the tapering point and carefully surround the wick with a heaped ring of table-salt. Then light up and the candle will burn very feebly, but it will go on doing so for a considerable time.'*

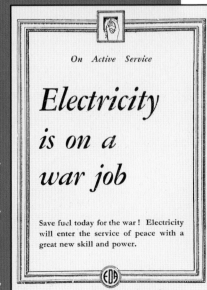

On Active Service

Electricity is on a war job

Save fuel today for the war! Electricity will enter the service of peace with a great new skill and power.

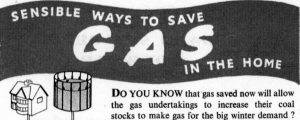

SENSIBLE WAYS TO SAVE
GAS
IN THE HOME

DO YOU KNOW that gas saved now will allow the gas undertakings to increase their coal stocks to make gas for the big winter demand? Gas wasted now may mean there will not be enough to go round in the cold weather. What are you going to do about it? Of course you're all going to see that not a single therm of gas is wasted—not if you know it! The hints that follow will help you to beat your own record in saving.

KNOW YOUR GAS COOKER

About ⅓ of the gas used for cooking is burnt on the boiling rings on the top of the cooker, so the greatest saving must be effected here.

1 Use a small ring instead of a large ring whenever possible. It may take longer, but it saves gas.

2 Never let the gas flare round the sides of kettle or saucepan.

3 Toast-making under the gas grill is a luxury in war-time. Give it up.

4 If the grill is in use, the heat rising from it should be used to heat a saucepan or kettle.

5 Remember it is more economical to fry than to use the gas grill. Cover the frying pan to save heat.

6 The oven is economical for cooking several dishes at once, but extravagant for single dishes.

7 Turn out the gas as soon as cooking is done. The heat remaining in the oven will keep food warm or heat water for washing-up.

DOUBLE DAY
COOKING

Plan ahead before you start your cooking. Another pound or so of potatoes—a bigger batch of pastry—an extra tier on the steamer may save that gas in to-morrow's cooking.

READ YOUR GAS METER REGULARLY

The golden rule for saving gas is to keep a check on your consumption by reading your meter at regular intervals—say once weekly. Make it a regular week-end job to read your gas meter and enter the figure on a record sheet kept beside the meter. If you're *still* not sure how to read your gas meter, very simple instructions can be obtained from your local Gas Showrooms.

gas

In 1941, **The Little Less** gave its readers four ways to save gas: '*1. Turn down the gas fire as soon as the room is warm enough. A smaller fire will keep it warm. 2. Never put a quart of water in the kettle when you need only a pint; never let the gas flare up round the sides of the kettle or saucepan. 3. Keep your cooker clean and your utensils clean. Dirt wastes gas. 4. Use less water in the bath. You will save both gas and water (water needs fuel to pump it at the waterworks).*' In December 1943 **Ideal**

Home magazine supplied more gas-saving hints: '*Keep lids on saucepans, even when boiling an egg. A small burner, though slower, is more economical than a large one. Use wide-based pans if you can, and if you have no steamer, improvise one by putting a colander in a saucepan.*' **1001 Household Hints** took up the idea: '*To economise on gas bring the potatoes to a boil, then lift them out and place in a colander. Put your greens into the potato water which should still be boiling. Place the colander with the potatoes over the saucepan and cover with a tight-fitting lid, thus steaming the potatoes and cooking the greens over the same gas ring,*' and '*When serving potatoes baked in their jackets scrub them and parboil them first. Prick them and put them in the oven for 20 minutes only. The result is excellent and you save on gas and electricity.*'

Home Notes of September 1942 suggested another way of saving gas in cooking: '*Take a fairly large biscuit tin, or old cake tin. Cut off the bottom, stand this over the gas and put your saucepan inside; the space between the ring and the saucepan will collect surplus gas and heat; and a saving of one-third of the gas usually burned can be effected.*' The Brown & Polson **Book of Wartime Recipes** recommended: '*When planning menus, try to cook a complete meal either in the oven or on the top of the stove, e.g. when making a stew, steam a pudding over it, and when using for roasting meat, arrange to have a baked pudding,*' and '*When using gas, do not allow flames to burn up the sides of a pan, or kettle. When using electricity, switch off the current before cooking is completed. Some dishes, e.g. stews, fruit, vegetables etc., cooked in the oven and milk puddings do not need the oven to be pre-heated.*'

Home Companion of May 1943 suggested: *'Of course, you only use your oven when you're having a real baking day. When you do, here's a way to get hot water for the washing up. After you take out your baking and turn off the gas, put a panful of water in the oven. And put a cake-tin instead of a lid over big saucepans and boil up the kettle in the tin. That kettle soon boils, and comes in wonderfully handy for making gravy, and that after-lunch cup of tea,'* and *'Have you ever thought of soaking dried peas and lentils overnight in a "thermos" of hot water? Wisdom in it is that those peas are gently cooking*

WOMEN WHO WORK

Air Raid Wardens appreciate the Super-Fast Burner

Not the least of the time-saving features of the modern Regulo New World Gas Cooker is the super-fast burner which boils 1 pint of water in 125 secs! Other refinements for better, quicker and more economical cooking include a high-speed grill reaching toasting heat in 60 secs.; unique oven design with single burner; and, of course, the *genuine 'Regulo'*—which automatically saves gas and enables a complete meal to be perfectly cooked all at the same time.

OVER 2 MILLIONS IN DAILY USE

See the Cooking Number in the REGULO TRIANGLE ▲

REGULO NEW WORLD

GAS COOKERS

SEE THEM AT YOUR GAS SHOWROOMS

A **Radiation** product

overnight, so need far less gas next morning. And doesn't this little notion get you thinking about sago and rice?'

An extension of this idea was the hay box, developed in the First World War. It was made from a stout box with a lid, lined with about twenty sheets of newspaper, with 5 inches of hay placed in the bottom. Food needing long-boiling or simmering was placed in a saucepan and brought to the boil on the stove, then the saucepan and contents (with a lid on) were placed inside the hay box, and straw packed around the sides and top and the lid closed. The food would be kept hot, slowly simmering.

Far Left

Another government leaflet, this time advising members of the public on how to cut down their gas consumption.

Above

The war was used to sell many items, including these cookers, which, according to the advert, saved time and gas.

Left

Advert from the Ministry of Fuel and Power from December 1944, pointing out that electricity and gas were both derived from coal.

matches

Even lighting a fire became difficult as matches joined the list of shortage materials. Tips here included splitting matches in two with a razor blade. **Practical Hints in War Time** pointed out: *'It is wonderful what we can do without. Take matches. We used to buy a packet of a dozen boxes every few days. Now, if our grocer obliges us with a single box, we regard it as a favour. When matches first ran short, it was something in the nature of a minor catastrophe, but ways and means were soon found in our home and, now, it often occurs that only one match is struck in the house per day and that is the first one in the morning. In winter time, it is not so difficult because there are fires going and close to each fireplace is a supply of paper spills, These are made for the most part of the envelopes that come into the house. An average envelope folds into eight spills and each spill serves for two lightings, so nobody could complain about the paper that is used. In summer, when there are no fires, a small homemade lamp is brought into commission. It consists of a glass jar with a metal screw-on lid. In the centre of the lid, a hole is punched and the wick of a cigarette lighter threaded through it. The wick only peers above the lid sufficiently to provide the tiniest of flames and the other end floats in paraffin. This lamp is kept going all day at a cost of less than a halfpenny. A supply of paper spills is stood near it and anyone who wants a light uses the lamp to light a spill.'*

Tit-Bits, in July 1942, suggested a variation: *'In the home you can make an efficient and economical lamp by threading a wick through a hole pierced in the tightly-fitting lid of a tobacco tin and half-filling the container with methylated spirit or paraffin oil. Some people pack it with cotton-wool.'* Spills themselves became a problem, as waste paper was needed for the war effort. **Tit-Bits** continued: *'the dearth of matches has tempted thousands of people to convert some of their waste paper into spills. They have been lighting gas, pipes, and cigarettes by means of these spills. The total amount of paper burned in this way throughout the United Kingdom represents many hundreds of tons, and the wastage is completely unnecessary. This does not mean that you should abandon your pipe or your cigarette. There are several substitutes for matches without consuming vital supplies of paper.'* These included waxed bread bags, or string dipped in melted candle wax.

Above
Wartime matchboxes exhorted you to 'Use matches sparingly', as they too were in short supply.
Right
Oxydol advert, June 1942. All forms of soap had gone 'on the ration' in February that year.

firelighters

Lighting fires without using much-needed paper was yet another problem. **Practical Hints in War Time** commented: *'It was easy to light fires when paper was plentiful because newspapers consisted of 24 pages and everything came into the house wrapped. But now that paper is wanted for munitions, it seems wrong to use it for lighting purposes. Why not imitate the Boy Scouts and forego paper entirely? Their plan is to take sticks of wood and fluff up each one of them in the centre. They hold the sticks and cut slantingly into them with a sharp knife. Each stick is given about a dozen small cuts. When the sticks are laid, the shredded or fluffed parts catch light readily.'*

1001 Household Hints suggested that *'Useful firelighters can be made by breaking bathbricks into four pieces. Place pieces in a tin and cover with paraffin. The bricks are not affected by the heat and can be replaced in the paraffin,'* or *'Dry all potato peelings and use for kindling the fire with a small piece of paper and a very few sticks.'*

cleaning

On 9 February 1942, a rationing scheme for soap was introduced. This was done in order to divert fats and oils, used in the manufacture of soap, to food use. Like clothes rationing, it was brought in overnight, with no prior warning. In his memoirs Lord Woolton recalled what happened: *'For security reasons we could not label the papers "Soap Rationing", so we gave the file the code name of "Nutmegs". Nobody was particularly interested or*

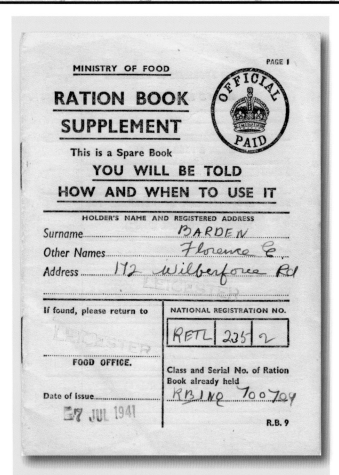

curious about nutmegs and there was no sign of any leakage of information on this subject until the Saturday afternoon before I was going to make the announcement on the Sunday. Then, somehow or other, the story leaked that nutmegs were to be rationed; reports came in to the headquarters of the Ministry that there had been a sudden rush in the shops on nutmegs. I wonder what happened to all the nutmegs that the credulous people who cleaned up the market purchased on that Saturday afternoon.'

There was one major problem: bars of soap were not made in uniform weights, which made it difficult to allot a coupon value to the various brands of soap and soap powder. Later, manufacturers would alter the size of their soap bars so as to offer the maximum amount for coupon economy. Every-

body was given 4 coupons a week which could be used for toilet soap, hard soap, soap powder or soap flakes, each of which would be given a coupon value which could change to suit supply. The coupons were from the yellow ration book, R.B.9, and were cancelled on use, rather than cut out. As with clothing, there was no need to register and coupons could be used in any shop.

You had a choice: either 4 ounces of household soap or 3 ounces (later 2) of toilet soap, or 3oz soap flakes or chips, or 6oz soap powder no. 1, or 12oz soap powder no. 2, or 6oz soft soap per person per week. Shaving soap, scourers, shampoo powders, liquid soap and dental soap were not rationed. Within a couple of months the ration for children under twelve months was doubled, and extra coupons were supplied to those with particularly dirty jobs.

Tips abounded for economising on soap. **Mother & Home** that February told its readers that *'When a cake of toilet soap was wearing thin, my mother always stuck it on to a new bar. (Just wet the two pieces and they'll stick all right.) Over a year, it mounts up as a really important soap-saving idea.'* The **Home Companion** of August 1943 asked, *'Have you ever thought of using the fluted cap of a lemonade bottle to stick on the bottom of your cake of soap? Wisdom here is that the cap raises your soap an odd quarter of an inch, and keeps it high and dry so that you can use it right down to the last little sliver.'* Even that last sliver was precious; **101 Ways to Save Money in Wartime** suggested: *'Never throw scraps of soap away – keep them in a jar, boil them into a soap jelly and use for your lather on washing day.'*

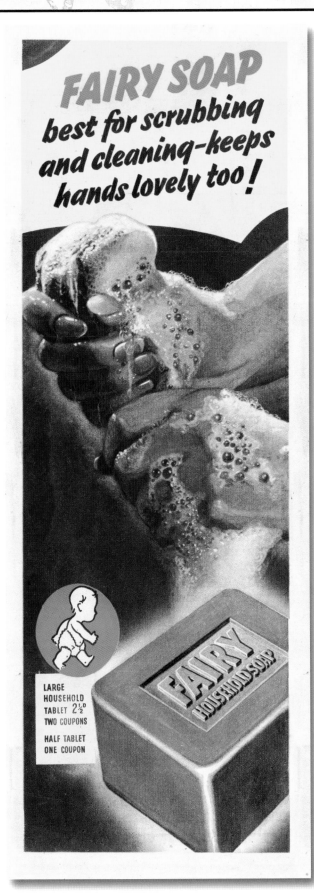

FAIRY SOAP
best for scrubbing and cleaning-keeps hands lovely too!

LARGE HOUSEHOLD TABLET 2½ᵈ TWO COUPONS

HALF TABLET ONE COUPON

FAIRY HOUSEHOLD SOAP

Similarly **Ideal Home** magazine recommended that you *'Grate on a cheese or coarse grater half a tablet (not a bar) of Sunlight soap and put the flakes into a 2lb stone jar. Fill jar with boiling water and leave overnight in a cool place to set into a jelly. This jelly is excellent for washing up and for washing household linen and underclothes. Use a teaspoonful of the jelly to a bowl of very hot water.'* **The Little Less** suggested that *'Scraps of soap that have become too small for ordinary purposes are useful for washing up, etc., if put into a little wire cage or cheese-cloth bag, and stirred in the dish water.'*

Practical Hints in War Time informed its readers that: *'Soap that has been kept some little time is usually harder than soap just bought. Hard soap is more economical than soap that is soft. Therefore, buy your soap as long as possible before you need it. Like that, you will save several tablets in the course of a year.'* Alternatively, the **Home Companion** of October 1943 suggested that *'It saves the kitchen soap if you bore a hole through it, thread it with string, then tie a knot. When the soap isn't being used hang it up. The air gets to it and hardens it off so that it lasts almost twice as long. Also you will find less soap will be needed if you add a teaspoonful of borax to every quart of water. Borax is a grand water softener, and besides saving soap, it saves your hands, too!'*

101 Ways to Save Money in Wartime suggested that you *'Use an old spoon for measuring soap*

flakes and washing powders. The packet will last much longer than if shaken indiscriminately,' while **The Little Less** advised that *'Less soap flakes are needed if they are first dissolved in very hot water and cold water added after the lather has been made, until the right temperature has been reached.'* For washing clothes, **Make Do and Mend** recommended: *'Use soft water or rain-water wherever possible. Water can be softened with a few drops of liquid household ammonia,'* and *'Put very dirty clothes to soak in semi-dirty water left over from washing and rinsing lightly soiled ones'.*

Alternatives to soap were investigated. **Practical Hints in War Time** recommended that: *'If you have been accustomed to using soap for washing up greasy plates and dishes, try whitening instead. Buy a lump of whitening, dry it in the oven, then crush it to a powder and store it in a carton with holes punched in the top to serve as a sifter. Sprinkle a little of this on the greasy plates, etc. and they will be easy to wash, but they must be given a good rinse after.*

Use whitening for cleaning aluminium saucepans. Prepare in the same way as above, but add one part of silver sand to three of whitening and mix well. Enamel saucepans may be cleaned with the same preparation. For them, mix in twice as much silver sand as before and add a little powdery soda.'

1001 Household Hints suggested: *'Don't throw away left-over tea. It will wash the dirtiest hands quite clean and save the cost of soaps,'* and *'Collect tea leaves in a pail for a week, then add a quart of boiling water. Leave for an hour, strain, and bottle. It makes mirrors, glassware, or windows shine and wards off flies. It's handy, too, for cleaning perambulators, motor car bodies, and bicycles.'*

Not only soap was short; although not rationed, most proprietary household cleaners were among the growing list of hard-to-get products. **Mother & Home** in February 1942 suggested a free alternative to scouring powder: *'One day, burn logs only on your open fire, and you'll find you'll have enough wood ash to last you for a month. We children used to shake the ash through an old kitchen sieve to make sure that it was thoroughly powdered. Then, with a little soap powder, it was put in an old saucer into which my mother dipped her cloth. You have no idea how good that wood-ash cleaner is for pots, pans and non-stainless steel knives. As it doesn't scratch the surface, you can use it on the kitchen sink.'*

The **Home Companion** recommended corks: *'Have a go at a splashed window with a dry cork – it knocks spots off that window every time! And corks make great pan-scourers, too – dip in your scouring powder, then scrub away with a will. In no time that saucepan winks back at you. Most of you know the knife-cleaning dodge with a cork dipped in knife powder, but next time your grocer runs out of your pet brand of knife powder, dip that cork in a drop of paraffin instead. Paraffin does a grand job of work on badly rusted knives you'll find.'* In October 1943, the magazine advised: *'Remember that a thin, flat bone makes a good pot scraper for iron saucepans, and that string and florists' wire knitted up together into a square as a first-class second-best to a ball of steel wool.'* **1001 Household Hints** recommended: *'Soak a ball of silver paper in water, squeeze it well, and use it for cleaning chromium articles which have been stained.'*

Home Notes of September 1942 suggested a traditional cleaner: *'Heather brushes have always been used in the north of Scotland, and I still find they are better than any pan scrubber that is to be bought now. So if you live near a common or a heath, gather a bunch of heather, cut off the flowers and the very young green bits, leaving the stalks and branches about 7 or 8 inches long, bind with wire or strong thread very tightly, about 1¼ inches from the top to form the brush, which should be about 2 inches across.'* Alternatively, **Home Companion** recommended *'the best bits of an old loofah'* as a scourer, while for aluminium pans, *'scouring isn't the thing, but boiling up apple peelings in that saucepan is!'* or *'Aluminium pans need specially cherishing. No soda for them, please! If they're burnt, boil them up, adding a little salt and a little vinegar to the water. Now rinse and rub away at the burnty bits with a coarse cloth dipped in salt. Never scrape and scratch away at aluminium – it's fatal.'* For pots which had gone rusty *'boiling them for half an hour in a panful of water to which you've added the day's potato peelings and a lump of soda'*. Home Notes advised *'If you have a burnt saucepan, put in a few potato peelings, cover with cold water, bring to the boil and simmer for a while. Brush round and rinse, and you will find all trace of black gone, however badly burnt it was before.'* **Home Companion** of October 1943 suggested a method for cleaning frying pans: *'Pour off the left-over fat while it's still hot, then wipe out with a pad of paper dipped in salt,'* and *'Have a go at really grubby baking tins and cake tins by putting them in a zinc bath and boiling them up with soda. Rinse, dry and polish with a soft cloth. Now, they sparkle just as much as when they were new.'*

Far Left Above

Soap rationing meant that staying clean became a problem. One answer was the three-inch cut, a much shorter hairstyle for women, which came into fashion, and needed, as this advert shows, much less shampoo.

Far Left Below

To save fuel, the government had introduced the 5 inches of water scheme, that being the depth of hot water recommended for bathing.

Above

Once again, the war is being used as a selling point; evacuees leave finger-marks on furniture, and furniture will be hard to get after the war (quite true, as it turned out).

1001 Household Hints advised: *'Save eggshells and tie them in thin cloth. Boil them with white clothes, you will find them better than bleach.'* **Home Companion** of January 1943 suggested that to get rid of tea stains, *'Soak the stained part in water in which potatoes have been boiled, then wash in the usual way.'* That July the magazine advised not to rinse the soap out of your dusters after washing: *'because leaving those dusters slightly sticky is just what's wanted – so that the dust will cling to them instead of blowing from one place to another! A drop or two of precious paraffin sprinkled on your duster is another wheeze, as again this collects the dust.'*

In September 1943, **Home Companion** gave a tip for cleaning carpets: *'After you've brushed them in the ordinary way, sprinkle down coarse salt and brush them all over again. Shades cleaner now, but even better still if you have a final scrub at them with an old nail brush and hot water to which you've added a dash of vinegar. When the carpet dries it looks almost too good to be true.'*

When things got grubby you could not just replace them; they had to be reconditioned – even playing cards. Once again, the **Home Companion** comes to the rescue, this time from October 1943. *'Give these cards a brisk rub over back and front with spirits of camphor. It works like a charm because those cards come up so fresh and clean that you hardly know 'em!'*

Mother & Home magazine of February 1942 gave instructions for floor polish: *'put the wax polish in a jar and add four times the amount of paraffin. I leave the wax to soften, shake the mixture to blend it, and rub*

a little on my floors once a month.

The secret of keeping my floors looking like new is – in addition to the cream – a small stiff handbrush like a black-lead polishing brush (which, by the way, also serves perfectly well). Using that brush is not tiring – and it's a good waist-slimming "exercise".' **101 Ways to Save Money in Wartime** had another tip for saving polish: *'When applying floor polish, first wring out a piece of old rag in cold water and apply the polish with this. It will go much farther.'*

1001 Household Hints advised cleaning silk upholstery by making *'a paste of breadcrumbs mixed with methylated spirits. Spread this over the surface with a knife, leave until dry, then brush off.'* Further, *'When the kitchen woodwork looks dirty and greasy, run a piece of flannel soaked in linseed oil over the wood. It will look as if it had been repainted.'* Meanwhile **Cheerful Rationing**, of April 1944, recommended that *'To clean varnished paper or paint, wipe with a flannel dipped in cold tea and polish with a dry cloth.'*

starch

Well-known brands of starch disappeared to be replaced by pooled 'National Starch', but even this became scarce. This brought on the usual saving tips and substitutes. **1001 Household Hints** gave instructions for saving cold water starch: *'after use, let it stand for an hour or two, then drain the water from it. The starch will dry and be fit for use again.'* In June 1943 **Home Companion** suggested washing items

MAKE-DO AND MEND

ISSUED BY THE BOARD OF TRADE

HOUSEHOLD ADVICE CENTRE

BRING YOUR PROBLEMS HERE

MEND AND MAKE-DO TO SAVE BUYING NEW

needing starch in hot sudsy water, rinsing thoroughly, then rinsing again in warm water to which was added water in which rice had been boiled. Allowed to soak and ironed while still fairly wet, *it crisped them up beautifully and put such a nice gloss on them*. **1001 Household Hints** recommended milk as a good substitute, or milk and water, *if you do not wish to make the articles very stiff*.

rubber

With the rapid advance of the Japanese forces in Malaya, Britain's supply of rubber was badly hit; at the end of December 1941 manufacture of many rubber products was banned, including such items as bathing caps and corsets, and in July 1942, the

government was forced to perform a U-turn. The old slogan, 'Carry Your Gas Mask Everywhere', no longer applied; to save rubber most people were now exhorted to leave them at home, but anyone sleeping away from home should take their

Mrs. SEW-and SEW suggests :

8 ways to make Corsets wear longer

1 BE SURE OF YOUR SIZE. Good fit not only gives better support and more comfort, but increases serviceability. So before buying new corsets, run a tape measure over yourself. Don't forget to measure your hips as well as your waist. If corsets are too small on the hips, they develop that worst-of-all faults—riding-up.

2 ALWAYS WEAR A THIN VEST beneath your corsets. Perspiration soon weakens and rots elastic and rubber fabric, and the vest will help to absorb it. At night, spread your corsets over a rail or chair-back and air them well.

3 WASH THEM OFTEN. It's a mistake to think that washing harms corsets. On the contrary, it preserves the fabric and restores elasticity, so wash once a fortnight. Just squeeze them in warm suds. Never scrub or rub. Rinse well, pressing out moisture in dry towel.

ISSUED BY THE   BOARD OF TRADE

Below Left

The war's demands on people's time is the theme of this Mansion polish advert of May 1943; what with fire-watching, digging for victory, the ARP, WVS, and so on, this was a very real problem for many.

Above

Shortages meant that things had to be repaired instead of replaced, often by wives and mothers whose now-absent husband had done such work in the past. Make Do and Mend household advice centres were set up to help them.

Right

Even corsets had to be repaired as rubber was so short. The Board of Trade in the form of 'Mrs Sew-and-Sew' stepped in.

respirator with them.

Prolonging the life of rubber items became vital; **Home Companion** in January 1943 advised: *'One enormously important resolve is to pamper anything and everything that's made of rubber. That hot-water bottle that looks limp and flabby, the bath mat that's been down for years – both bounce up again most wonderfully restored, if you soak them in a solution made of one part of ammonia to two parts of water. Time for the beauty bath is anything up to half an hour, depending on how many wrinkles and puffs need removing.'* In June that year the magazine gave directions for making a waterproof sheet for a baby's cot from brown paper: *'Three stiff, stout sheets of it sewn together give splendid protection. Fold a double thickness of clean old sheeting over it, and there you are. The paper can be changed from time to time, and in this way you will always be able to keep the little mattress sweet and clean.'*

general household hints

Oven gloves could be made from sacking, while the pieces of a worn-out sponge could be collected up and stuffed into a 'pillow' made from bits of old towelling making a cross between a sponge and a flannel, both hard to get. **Home Companion** in July 1943 recommended: *'Useful household gloves made out of the best bits of your worn locknit petties and vests and nighties. Had you thought of it? An easy enough job if you unpick one of hubby's old gloves and use this as a pattern. Hubby's would be about the right size, you see, because, of course, those work-a-day gloves need to be very roomy. If the glove is a left one, reversing it will give you the pattern for the right hand. Use strong, firm back-stitching and double crochet cotton when you come to the sewing, and if you're wise you'll make your-self two pairs for working round the house in and a third pair for bed – these to pull over your well and truly creamed hands.'* Worn-out stockings could be cut in fine strips, *'starting at the top and making one long spiral. Stretch it out well and truly, join three or four stocking spirals together, then work them into a square, using a big coarse crochet hook. Present hubby with one of these squares for polishing his shoes, and they'll be bright as his smile is.'*

In 1940 the government had appealed to the nation's housewives to give up their aluminium pots and pans to be made into Spitfires, although in fact the metal was too poor-grade to be used as such. Still, the morale-boosting effect of the exercise was huge; people felt that they were doing something to hit back, and it was not unknown for better-off people to buy new aluminium saucepans to give to the collections. How many would regret the sacrifice within a few years, as, inevitably, kitchenware of all descriptions became scarce?

Mother & Home magazine, in February 1942, suggested that *'Kettles are hard to buy these days, so we must preserve our old ones. If yours is furred, rectify it by boiling a pint of water in the kettle and adding a tablespoon of borax.'* In September 1943, **Home Companion** asked, *'Have you painted with enamel the bottom of your dustbin both inside and out? So worth-while doing this, because it won't rust now, and so consequently lasts very much longer. And, of course, any old enamel will do for the job.'*

While there were never any specified designs, a lot of pottery manufacturers produced ranges which might be referred to as utility, as they followed the Board instructions. In April 1942, the Board of Trade ruled that pottery designs had to be chosen for simplicity of design and resistance to breakage. From June that year the manufacture of inessential items of domestic pottery was banned, while what was produced was restricted to a plain white, cream or brown finish. **Picture Post**, in April 1943, advised its readers how to brighten up their kitchen by using *'odd pieces of coloured china to supplement your white Utility – a coloured teapot with your white cups, or coloured vegetable dishes with a white dinner set'*. With production severely limited, items had to be multi-functional; with Wedgwood's 'Victory Ware' serving dishes, for instance, one could be inverted to fit over another, becoming a lid for it, to form a casserole dish, while Spode's utility teapot doubled up as a jug, and utility kettles doubled as saucepans.

With pottery so hard to come by, it had to be made to last; **101 Ways to Save Money in Wartime** suggested you *'Fill up cracked cups, jugs and basins with milk and stand in a cool oven until they boil. They can be used for years afterwards, and the milk can be consumed in the ordinary way.'* And in a similar vein **Home Companion** of August 1943 suggested: *'Make a thick spready mixture of pea-flour and water, paste it generously all over the sides and bottom of your dish where the cracks are, then stand the dish for twenty-four hours on the coke stove. This gives time enough for the flour to soak well into the cracks, and there it stays, making your dish watertight once more.'*

Anything made from wood was in shortage. Even clothes pegs were difficult to get. **Housewife**, in October 1940, advised: *'She doubles the clothes line equally, and twists the two ropes fairly*

Above Left
Even razor blades were in short supply and had to be re-sharpened.
Left
An alternative to re-sharpening blades was to buy an 'auto-strop' razor, which sharpened itself.

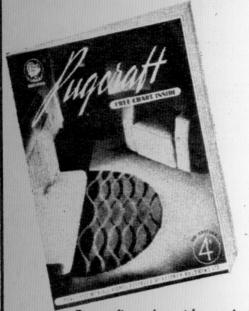
tightly before hanging the line up. When putting out the washing, she separates the twists and slips in a corner of the garment. The line holds the clothes safely, and they are easily removed when dry.' Brooms too were in short supply. **Practical Hints in War Time** reported that *'Brooms and brushes are difficult to replace now, but they wear out just as quickly as ever they did. That short handled floor broom for which you had a preference is probably getting the worse for wear. The hairs at the tip have worn away and now the wooden part projects so that you cannot sweep with it into the corners. Take a saw and trim away an inch or two of the wood at the front. You will then find that, having shortened the wooden part, a new set of hairs comes into use and you have practically the equal of a new broom. A scrubbing brush that has worn down at the tip may be treated in the same way.'* **Home Companion** of June 1943 had other ideas: *'Cut off the handle at the good side, and reverse it to the "baldy" side. Good strong glue and a couple of long nails without heads do the fixing for you, and that brush gets exactly twice as long to live. Of course, you wash your brushes from time to time, but do you ever give the bristles a good old soak in soap and water? It stiffens 'em up beautifully.'* And **1001 Household Hints** suggested that *'Your old broom will make a good polisher. Bind the head with pieces of old cloth, cover with an old piece of velvet and fasten securely.'*

Left
Rug-making had been a pastime many had enjoyed pre-war, now it became a necessity.

decorating

In the first part of the twentieth century, decorating the house was a job for experts, as the materials involved were certainly not designed with do-it-yourself in mind. Even paint had to be mixed and blended, and it was a brave man who would try to do anything more than dab on a bit of whitewash. However, as home ownership mushroomed throughout the interwar years, so what we would call DIY manuals began to appear, and a spot of home decorating became respectable.

Even with the outbreak of war, DIY decorating continued; indeed it became more common, as younger building workers were called up, and a rash of conversion work, shelter building and the like meant that the remaining builders were kept extremely busy. **The Times** of 27 March 1940 carried an article on 'Painting and Repainting – Making a Good Job of It', advising its readers that: *The wood must first be smoothed, then its absorbency must be reduced. Knots are covered with knotting varnish, and the whole is then primed with a special paint called pink priming. This, and all subsequent coats, must be lightly smoothed with sandpaper on a flat block when entirely dry, and then well dusted.*

Painting is an infuriating pursuit to the slap-dash, but a soothing recreation to the methodical. He assembles everything he wants on a tray, lays newspaper on the swept floor, and carefully dusts the work and all its surroundings. He has fixed a wire across the can against which to drain the brush, and he has fixed a rubber brush-collar to

The fashion in wallpaper in the 1940s tended to be very colourful.

Floral designs, in bold colours, were popular.

Art deco-style geometric patterns.

Another fashionable geometric wallpaper.

A second rich foliage pattern.

A sort of hybrid pattern: foliage, but with a geometric feel.

SOFTLY SCREENED WINDOWS

Not the white starched curtains of other days but soft folds and frills and delicate patterns. In fact, the new lace curtains are very feminine indeed. You may have them hanging across the windows with draw curtains as in the top picture, or frilled and tied back with blue as shown on the right. Both are very pretty. Roller blinds must be drawn closely behind them.

To go with them there is this blue starred shadowy patterned paper, and blue paper border.

This dainty wall-paper (No. 72023) with border (No. 69020), from Messrs. Arthur Sanderson & Sons, Ltd., 52 Berners Street, London, W.1 or leading decorators.

Nottingham Lace in many pretty designs may be obtained from leading stores.

This is the wall paper.   *This is the wall paper border.*

This lovely material is Sanderson's Indecoior "Flower" Cretonne No. A714. It is sun-resisting and washproof. 31 inches wide. Price 1s. 11½d. per yard. From leading stores.

FIRST IMPRESSIONS
Warmth and a Good Colour-Scheme

When you come into a hall like this the first thing that you would notice would be its pleasant warmth. The whole house, in fact, would be pervaded by this sense of well-being, as the "Courtier" stove is capable of circulating warm air day and night throughout the whole winter.

Model "K" shown here is eminently suited to a hall, being higher than other models. It is low in cost, inexpensive to instal, and easy to light and maintain. In it ordinary household coal mixed with broken coke burns satisfactorily.

It is a national duty to economise in fuel; the "Courtier" will help you to do this.

Your local ironmonger will give you further details of the "Courtier" stove. Or write for a free colour booklet, No. C.S.36, giving full particulars to Messrs. Mitchell, Russell & Co., Ltd., Chatlan Foundry, Bonnybridge, Scotland.

This is a Courtier stove, Model "K"

By simple planning and a good colour scheme, this little hall has been transformed into a very attractive lounge entrance.

The green enamel stove is the keynote of the scheme. The pretty green walls match the background of the cretonne. A Persian carpet is one of the best floor coverings for a position of this kind, as it is so strong and durable, and its colouring is particularly fine and bright.

---

keep the handle of the brush clean. He arranges the work so that it need not be moved again till it is dry, he sees that he has as good a light as possible, and then he is ready to start.

He goes smoothly on, painting slowly with rhythmic strokes, first with the grain, then against, and then smoothing lightly with the grain. When it comes to the finishing coat he floats it lightly on, brushing with the grain only, but watching very carefully the fullness of each brush-load. In between the coats the brushes are suspended in cold water, and the lids of the cans carefully sealed on with a lick of wet paint.'

Such advice would soon become almost irrelevant as, along with everything else, paint went into shortage, so much so that by August 1943 the government was announcing that for the next three months 500,000 gallons of *'war-time emergency paint'* were to be made available by the Ministry of Works for *'essential external maintenance repair work of private dwellings and other civilian property in Britain and Northern Ireland'.* Before people got too excited however, they further announced that the paint was to be used only for *'patch painting exterior work where the paint film has perished',* and to this end would be issued, ready mixed for use, in dark brown only. It sold in tins at 1s 9d a pint and 3s 6d a quart.

It was a similar story for wallpapers. Once again **The Times** in the last days of the Phoney War,

March 1940, was advising its readers that: *'Gone are the days when nudity was the fashion in wall decoration, and gone, too, are the times when one's only difficulty was to decide between "a pretty pink trellis of roses" and the pimpled type of paper which "might almost be leather". Nowadays manufacturers have combined with artists and decorators to provide a great variety of designs, to suit every type of house, every style of furnishing, and every taste in colour schemes, and it is for the discriminating to choose the papers which will exactly suit each room.*

Broadly speaking, the new designs can be divided into two categories – the flamboyant, which are carried out in bold designs and rich colours, and which will "furnish" bare rooms, reduce the scale of over-big rooms, and give decided character to certain period rooms, particularly the Victorian; and the delicate papers, which are beautifully designed in pastel shades, and may have finely drawn leaf and flower motifs, delicate flute, ribbon, and lace designs, or the ever-popular polka dots or stars on a pale dove-grey, apricot, or lilac ground.

These delicate papers are intended for women's bedrooms, elegant drawing-rooms, and intimate boudoirs where space is restricted and scale can be given by a clever use of upholstery and wallpaper in the same colour and design.'

For a drawing-room they suggested a wallpaper *'in an oak-leaf design patterned in complicated columns from floor to ceiling and echoing the colour scheme of, say, mulberry and sage-green'.* A modern living-room which had a wall with a fireplace and niches either side might be papered *'in a bold mural design of figures and trees, and the other walls carried out in the same background colour, but a perfectly plain paper'.* A woman's bedroom might have its ceiling *'papered in scattered stars, the walls in a delicate lace design, and the scheme completed by a lace bed-spread, and very fine lace, star-patterned, at the window'.* A smaller bedroom could be given the illusion of space with *'a gay paper in a chintz design that covered both walls and ceiling, and exactly matched the chintz curtains and upholstery'.* And *'A bathroom can be emphasised by the new glossy finished papers patterned in crest of the wave designs or saucy little fishes.'* Finally, for the nursery, the paper recommended *'Mickey Mouse and nursery tale cut-outs, which are inexpensive and can easily be stuck on the nursery walls. For older children there is a host of good designs in which policemen, soldiers, animals, and little Christmas trees figure.'*

1001 Household Hints further suggested that you paste wallpaper on the inside of your blackout blind, as *'It is cheery to look at and no chink of light will be seen outside.'*

However, within weeks the German blitzkrieg had swept over Europe, and with it had gone Chamberlain. In his place had come Churchill, and with him a new reality: total war. By the end of June 1940, new paper controls were brought in; no new newspapers were allowed and strict controls applied to the number of pages in existing ones. Wrapping paper was soon banned too, and wallpaper no longer widely produced. Paper supplies for wallpaper manufacturers were severely cut, and for long periods, non-existent.

Left
Bedroom and hall designs from **My Home** magazine, November 1939.

It was normal to keep left-over pieces of wall-paper for use as small patches later on. Now even those had to be stretched; advice was to cut pieces out from behind pictures, leaving a hole which was masked by the picture. Further advice was to tear roughly, rather than cut, round the edges of the patch, as a ragged edge would blend in better than a straight one. Or you might use paper with an entirely different pattern: **Home Companion** in September 1943 suggested: *'You know how thumbed and grubby the wall around the light switch can become? Most depressing to look upon it is, and if you don't want to see it any more, do what I've done. Used a saucer to cut out a round of gay flowery wallpaper. I cut a hole in the middle to accommodate the switch, pasted the wallpaper over the grubby bits, and fine it looks. Or if your light switches are square, make neat little "frames" for them – mitred corners look best you'll find, so make your frame from four little strips. Flowery wallpaper pasted under a glass door-plate would take up the notion, and it certainly is a charming way of fresh-ening up any bedroom.'*

But there was no chance of repapering; some-times walls could be painted, although the paint was often thin, and the results blotchy, so the old skills of rag-rolling and stippling were widely used. But even this was not always possible; **1001 Household Hints** meekly suggested: *'Never mind if you can't have the bedroom papered. Brush down the walls thoroughly. If there are any stained patches on the paper, put some oatmeal in a muslin bag and rub gently over the stains. Repeat until the marks are less noticeable.'*

Brightness, contrast and colour might be added

Above
Old dark-wood furniture could be made to look modern with a coat or two of lacquer.
Right
Picture patterned net curtains such as this were fashionable in 1941.

in other ways. If you could not get large tins of paint to redecorate the walls, small tins could be used to smarten up the furniture. **War Time Household Repairs** recommended enamelling whitewood furniture: *'In selecting the colour for the enamel there is no reason why you should not be somewhat daring as this is a case where a note of cheerfulness can be useful. Consider such colours as fuchsia, primrose, apricot, turquoise blue, eau-de-nil, tangerine and old rose.*

Sometimes a slight amount of decorative work done in a second colour makes the piece more attractive. This should never be carried to excess for while a line of colour here and there may act as a pleasing foil a great deal of colour work is likely to appear gaudy. The paint used for the second shade should be of the same brand as that employed for the first.' **1001 Household Hints** advised, *'Even if you can't do as much painting as you would like, you'll find skirtings all the better for a new coat. Wash well in a soda solution before putting on new paint.'*

Often even this was not possible. **Home Companion** in March 1943 had a suggestion for cheering up your rooms without the need to spend money or coupons: *'Something for a change is the notion of lending your pictures. Ever thought of it? Certainly if you're one of the folk who pines for something fresh to look at, there's an idea in it for you. Loved and familiar things often become so woven into the pattern of our lives that we forget to look at them, so if you feel you aren't appreciating the pictures in your sitting room enough, make a temporary swap with your neighbour and see what a change of scene her pictures give you. She'll be just as refreshed by the pretty "flowery" pictures you've gone in for, as you are by her sunsets and heather-clad hills. Fresh pictures make a room strikingly different and perhaps this swapping notion is the next best thing to new curtains this spring.'*

A room might be brightened up by using the old remedy of new cushions or curtains, though clothing rationing made this difficult. **Home Companion** of July 1943 told its readers that: *'Your clothing coupons are probably all on your back, but you long desperately for new curtains to cheer you up in the sitting room, so either you put up pastel-tinted butter cloth, as I suggested last week, or else you make gay patchwork ones! Easy enough to hunt up all your oddments of sprigged cretonne, checked gingham and anything else you can find. Arrange them as best you can in broad bold stripes, stitching one above the other till you've got the length required for your windows. Save the boldest, most colourful design for the bottom, and if possible make it broader than the other strips, and finish off the bottom with large scallops. Scallop the inside edges of your patchwork curtains to match, then loop them back with bright coloured braid. The effect is gay as a market stall and really does the heart good.'* Alternatively, to brighten up blackout curtains, *'my notion is to stripe them gaily with brightly coloured ribbon or braid. Set the stripes lengthwise and four inches apart, and you'll have a transformation, because the effect is most attractive.'*

New Shade Art. Silk Panel Curtains, 6/- Pair

Woven in delightful pattern that looks well at the windows, and a splendid-wearing quality, these curtains can be chosen with full confidence in their value, their effectiveness, and their service.

Approx. 26 x 36 ins.

HONEY
No. 57/0

MRS. D IS WINDOW-WISE!

She knows that the heavy framework of a window needs softening and veiling . . . that thick black-out curtains must be relieved with something light and dainty. So she chooses panel curtains of British Lace, delicately patterned and so fine that they obscure none of the Spring sunshine. She knows that Lace is a real "window charmer" and yet so economical, so easily laundered, so long-lasting. In fact, she's "window-wise." If you would be, too, send to the address below for a lavishly illustrated Free Booklet "Lace Loveliness for the Window-Wise."

BRITISH LACE FURNISHINGS LOOK LOVELIER . . LAST LONGER

ISSUED BY THE BRITISH LACE FURNISHINGS ADVISORY BUREAU, P.P.6, 69 NEW OXFORD STREET, LONDON, W.C.1.

BE SURE IT'S LACE Genuine British Lace Furnishings are firmly twisted and tied at every intersection. That's why they are so hard-wearing and can be relied upon to last.

HAVE YOU TRIED KNITTING A LAMPSHADE COVER?

With Some Cream Dish-Cloth Cotton And Odds And Ends of Wool, You Can Make A Very Gay Cover

---

In March 1943 the magazine had told its readers, *'Of course, we're all agreed that there's a tremendous lot of red-tape about the blackout; none of us want to get entangled in that – but scarlet braid is quite another story! Buy it and try it. Zig-zag one row of it along the bottom of your pelmet, and three rows along the bottom of your dark curtains. Effect is wonderfully cheerful.*

If you can't get braid, fringing is fun. Loop it up in deep scallops and scallop the bottom of your curtains to match. This is a notion that war-time brides among you might like to copy, because if you're clever enough you can "pretty" up your black-out curtains (they can be dark brown, blue or green, by the way!) so that they're nice enough to hang solo at your windows. And that, of course, would be a wonderful saving in cash and coupons, wouldn't it?'

Picture Post in April 1943 suggested: *'Plenty of fabrics are still to be had without coupons or at a low coupon rate. Besides net and lace, there's a new uncouponed Hessian dyed in lovely colours*

for 6s. 11d. a yard. For bedroom curtains, it's worth spending a few coupons on chintz. But the best curtain idea of all is to use dark blue or green blackout material, if you can manage to get it, and to edge curtains and pelmet with white fringe or ruffled ribbon.'

On a smaller scale **Home Companion** that July advised that *'you could save snippings from the broad stripes and patchwork a shabby parchment lamp to match. An easy matter to paste the strips in squares over the shade, and for a bold finish you could gum scarlet braid round top and bottom. When the lamp is lit the shade will look specially bonny. It's brave little touches such as these that*

Quilted Cushions from Hankies

They also make very smart night-dress sachets.

Page Seven

keep our homes "homey" don't you agree?

A frilly "petticoat" of curtain net for the shabby silk shade in your bedroom is another dainty renovation idea. Gather the net round the top nice and fully so that it hangs in loose folds. A lace border to the frill would look dainty as you please, or a big velvet ribbon would be attractive too.'

Picture Post suggested that you *'Provide colour with plenty of cushions. Cover them with patchwork, if you can do it, made from old clothes or odd bits of stuff. You can even save buying cushions by stuffing your pillows into covers by day.'*

Floor-coverings were difficult; a Board of Trade leaflet on Utility furniture issued in November 1944 pointed out that: *'There is very little real linoleum and it is all needed by hospitals, etc., but the manufacturers are making substitute linoleum and felt-based floor coverings'*, although this too was short unless you had a 'priority docket' (see furniture section).

Carpets, too, were impossible to get new; even small second-hand carpets would fetch a high price. **Picture Post** in April 1943 wrote: *'Carpets are getting just as scarce, and alternatives, such as linoleum or felt, are rarities, too. But a poor carpet is always a bad buy. Rather than this, it's better to stain your floors and buy the largest secondhand rugs you can afford. A secondhand department or country auction may still provide a good Persian or English rug, though there are no more "incredible bargains". Even at the most obscure country house sale, you won't find a good rug of any size for much less than £15.'* This would be about £400 at today's prices.

As early as December 1940 **Modern Woman** suggested, *'Halve a grey army blanket lengthwise, bind the edges with emerald – or another bright, clear colour. Use as a stair covering. It is warm, durable and unusual.'* On a similar theme **Home Companion** in January 1943 suggested: *"fishy" bath mats shaped like a giant plaice! I thought at once that some of you, whose bathroom is your special pride and joy, might like to copy this attractive idea. Bath towels worn badly at the edges will go to make your mat. Use two thicknesses from the good middles to cut out your fish, then bind round the edges with braid to match your curtains. To make your fish look even more at home by the side of your bath, give him a neat little fin, a bright eye,*

and speckles on his tummy! Work all these in coloured embroidery cotton. You'll love the finished effect.'

101 Ways to Save Money in Wartime recommended, *'Instead of replacing lino and carpets, sandpaper the floorboards, stop up holes and cracks and paint with a good brand of hard floor enamel. When dry, polish with floor polish. This will preserve the floorboards from rot, germs and insects, and makes a delightful and artistic surface, cool and dustless in summer, cheerily glowing with reflected light in winter.'* **War Time Household Repairs** went a stage further, suggesting covering a floor with plywood to imitate parquet: *'There are various grades of plywood and it is advisable to choose a kind that is faced with a wood possessing an attractive grain. Birch, ash and oak are suitable, but ordinary deal though cheaper is not recommended as it is not hard enough and will not wear so well . . . do not make the mistake of having the squares too small. Nothing smaller than 12 in. squares should be decided on and 15 in. is perhaps preferable. It is not necessary to have squares if oblongs can be cut from the sheets with less waste . . . set out the squares temporarily on the floor starting at the centre of the room. It may be that by slightly altering the mass of squares you are able to get a better arrangement. In any case it is unlikely that the squares will exactly cover the floor, nor is it desirable, since the best effect is provided by having strips of wood beside the skirting boards to act as a surround. These strips should be approximately the same width all round the room. . . . Having made the whole of the floor smooth and level, stain it and, when the coating has soaked in, give the*

alternate squares a second covering. This will make them stand out in a pattern and provide a very pleasing effect especially if it were remembered to lay the squares alternately with the grain running across the room and down it. As soon as the stain has dried give the surface a wax finish.'

As with everything else, events intervened. Wood shortages meant that in January 1942 plywood, used extensively for aircraft production, was no longer available for civilian use. The shortage of wood generally meant that every scrap needed to be utilised. **Modern Woman** of December 1940 suggested *'Old cotton reels, painted or stained, make excellent door stops or makeshift handles on doors or drawers. Fix with large screw through centre hole.'*

furniture

From the very beginning of the war, wood was in shortage; on 5 September 1939 timber was brought under government control, and one week later it was announced that, as of that date, no further timber would be available for house building, bringing any further construction to a halt.

In July 1940 all supplies of wood for furniture manufacture were halted; production trickled to a halt as factory stockpiles ran out, and availability of furniture in shops soon became tight. Even making your own became difficult, as timber supplies to

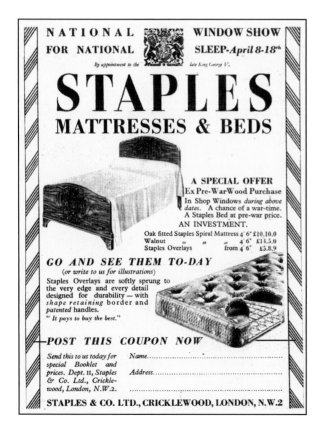

any civilian outlets were tightly controlled. In January 1941 **Hobbies Weekly** reported: *'One of the difficulties confronting readers to-day is the shortage of timber. We can no longer be too particular in either the choice of the kind of timber we want or the selection of its quality. Indeed, some items may prove impossible of construction owing to the amount of timber needed, especially those calling for a considerable amount of softwood. Fortunately a new source of supply has now become available, and readers will find it worth while to consider this for their work.*

Air raids have resulted in the destruction of large numbers of houses, and the various local authorities in their salvage work have stacked together large quantities of timber, most of which is available to anyone who cares to buy it. Much of it

Any handyman can make this

INEXPENSIVE HALL STAND

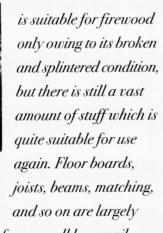

examination is necessary. Often the chopping out and plugging of the offending part may be better than the use of a stopping. Plastic wood, however, will have to be widely used. In any case, we have to be satisfied with a lower grade of timber than we would use in normal times. Access to these salvage timber dumps is usually through the local borough or other council, and readers living near them will certainly find a visit well worth while.'

is suitable for firewood only owing to its broken and splintered condition, but there is still a vast amount of stuff which is quite suitable for use again. Floor boards, joists, beams, matching, and so on are largely sound, though, of course, all have nail holes (and nails too). In addition are room and street doors, window frames, mantelpieces and interior fitments of all kinds.

For better class interior woodwork such as furniture, this rough timber is scarcely suitable. On the other hand the various doors and other fitments offer a source of good clean stuff. It is just a matter of knocking them to pieces. In some cases hardwood such as oak and mahogany is available in the form of shelves, mantelpieces, and so on. These items are invariably available at cheap prices, though a difficulty may be that of transport. Anyone who has the means of carrying timber will find the purchase of this timber economical. In some cases it may be possible to take advantage of lorries which, arriving in the district with a load, would normally be returning empty. Naturally one of the drawbacks of this salvage timber is the presence of nail holes and often of cracks. For rough outdoor work this may not matter, but for indoor use a careful

In that month (January 1941) came the first mention of Utility furniture. The 'Big Blitz' on Britain's towns and cities had begun in September and by now thousands had been 'bombed out' and there was a pressing need for emergency replacement furniture for them. One month later plans for the future manufacture of 'Standard Emergency Furniture' was announced; this was not Utility as such, and was largely made from plywood.

One year later, discussions about the manufacture of Utility furniture began. Utility clothing had begun to be introduced one month before, and the system, based on hard-wearing products produced with as little wastage as possible of materials and labour, seemed perfect for the hard-pressed furniture trade.

By now there was a real shortage of furniture. **Picture Post** magazine, in April 1943, wrote: *'After studying current prices, regulations, and the amount of merchandise available, I'm convinced that it's impossible – unless you're a millionaire or something really big in the Black Market – to furnish a home today from scratch. Only about 12 per cent. of young people getting married are even attempting it.*

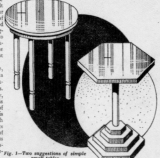
Put all you can afford into good armchairs; into good beds; into good carpets; into good men's furniture. (You will probably be perfectly happy with a rickety little dressing table so long as it's pretty, but your husband will be wretched with a ramshackle chest of drawers.) Unless you already have these big items, or can put down a considerable sum for them, it really isn't sensible to set up house during the war; for you can no longer buy good examples of these things cheaply, and inferior ones are not practical.

A good armchair, for instance, costing from £10 up, will give you fifteen years of comfort, but a cheaper one may give you two or three years discomfort and then give out. Good beds, too, are getting scarcer and scarcer, and you have very little chance of getting a double divan bed, either new or secondhand, for under £25.'

Poor quality pieces were selling for exorbitant prices, while the price of second-hand furniture rocketed, and that May prices of furniture including second-hand items came under government price control. Antiques, defined as anything made before the year 1900, were excluded.

On 3 July 1942, Hugh Dalton, President of the Board of Trade, announced that the Utility scheme was to be extended to include furniture, which would be made available from January 1943. The first Utility furniture prototypes were presented to the Board of Trade in September; these were deemed acceptable by the Board, which decided to show them to the public in the form of a 'Utility Furniture Exhibition' one month later.

Production began in November 1942. It was further ordained that all other furniture still being made had to be completed by the end of January 1943, and sold by the end of February, as only

Utility could be sold as new furniture after that date.

Utility furniture could only be obtained with permits, similar to ration coupons, which were issued to newly married couples and those who had been bombed out. From March 1943 this was extended to married couples, with children, setting up home for the first time.

A Board of Trade leaflet set out the scheme: *'Supplies of utility furniture are limited by the shortage of materials and labour; and have to be shared out fairly among the newly married, the bombed out and certain other classes of people with an urgent need to make a home. It is illegal to sell permits or units or to give or transfer them to any-one else.*

Utility nursery furniture (that is cots, play-pens and babies' chairs) can be bought without a permit; but there will only be enough for people who really need it, and you should not buy a new chair or cot if you have an old one that would do.

In order to make the best possible use of the limited materials available, production has been confined to a few selected designs, and the whole range of utility models can be seen in an illustrated catalogue which gives prices and general specifica-tions. The shopkeeper from whom you order your furniture may have a few pieces on temporary show, though he is unlikely to have a complete range. But he will be able to show you a copy of the catalogue.

The buying permit is valid only in the area named on it; you may order utility furniture from any furniture retailer in that area; but in order to save transport and possible delay, you should choose a shop near to the address at which you will be using the furniture. The prices given in the catalogue include delivery within a radius of 15 miles, but the retailer may charge for delivery beyond this radius. You need not buy all the furni-ture at the same time nor from the same shop, and if you wish you may order it by post.

Since supplies of utility furniture are limited, manufacturers will not be able to keep large stocks

Above Left
A DIY coffee table in a very modernist design. As well as being ultra-modern, such simple designs were far easier for the amateur handyman, or woman, to make.

Below Left
Not reproduction, but restored. Stores such as Harrods could no longer sell new furniture, so sold antiques instead.

Below
150 guineas was about £4,000 in today's money.

ARDING & HOBBS

famed for fine Furniture

Fine example of quality Secondhand Furniture in a set of 2 arm and 6 small dining chairs. Seats fully upholstered and covered morocco.

150 gns.

ALTHOUGH new furniture is now restricted to Utility Models, we can offer some choice Secondhand and Reproduction pieces which have a charm of their own and are a joy to possess. A visit to our Furniture Galleries will be found interesting and profitable.

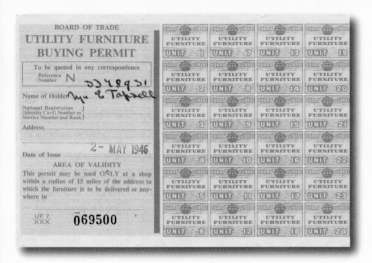

and there may be some delay before the furniture is delivered. The Board of Trade cannot guarantee that the factories producing utility furniture will be able to deliver the articles within any definite time after an order has been placed.

Maximum prices have been fixed for both new and secondhand utility furniture, and traders are permitted to sell under a hire-purchase or credit sale agreement subject to a minimum initial payment, to a maximum charge for the facility, and to full payment being made within two years from the date of the contract. The retailer from whom you buy the furniture will be able to show you a list of cash prices and give particulars of hire-purchase terms. The cash prices are also shown in the catalogue.'

Reactions to Utility furniture were mixed. **Woman & Home** magazine in March 1943 commented that *'Though "Utility" furniture was primarily designed for people who have lost their homes through enemy action, or for "newly-married" couples wanting to set up home in war-time – it is the kind of furniture whose simple lines appeal to every-one. It goes splendidly in the "tailored" rooms that modern couples like. The furniture is of oak or*

mahogany on simple strong lines.'

Picture Post observed: *'Utility furniture, in my opinion, is not a success. Most of the designs are downright ugly and some of the pieces, particularly the beds, don't look as though they would outlast the war. The prices are no cheaper than average second-hand prices, and I would consider a well-chosen second-hand chest for £9 a better buy than a Utility one for £9. 6s. 9d.*

The Utility dining furniture, however, is moder-ately priced and quite attractive; we chose it for the dining corner of this flat. If you like it, and are eligible for Utility furniture, apply for "points" at your local Fuel Office. They will allocate you a certain number of points according to your needs.'

Applicants would be assessed on their eligibility and needs and issued with the appropriate 'units' depending on the number of people in the family, how much furniture they possessed already, and so on, up to a maximum of 60. Units could then be spent on any items they wanted from the Utility catalogue. As the Board of Trade leaflet stated, shops could not keep furniture in store, having to order it from the manufacturers only on receipt of an order from a customer. Their windows would therefore only display those few pieces of second-hand furniture which they had available. It was not unknown for shops to pay customers ordering Utility pieces to allow them to keep the furniture for a month or two, so that they could display it in their windows.

For those who did not qualify for Utility units, second-hand was their only resort. **Picture Post** gave them advice: *'The other great source of cheap furniture is, of course, the second-hand shops.*

England seems to have an inexhaustible supply of old furniture, china and junk, much of it of beautiful quality and design, and some of it still cheap.

Old pedestals make good stands for lamps or vases. Old gilt mirrors can be bought for less than £1. Patterned candlesticks or vinegar sets dress up a Utility dining table. A second-hand couch for £10 or less may come cheaper than two armchairs. Little odd chairs can still be picked up cheap for painting or covering yourself. (Try to get the ones with loose seats; you can cover them in five minutes.) And the saleroom or junk shop now rivals the great Woolworths as a hunting ground for household cans, kettles, cloths, and carpentering tools.

Don't spend a vast sum on a dressing-table, but don't do without one. Either buy a pretty decorated table and stand a mirror on it or have a plain table or even a packing case or meat safe, and cover it with a drawstring skirt of uncouponed net, add a tray on top for your brushes and bottles, hang a mirror on the wall.

For the kitchen, a plain table with a piece of oil cloth (still obtainable) tacked on top is often cheaper than an enamel topped kitchen table. A trolley, provided your kitchen and dining table are on the same level, will save buying a sideboard, for you can keep your cutlery and china in the kitchen, and wheel it all in.'

Home Companion that July suggested: *'Every girl wants a dainty little occasional table for the sitting room, but because they cost pounds now how about letting an oval mirror*

do duty for one? Happily mirrors still abound in junk shops, and if you buy one and have it mounted on four little legs and enamel the wooden frame to tone in with your colour scheme, it'll look fine. Tea-pot and china will be reflected most attractively in it, and of course a bowl of flowers looks heavenly set in glass.'

In September 1943 the maximum number of Utility units was reduced to 30, increased once again in August 1944 to 60 units but with 30 deferred, and at the same time the scheme was extended to Ulster. Like many other austerity measures, the Utility furniture scheme outlasted the war; in June 1947 a second Utility catalogue was even published. Furniture rationing did not end until June 1948, while the Utility scheme continued until May 1952.

Above Left
Utility furniture coupons from 1946. Few qualified for such coupons; those that did were mainly newly married couples and those bombed out, and even for them, the number of coupons was far from enough to cover furnishing of all but the tiniest of flats.

Below
Table of coupon values of Utility furniture. Those lucky few who received coupons would have to be very careful how they used them.

ARTICLE		NO. OF UNITS REQUIRED	ARTICLE		NO. OF UNITS REQUIRED
Wardrobe	(4' 0")	12	Kitchen chair		1
"	(3' 0")	10	Kitchen cabinet (complete)		8
Dressing Chest	(3' 0")	8	(top)		3
"	(2' 6")	6	(bottom)		5
Tallboy		8	Fireside chair		5
Bedstead	(4' 6")	5	Arm chair		6
"	(4' 0")	5	Bed chair		6
"	(3' 0")	3	Divan	(3' 0")	6
Sideboard		9	"	(2' 6")	6
Dining table		6	Bed-settee		10
Dining chair		1	Shelves		3
Kitchen table	(4' × 3')	6	Occasional table		3
"	(3' 6" × 2')	4	Curb (Fender)		1

TABLE OF UTILITY FURNITURE UNITS VALUE

GROUPE DES PUBLICATIONS CONDÉ NAST   11, RUE SAINT-FLORENTIN

LE JARDIN DES MODES

19e ANNÉE. N° 290.   15 NOVEMBRE 1939.

NINA RICCI

Ensemble en Obanya

de MEYER

clothing

By the late 1930s fashionable clothes were available to a far bigger section of the population than ever before through mass-produced off-the-peg clothing, though the size of the average person's wardrobe was far smaller than today.

As ever, the most fashionable styles would only be worn by the younger and usually more affluent members of society, who could afford a dress whose style or colour would be out of fashion within a year. However, home dress-making - far more common then – meant that last year's frock could be altered or dyed to bring it up to date. Older women normally wore the house-wife's uniform of a pinafore, the 'pinny' being removed for more formal occasions, and the style of the dress often reflected the fashions of the wearer's youth.

Housewife magazine of October 1940 discussed a woman's wartime wardrobe:

'Well, the first item is likely to be a top coat. This is your most important purchase, and its line and colour will influence everything else you buy, so choose it carefully and well. Don't have it fur-trimmed, unless you feel you must. "Dressy" coats are out of touch with these strenuous times, and the money you would put into fur will be better invested in first-class fabric. Don't pick anything extreme in style, since you are buying for more than one season and all extremes are soon outmoded.

If your coat is plain, a check suit might well be your next investment. Add a tailored wool crepe shirt in the suit's predominating shade, and a crepe-de-Chine shirt that picks up one of the other tones. You'll knit yourself a couple of gay woollies, too, to add to the suit's scope.

Day-dresses? Probably two; a shirt-frock for workaday wear, and a frock of fine woollen with just enough formality about it to be right for a social lunch or tea, or a quiet evening with friends. (Your list contains no evening dress; if you decide that

No. 733

GOOD TASTE

FIRST IN FICTION FASHION & BEAUTY

8ᴰ

FEB. 1941

Inside

FREE Dress Pattern Offer *and* **Cut-out Offer** *of this* **Frock**

WITH CHOICE OF THREE SIZES

you really must have one, choose a simple style and run it up with your own needle.)

The shirt-frock – perhaps in check if your coat is plain – should have a high neckline with turn-down collar, and no more elaborate detail than pin-tucks or pockets.

The other dress, in plain colour, might have a rucked or shirred bodice and some soft fullness in its skirt front.

Both skirts will be short – the newest hems are from seventeen to eighteen inches from the floor – and narrower in silhouette than those of last season.

This slimmer line is partly the inevitable swing of the fashion pendulum away from very full flares, partly a natural result of wartime shortage of material; it is coming in gradually, and it doesn't preclude straight-falling gathered fullness, pleats pressed or unpressed, or even a moderate flare.'

Men's clothes, which apart from knitted items such as jumpers and scarves, were not made at home, remained far less the subject of fashion. The basic costume was made up of the three-piece suit,

shirt and tie, and outdoors, the almost obligatory hat. For informal occasions the waistcoat might be replaced by a cardigan or jumper, but the tie would almost invariably be worn.

Suits fell into two main categories; 'town suits', in wool or a similar cloth, and 'country suits' in tweed or similar, sometimes with plus-four trousers.

Most men would possess two or three suits; a 'Sunday best', replaced every two to five years, for a wedding or other occasion. Upon purchase, it would replace the previous best suit, which was then used for work, or everyday dress. Often the trousers would wear out first, which was why suits were often sold with the option of two pairs of trousers. The jacket could, of course, be worn with

separate trousers, often a pair of flannel bags, worn for sports or for holidays. Trousers were almost universally button-flyed, and held up by wide elastic braces. The better off you were, the more suits you were likely to possess: Chips Channon, a Conservative MP and businessman, claimed to own forty. These would probably include at least one evening suit, with dinner jacket, and a tail suit for very formal occasions. Few men owned the first, and very few the second – hire shops would do the job in the unlikely case that most men would actually need either.

The suit, or jacket and trousers, would be worn with a waistcoat or jumper, and a tie on all but the most informal occasions, usually in the summer, when the shirt collar would be worn open over the coat or, for the better-off, blazer. Ties, worn as they were under a waistcoat or jumper, were much shorter than today. A hat completed the outfit, usually a flat cap for working men or for sport, a bowler for business types, and a trilby-type for the better-off.

Children often wore what was basically a cut-down version of their parents' clothes. Middle- and upper-class boys wore a V-necked jumper over a shirt and tie, often a school tie, usually with ⅛in to 1in horizontal stripes in the school colours. These were worn with long shorts and long socks, leaving just the knees showing, and finished with a school or Cub cap. More working-class boys would wear a similar outfit, but the shirt would commonly be of the knitted cotton or wool, 'Fred Perry' type, though still worn with a tie. Older boys were often seen in school uniform, blazer, tie and cap, and from the age of twelve, long trousers. Girls wore a

frock, or school uniform in the form of the gym slip, worn with shirt and school tie.

War brought some immediate changes to people's dress; despite the official description of the gas-mask cardboard carrying box as 'sturdy', regular use soon gave them a battered appearance, and exposure to rain made them soggy. One

Above
Girl's knitted dress. Working-class children's clothes were often hand-made pre-war, and as shortages and rationing bit, the habit spread.

Right
A man's siren suit, or shelter suit. The most famous wearer of the siren suit was undoubtedly Winston Churchill, who often sported a red corduroy version.

answer was to cover the box with a waterproof material, such as 'American cloth'. The private sector offered for sale a range of gas-mask cases, from the cheapest cloth covers costing less than 2s, designed to take both gas mask and box, through to real leather cases, and in the most expensive range, leather handbags which incorporated a section for the gas mask. Other popular designs included metal boxes or cylinders, favoured by men and children. The box-type container had one big advantage: there was room in the box for extras. **1001 Household Hints** advised, *'Put a small first-aid dressing box inside your children's gas mask containers. Box should contain one 2-in. bandage and a small piece of boric lint.'* Chemists sold small first-aid packs especially for the purpose. It was, however, noted that not all cartons and carriers actually contained a mask at all, becoming a sort of replacement handbag.

In the first few months of the war, as deaths on the road at night showed a dramatic increase due to the blackout regulations, the government encouraged people through poster campaigns to 'wear something white at night'. Shops sold 'luminous' articles, including buttons, armbands, and artificial flower buttonholes, as well as white hatbands, belts, waistcoats, umbrellas and overcoats. Women were offered white stockings, although many rejected these as they made the legs look fat. Most did not bother at all, or carried a newspaper, or, in the case of men, pulled their shirt tails out. With the relaxation of the blackout rules from mid-September 1939, such ideas faded out.

Another early wartime fashion was the 'siren suit', otherwise known as the 'shelter suit'. When the warning siren sounded you had a few minutes to get to your shelter before a possible raid might start; if this was at night, as many raids would be, you would have to dress warmly, as well as quickly, as most shelters were cold and damp. The perfect answer was the siren suit, a one-piece overall, usually made of lined woollen material, and often incorporating a hood. These were normally worn by women, although children's versions were also popular.

Another air-raid fashion was the helmet. Children's versions were very popular presents at Christmas 1939, while for adults there were bakelite and fibre helmets sold which were guaranteed as effective as steel versions, although if they did not prove to be so, you would probably not be alive to claim your money back. More prosaic was the suggestion that a large metal basin or bowl, padded out by a towel, would do just as well. What this of course missed was that you might be safe, but it was difficult to maintain an heroic air with a bowl on your head.

There were also commercially produced 'gas-proof' suits which the manufacturers claimed were easily carried and could be put on in a few seconds.

In the first few months of the war controls were introduced on supplies to manufacturers of many raw materials including flax, hides, skins, jute, leather, silk, wool and cotton, as large amounts of these were needed for the war effort, and this had to come before 'luxuries' such as civilian clothing. It soon became clear that this would result in rapid price increases as the laws of supply and demand operated; in mid-September 1939, the **Daily Mirror** was predicting that 'prices of all clothing, including underwear and footwear, are likely to rise as soon as stocks now held by retailers are cleared'. In January 1940 the government responded by introducing price controls on a large number of items including clothes and shoes.

In April 1940 the government issued 'Limitation of Supply Orders' on cotton, rayon and linen goods. Under these orders manufacturers were only able to produce a limited quantity of goods based on a percentage of their pre-war production, in this case, 75%. It was only natural that under these circumstances they would protect their profits by cutting their less profitable, cheaper lines. **Housewife** magazine, of October 1940, reported that '*Your dress allowance has dwindled, is dwindling, and is likely to dwindle further still. The price of clothes has risen, is rising, and will continue to rise.*' Six months later, as the amount of clothing in the shops decreased, prices had increased to 72% above their 1939 level, and by 1942 clothing manufacture was down to 50% of the 1939 level.

Buying second-hand clothes had long been a common experience for the working class, but this practice began to increase as prices rose rapidly, and many of the goods on sale were found to be shoddily produced.

It became important to squeeze every ounce of use out of the clothes you had, especially in shortage areas such as shoes, and tips abounded in magazines and government leaflets. The booklet **101 Ways to Save Money in Wartime** gave the following tips for shoes: '*Try painting the soles of the family's shoes with Copal varnish. They will last longer without repair,*' and '*Uppers of shoes should be treated with a little castor oil occasionally*

and the welts waterproofed by the application of neatsfoot oil, linseed oil or vaseline,' or *'Lay shoes on their sides immediately after taking them off, and if you have no trees stuff them with newspaper lightly rolled.'* In addition, *'Silk stockings will not ladder easily if after washing they are dipped in water containing a little methylated spirit or common salt. Toes and heels of silk stockings rubbed very lightly with bees-wax will stand hard wear.'*

Two later fashions brought in by the war were the wearing by women of trousers and headscarves. Trousers on women had been regarded as almost scandalous in the pre-war years, and any women who did wear them for motorcycle riding or similar would often find themselves being refused service in cafés or bars. However, the vast increase in women working in factories saw the wearing of overalls and trousers mushroom, and similarly 'digging for victory' was much easier in trousers. The wearing of trousers thus became a badge of honour indicating that the wearer was doing her bit for the war effort, and many who were not actually doing jobs where you might need to wear them took up the fashion, until in some places it was almost the rule rather than the exception.

Hats were not rationed, and as such became very expensive, so many women took to wearing the headscarf, a versatile item which could be used as a turban or a shawl, both of which helped cover the hair, which, after the introduction of soap rationing in 1942, was often greasy, especially for factory workers. Headscarves made a splash of colour in an otherwise drab outfit, especially

those produced by Jacqmar. The firm of Jacqmar was based in Mayfair, where they produced a wide range of propaganda textiles, most designed by Arnold Lever, who continued to work for the company even after joining the RAF. They were produced as headsquares for women and neck scarves or cravats for men, especially in the forces; originally in silk, but after its use was banned for making civilian clothing, from cotton or rayon.

Far Left
A variation on the siren suit, the siren dressing gown, from November 1939.

Left
The epitome of the wartime look: the turban and the short-sleeved, square-shouldered, hand-knitted sweater. It's difficult to make out, but if she is wearing trousers, the look is complete.

Above
Headscarves were everywhere; most fashionable were the 'pro-paganda' scarves produced by Jacqmar of London, many of which were designed by Arnold Lever. This one depicts salvage.

Knight's Castile

FOR *Face* APPEAL

austerity

Throughout the war the government was determined that the sacrifices which the nation would clearly have to make should not be seen to fall unfairly on the poorer sections of the population, as had, to a great extent, been the situation in the First World War, when calls for food rationing had been rejected until the very end. This had seen prices rocket, and the rich were able to ride the storm while the poor went hungry.

The government's first weapon against the repetition of such a situation was price control, but this could be difficult with clothing; while the cost of a loaf of bread could be easily fixed, two suits could be hugely different, in terms of fabric, cut, off the peg or made to measure, and so on.

The government, in the form of the Board of Trade, introduced other weapons: control orders which dictated what could be made, in what quantities, the materials which could be used, and even the specifications of their design and construction. These various orders became known as 'Austerity', creating, as they did, an austere, uniform look with few fripperies or extras.

In November 1941 an order banned the setting-up of any new clothes manufacturing businesses. One month later, rubber, in great shortage as the

Above Left
The snood. A medieval-type hair net, popular in the early years of the war, before soap rationing and factory work led to shorter hairstyles.

Left Below
Uniform became the smartest fashion of all, and for those not in uniform, working clothes demonstrated that you were 'doing your bit'.

Above Left

Austerity spread to every type of clothing, including baby clothes.

Above Right

The austerity man's suit, three button, single breasted, no waistcoat and no turn-ups.

Below

With leather becoming short, wooden-soled shoes arrived. Clogs had long been worn in parts of northern England and Wales, but for women who were not used to wearing clogs, the government had to issue advice on how to walk in them.

Japanese forces overran Malaya, came under Board of Trade control, and a long list of items which were no longer allowed to be made was published, to include various items of clothing, while Wellington boots and rubber gloves could only be purchased with a permit.

At the beginning of May 1942 the first 'Civilian Clothing Restriction Order' placed severe restrictions on the manufacture of clothes. Men's suits had to be single breasted with no slits or buttons on the cuffs, and no flaps over the pockets. The trousers could have no more than three pockets, no elastic in the waistband, no zip fasteners and no turn-ups, although if off-the-peg trousers were too long, the tailor was not allowed to cut off the extra, and could turn them up.

Women's clothes were limited as to the number of buttons that could be used, and the number of pleats on a dress or shirt; turned-back cuffs on sleeves and flap or button-down pockets were banned, as was the use of embroidery. The depth of hems was regulated and certain materials prohibited. For both sexes the amount of stitching was limited.

In August 1942, crepe rubber soles were prohibited, while in September a restriction order was applied to the manufacture of shoes: this prohibited the use of cut-outs such as open toes in footwear, while heels were limited to a maximum height of 2⅛ inches and could only be made of wood without any leather covering. Further, metal buckles and rubber adhesive were banned in shoe manufacture.

The following year came a control of use order for elastic, using, as it did, scarce rubber. Elastic could no longer be used in the manufacture of clothes other than women's corsets and knickers, and even then could only be used in very small lengths, rather than around the whole waist. Elastic soon became the province of black-market 'spivs', such as private Joe Walker in **Dad's Army** who is always able to offer some buckshee knicker elastic.

clothes rationing

Food rationing, which was introduced in January 1940, was overwhelmingly regarded as a success. That is not to say there was no moaning about the levels at which rationing was set, but at least the suffering was being shared by everyone, rich or poor – 'fair shares for all' was the phrase repeatedly used by the government to describe it. Indeed it was in the areas where there was no rationing, such as offal, that the biggest criticisms came as some shopkeepers favoured 'special' customers, and this often meant the better-off, through the 'under-the-counter' system, by which scarce or hard-to-get items were kept to one side for the select few.

Government-enforced cutbacks in the quantity of civilian clothing produced during the first 18 months of the war, and the ensuing rapid rise in its cost, led to calls for a similar system of rationing to be introduced for clothing and shoes. The latter were especially hard to get as there existed a severe shortage of leather, so much so that supplies of leather to manufacturers had been rationed in February 1941. The wealthy, like Chips Channon with his forty suits, could always afford to buy more as prices rocketed, whereas the least well-off, who had the fewest clothes in their wardrobes, could not.

Oliver Lyttelton, President of the Board of Trade, had tried to introduce clothes rationing, but Prime Minister Winston Churchill was deeply set against the idea and vetoed it, being convinced that the public would hate it. Finally, early in 1941, Lyttelton reintroduced the idea when Churchill

COUPONLESS LASS—
—NOT IN THE SWIM

"What can I do?"
"Use moth-balls next time!"

had his mind on other things, and the former was able to slip the proposal through, much to the annoyance of the Prime Minister when he realised what was going on.

On 1 June, Lyttelton announced in a wireless broadcast that clothes rationing would be introduced the following day, to be followed almost immediately by the rationing of furnishing fabrics and carpets. That such a huge undertaking could be accomplished without any hint escaping to the general public was a master stroke. Food rationing had been heralded by an official announcement made almost two months before its introduction, allowing

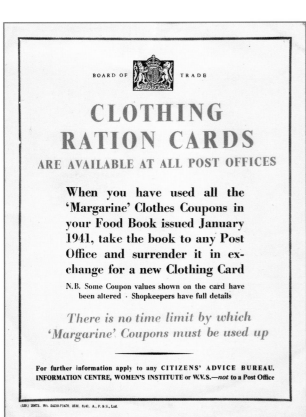

BOARD OF TRADE

CLOTHING RATION CARDS
ARE AVAILABLE AT ALL POST OFFICES

When you have used all the 'Margarine' Clothes Coupons in your Food Book issued January 1941, take the book to any Post Office and surrender it in exchange for a new Clothing Card

N.B. Some Coupon values shown on the card have been altered · Shopkeepers have full details

There is no time limit by which 'Margarine' Coupons must be used up

For further information apply to any CITIZENS' ADVICE BUREAU, INFORMATION CENTRE, WOMEN'S INSTITUTE or W.V.S.—*not* to a Post Office

(120.) 20675. Wt. 24210-P1470. 25M. 8/41. A., P. & S., Ltd.

those who could afford it to stock up.

Such a grand scheme as national rationing of clothes could hardly be kept secret, many thought, as the printing of over forty million ration books alone would involve hundreds, if not thousands, of printers, drivers, warehousemen and minor officials. The Board of Trade side-stepped this problem by the ingenious ruse of *not* printing ration books.

Everyone, of course, had a food ration book. These had to be printed months in advance, and also had to be capable of taking into account changes in the rationing system – new items added and so on. To do this, a number of spare coupons were included in the books, as well as coupons for items likely to be, but not yet, rationed. Among these were 26 spare 'margarine' coupons, and it was decided to use these as the first clothing ration coupons while proper ration books were printed.

Unlike food rationing, the element of choice was foremost. Items to be covered by the scheme were allotted a coupon value, and consumers given a set number of coupons, 66 in the first year. They could use these coupons for any rationed goods they chose, in any shop, or shops, whenever they wanted. The main problem with the scheme was the wide range of goods covered, from shoes to suits, underwear to swimwear, children's clothes to sportswear, a tutu to a vicar's cassock. The Board of Trade issued lists of clothes and their coupon values, and a booklet, the **Clothing Coupon Quiz**, which listed most items

Far Left
As with everything else, clothing rationing became a source of humour.

Above
Planning for clothes rationing had been carried out in virtually total secrecy, by the simple expedient of using margarine coupons from the food ration book, instead of printing special books.

Right
The intricacies of the clothes rationing system: the number of coupons required for various items, and which items were coupon-free, were so complicated that the government issued booklets like this every year, this one from 1943.

ISSUED BY THE BOARD OF TRADE

Your Questions Answered

THE 1942-1943 CLOTHING QUIZ

(REPRINTED WITH AMENDMENTS—JANUARY 1943)

CROWN COPYRIGHT RESERVED

HIS MAJESTY'S STATIONERY OFFICE 2ᴰ

and their values, as well as answering 101 questions, such as *'May I sell coupons I don't need, or may I buy other people's spare coupons?'* answer – no, or *'Are coupons required for knitting yarn?'* answer – yes, or *'Are coupons required for a domestic servant's uniform?'* answer – yes, and so on.

And what could you get for your 66 coupons? For a man, a woollen, lined overcoat would be 18, a three-piece suit 26, a shirt 5, a pair of shoes 7, a set of combinations 7, and a pair of socks 3, making a year's supply of 66.

For a woman, a wool-lined overcoat would be 18, a woollen dress or siren suit 11, blouse 4, nightdress 6, 2 changes of under-wear, petticoat, suspenders, brassiere and pants 18 in all, one pair of shoes 5, leaving enough for two pairs of stockings.

Knitting wool for service comforts, along with uniforms for certain civilian groups such as the Red Cross, and some working clothes were exempted, although other wools and cloths were both rationed, although not as much as the finished articles. Second-hand clothes were also covered to prevent unscrupulous people avoiding rationing by selling new clothes as second-hand. This worked on a fairly complicated scale. The **Clothing Coupon Quiz** explained that *'Secondhand goods require coupons if sold above fixed prices. These prices are fixed by multiplying the number of coupons that would be required for*

" BUT ANNE, THIS COUPON BUSINESS ISN'T TOO BAD IF YOU PLAN! I BUY 'CELANESE' – I KNOW HOW MARVELLOUSLY IT WEARS, HOW WELL IT WASHES, HOW GOOD IT LOOKS YES, OF COURSE, I HAVE TO LOOK FOR IT, BUT IT IS WELL WORTH WHILE!"

In UNDIES, NIGHTIES, PYJAMAS, DRESSES, DRESS LENGTHS, MENS SHIRTS, DRESSING GOWNS, PYJAMAS, TIES *and* CHILDREN'S THINGS . . .

'Celanese' TRADE MARK
Signifies Quality

the article if new by the price given in the list below.
(1) Hand-knitting yarn, cloth and stockings and woollen socks for men and boys – 8d
(2) Undergarments, stockings and socks other than those in the preceding item – 1/-
(3) Boots, bootees, shoes, overshoes, slippers and sandals – 1/6
(4) Other rationed goods – 2/-

If sold above these prices rationed goods, even though genuinely secondhand, will require the full number of coupons.'

Thus in the case of a man's suit, rated at 26 coupons, the tariff would be 2s per coupon, i.e. 52s, or £2 12s. So if a second-hand suit cost this amount or more, 26 coupons would have to be surrendered.

Using non-rationed materials to make your own clothes would, of course, mean saving coupons. In 1941, unrationed furnishing fabrics and curtain material were used for this, so these were added to the list of rationed goods. Housewives responded by using dust sheets, sugar bags and blackout material. In September 1945, with the end of hostilities, black-out cloth too went on coupons.

Children's clothes required fewer coupons than the same items for adults, to take their size into account, and children also received extra coupons, based on a very complicated system of age, height and weight.

In August 1941 ration cards containing the remaining 40 coupons for the year were issued at Post Offices; these replaced the margarine coupons which had confused some people – there were stories of shoppers who, having used up all their spare margarine coupons, tried to use their butter coupons instead!

In March 1942 it was announced that clothes rationing for the next year would be tighter. Coupons would be reduced from 66 to 60, and for 14 months instead of a year, making a yearly total of about 51 coupons. These would be issued in a small grey ration book, as opposed to the previous year's green card. Hugh Dalton claimed that the coupons it contained would be almost impossible to forge, unlike the cards, and the supplementary coupons given to children and certain manual workers, which had sold for as little as 10s a sheet.

Those who had received supplementary allowances, children and some manual workers, continued to get them, though the number of coupons altered. Most industrial workers got 10 extra coupons, as did children up to seventeen.

The reason that the 1942 allocation of coupons was for fourteen months was to bring the clothes

Left
Rationing meant that manufacturers began to advertise their products as hard-wearing, long-lasting and run-resisting.

Above
One of the biggest headaches for mothers was the fact that children outgrew their clothes. For this the WVS set up clothing exchanges, where children's clothes could be swapped, depending on condition, for other garments.

rationing year in line with that of food rationing. Thus many thousands of man hours could be saved by issuing the two books together, and indeed from 1943 the (now red) clothing ration book was issued as part of the food book, and had to be detached from it.

Expectant mothers received a supplementary book containing 60 coupons. These books were issued on production of a special certificate supplied by their doctor after the fourth month of pregnancy. After birth, the baby would be issued its own book containing the proportion of the year's coupons remaining as of the date of birth.

By 1943, the allocation of coupons fell yet again, this time to 38 coupons a year, although the

number of coupons required for an item of clothing remained largely the same. As with food rationing, clothes rationing would outlive the war, continuing until March 1949.

utility

With clothes rationing so severe it was important that what clothing you bought would last, as it could not be easily replaced. Austerity rules dictated the maximum work that went into making clothes, but not the materials used. As early as March 1940 the cabinet were discussing a 'standard cloth' for making men's suits.

The first discussions on Utility concerned furniture, which included furnishing fabrics. To save waste it was soon realised that large, bold patterns, incorporating large repeats, were wasteful when it came to matching up separate pieces. Small patterns, involving as they did small repeats, produced far less waste, and, if well made from good material, would, through their longevity, prove even more economical. Thus the concept of Utility cloth was born, and the idea applied equally well to clothing.

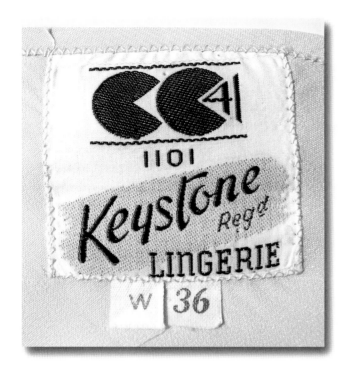

material, on which the sign is sewn.

At first the scheme suffered setbacks due to the fact that no standard specification of quality was laid down for the clothes themselves, and some early Utility products were very shoddily made, especially shoes. Efforts were made to put this right; specifications were drawn up and the quality of materials used regulated. Only when the Board of Trade was satisfied could the Utility mark be attached to a line. In August 1942 the scheme received a great boost when Utility cloth was made exempt from purchase tax.

In October 1941 adverts began to appear in the press for women's Utility clothing, and three

On 2 September 1941, the Limitation of Supply (Cloth and Apparel) Order was brought in. Its main effect was to introduce the Utility mark, CC41 (standing for Civilian Clothing 1941), although the term 'Utility' was not actually introduced until one month later by the Utility Cloth (Maximum Prices) Order. The mark, designed by Reg Shipp, became one of the most recognised symbols of all time in Britain, yet Shipp only received five guineas from the Board of Trade for the idea. The mark was intended to be a sign of quality at a fair price.

Utility cloth was not only used for clothes, it was also employed for household textiles including sheets, pillow cases, towels and blankets, as well as tea towels, tablecloths, furnishing fabric and black-out cloth. Only items of clothing made from Utility cloth could carry the Utility sign, as long as they conformed to certain specifications. It was the cloth that made an item 'Utility'. I have seen fur coats with Utility marks; these refer to the lining

ON THE WAY . . . Clarks, who have been making beautiful shoes since 1825 have in production a range of Utility Footwear. All manufacturers have to conform to a standard of quality in the materials used for Utility Footwear, but when you buy Clarks Utility shoes you are assured of more than this. You are assured also of that skill in designing and workmanship which has been their pride for over a century. MADE BY C. & J. CLARK LTD., (WHOLESALE ONLY), STREET, SOMERSET, *and by Clarks (Ireland) Ltd., Dundalk*

months later the first men's suits with Utility marks started to be sold. Meanwhile the Board of Trade had contacted eight top designers: Hardy Amies, Charles Creed, Norman Hartnell, Digby Morton, Bianca Mosca, Peter Russell, Victor Stiebel and Charles Frederick 'Worth', and invited them each to design four women's Utility outfits, to include a top coat, a suit, an afternoon and a cotton overall dress. The best of them were chosen and began to appear in the shops in the spring of 1942; they proved a great success.

In June that year the Utility scheme was widened to include hosiery, footwear and bedding, joined in August by gloves, and in June 1943 men's braces were added to the scheme, because of the rubber shortage.

By the end of the war about 85% of all civilian clothing and materials sold by the yard was Utility. The Utility symbol became syn-onymous with long-lasting clothes, but therein lay its downfall. With the upturn in the economy in the 1950s people no longer wanted clothes to last for years, they wanted new dresses or suits every season, and the final items of Utility clothing were made in 1952.

One other item generally thought of as Utility wear was wedding rings. In 1942 a government order restricted the manufacture of wedding rings to 9 carat gold, and while strictly speaking not Utility, such wedding rings were stamped with a special symbol comprising two intersecting circles alongside the hallmark. They cost 30s 9d, while black market 22 carat gold rings fetched £10 each.

make do and mend

Economising in clothes, by mending, passing down or making them yourself, had always been the practice of the less wealthy, or more thrifty, sections of British society. In the first year of the war, as the prices of clothes rocketed, more and more women turned to such means to stretch their clothing budgets.

In October 1940, for instance, eight months before clothes rationing began, **Housewife** magazine printed this letter from Mrs Matilda Mackie of Lanark: *"I thought it over, and realised that the front of a jumper is really all that is seen with a suit,"* she says. So, rummaging in her wool bag, she found enough brown wool to knit the front of a jumper with a plain, high neckline; the back she knitted in stripes of navy, grey and red. One half of the neckband was knitted in brown, the other in navy, and the sleeves were knitted in oddments of all shades. Worn brown side foremost, the jumper is smart with one suit; the stripey side is equally smart with the other suit, and in the house it is worn covered with a smock.'

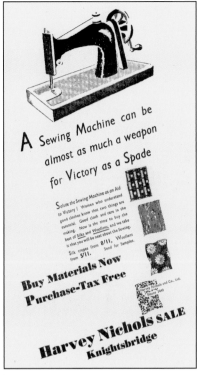

Far Left
One of the original Utility designs, incorporating austerity and style.
Above
Rationing meant that people could not get a new outfit whenever they wanted; the answer was to upgrade an old one.
Left
Even before clothes rationing, making your own clothes was seen as a patriotic act.

Such tips, which had always appeared in the pages of magazines aimed at a working-class readership, progressively became part of more middle-class periodicals, but with a new slant; such measures were a case of doing without for the nation, sacrifices for victory as they were sometimes grandly called, and were to be worn as badges of honour.

With the advent of clothes rationing in July 1941, prolonging the life of clothes became not only a national duty, but on a personal level, a necessity. There were calls for a 'National Campaign to Remake, Mend and Renovate', and the Board of Trade began meeting groups such as the Women's Institutes to try to organise such a campaign.

There would be several strings to this particular bow. For those women who had always made or repaired the family's clothes, the campaign would act as the hub of ideas, collecting and transmitting useful tips, such as: *'Don't throw away your old raincoat, it can be made into a useful apron for washing days'* (**1001 Household Hints**). This was purely an idea: how you could turn it into an apron is not mentioned – obviously the women at whom this was aimed were assumed to have the cutting and sewing skills needed to carry out the task.

For others such skills would be a mystery; for them instruction in the basic skills would need to be arranged, and this is where the established women's organisations came in, first with displays of work to get people interested, and secondly with classes.

In the summer of 1942 the 'Make Do and Mend' campaign was launched, with local exhibitions, cinema shorts, and adverts in newspapers and

Be Deft with Your Needle

And Try These Effective Renovations

This lovely new nightdress can be made from straight pieces of material—no pattern is needed.

Two squares of material were used to make the dainty French knickers shown on the right.

Make-do and Mend
SEWING CLASS

MEND AND MAKE-DO TO SAVE BUYING NEW

ISSUED BY THE BOARD OF TRADE

Left
Magazines gave their readers advice on making and renovating items, like this from **Woman & Home** of March 1945.
Above
Poster for a Make Do and Mend sewing class; these were set up to help those new to the art to acquire the skills of home dressmaking.

magazines, *'designed not merely to revive the lost arts of darning and patching, but to raise morale by showing how old clothes can be turned into really smart and attractive new ones'* (Board of Trade). Little of this was new, as such campaigns were a regular feature of ARP awareness, food rationing and so on, and the public was tired of them. It did not help that the campaign was unfocused; many of its exhortations to 'make do and mend' were regarded as an insult by working-class mothers who had always done so, and the tone of the adverts was often patronising and dull.

However the cause was duly taken up by the women's magazines, which, run by the professionals they were, adjusted their tone and direction to appeal to their readership, while Make Do and Mend exhibitions sprang up in village halls and in large city stores, where advice centres were also organised. Here women could consult experts for advice on every aspect of the subject, while mobile versions toured factory canteens. Make Do and Mend classes were set up; by the end of the war,

50,000 of them, and the Board of Trade booklet, **Make Do and Mend**, sold one-and-a-quarter million copies. It began *'Clothes have simply got to last longer than they used to, but only the careful woman can make them last well.'*

In the same way that wearing trousers had become almost a badge of honour among women, so, people were told, would patched and mended clothes. *'Nowadays, every re-made garment becomes a uniform of honour and every darn a "decoration",'* announced **Home Companion** in July 1943, and the following month the same magazine stated that *'Patched elbows these days are no disgrace'.*

Clothes made of patchwork were heavily pushed, but it was soon realised that the real secret was not to flaunt it but to hide it creatively, as in this idea from **Needlewoman** magazine for 'Make Do and Mend Decorative Patches': *'Very often it is not possible to find pieces of matching cloth to mend garments and then it is a good idea to turn the patch into a decoration so that it will not be unsightly. You must, of course, select a contrasting*

MAKE-DO AND MEND EXHIBITION

colour and use suitable materials. Obviously you would not put a cotton patch on a woollen frock or vice versa but a velvet patch on a woollen ground would be most effective; this latter need not be in a contrasting colour if you can match your garment.

Measure the hole to be covered and make sure the shape you are going to use will cover it. In the case of elbows include the thin stretched part; press these on a sleeve board, using a damp cloth in order to shrink the fabric as flatly as possible. Cut out your patches.

For all fabrics which fray use either close button-hole stitch, satin stitch, or make a turning all round and sew down; over this preliminary sewing feather or herringbone stitch can be worked. Whether turnings or not are made a previous tacking and stitching down of the edge must be done. The patches can of course be machined down all round close to the turned-in edge if preferred. On the flower heads an appliqué centre of a different colour can be sewn. Outlines of teddy-bear, yacht and ball can be in chain or stem stitch.'

The booklet **Make Do and Mend** pointed out: *'Don't forget that old skin gloves and the good parts of worn ones, and of worn leather belts will provide hard-wearing and smart leather patches for heavy materials.'* Such leather patches were often worn on tweed jackets, and were sold at the time with the slogan 'Save coupons'. Here is another treatment

for elbows, from **Practical Hints in War Time**: *'We now have to wear our suits much longer than formerly and certain smooth cloths show patches of shine at the elbows, knees and elsewhere before we can reasonably discard the suit. The thing to do in such cases is to rub gently on the offending parts with a clean piece of coarse glasspaper. Don't be vigorous and wear a hole through the cloth; merely stroke the material and roughen it on the surface. You can get rid of all the shine in this way'* – 'I've just got to sandpaper my suit' sounds like something Tommy Handley might have said!

Knitting was a very popular way of stretching the clothes ration. Even before rationing, knitting 'comforts' for servicemen and women had been a popular pastime. Knitting wool was rationed at the same time as clothing, at one coupon for two ounces, but this usually worked out at less than the coupons required for the finished article. Knitting became a national obsession; every women's magazine had

shake gently.' Of course, this did not always produce the amount of wool needed for the desired garment, so it became the fashion to knit garments in stripes of different colours, or better still in Fair Isle; being made up of lots of different colours, it was the perfect pattern for Make Do and Mend, and the Fair-Isle jumper became a symbol of the home front.

In 1944, the Board of Trade, taking its cue from the Ministry of Food's Potato Pete, introduced its own cartoon character, 'Mrs Sew-and-Sew', a patchwork doll, in an attempt to brighten up its worthy but rather dowdy leaflets. She was a great success.

directions for knitting something, and there were dozens of books produced with titles such as **Practical Knitting in Wartime**. However, many people realised you did not need to use up your coupons at all if you found old pieces of knitwear and unravelled them.

As usual, **Make Do and Mend** gave advice: *'Carefully unpick the old garment and wind the wool round a book or a piece of stiff cardboard. Then wind it into skeins, tying tightly in several places. Squeeze gently in lukewarm suds, made from a good soap, until the wool is quite clean. Rinse twice in lukewarm water. Lay the hanks in a towel, roll up and press gently. Then shake and hang up to dry, preferably on a piece of stick in the open air. If it is impossible to dry outdoors, dry over the kitchen rack but not close to an open fire or on a radiator. Occasionally*

ISSUED BY THE BOARD OF TRADE

A GUIDE TO *Woollies* by Mrs. SEW-and-SEW

Woollies can grow old gracefully. They can keep their shape. They can go on being soft and warm and colourful even after long use and repeated washings. "But," warns Mrs. Sew-and-Sew "you have to take care of them properly to get the best wear."

FIRST STEPS

If wool is not guaranteed pre-shrunk, wash skeins in fairly hot soap suds. Rinse thoroughly. Peg on clothes line away from heat or sun. Shake frequently while drying. Wind into loose balls so as not to strain wool.

TO JOIN WOOL

Join ends in wool by knotting at end of row, by knitting about 2 inches of new piece together with end of last piece or by darning end of last piece about 2 inches into new knitting with darning needle. Avoid knots in the middle of a row.

March 23, 1940.   Registered at the G.P.O. as a Newspaper

The Light Car

3D EVERY SATURDAY

HPA 137

transport

By the start of the Second World War ownership of private cars in Britain had grown massively. In 1904 there had been fewer than 9,000 (with family cars costing the equivalent of about £20,000 in today's money), but by the time the First World War broke out just ten years later this had risen to 132,000 (and the comparable price had dropped to £10,000). This shrunk to 75,000 (£5,000) by the end of the war, but soon accelerated and had reached one million by 1930 (£4,000), when 2.7 million driving licences were distributed, and two million in 1939 (£4,000), when almost 5 million were issued. Car ownership was still the exception, but with 10% of households having a car, it had become far from rare in middle-class suburbia.

At the beginning of September 1939 the government issued a leaflet entitled **War Emergency Instructions and Information**, which contained a section entitled 'Instructions to Drivers of Vehicles and Cyclists'. This set out many of the changes that the war would bring to motoring, including the blackout and petrol rationing. *Traffic on the roads will be specially controlled and you must obey immediately any orders given you by the police or any other authorised persons. If you are driving a vehicle when an air raid warning is sounded you must stop as soon as you have parked your vehicle so that it does not cause obstruction. If you are in a wide road you must pull in to the nearside kerb. In a*

Left
Early wartime private car – one headlamp has a blackout shield, the other has its bulb removed and the bumper is painted white for added visibilty.
Right
Humber advert from March 1940. Soon new cars would be impossible to get.

HUMBER

The comfort and quiet distinction of a Humber car are no sudden achievements. They are characteristics which have been developed and fostered through over forty years' insistence on quality.

THE 1940 MODELS ARE NOW AVAILABLE

| THE SIXTEEN £415 | THE SNIPE £425 | THE SUPER SNIPE £455 | THE PULLMAN £865 |

narrow road or congested area you may have to park the vehicle in a side street or as directed by the police or air raid warden. You must not drive or cycle at night unless your lights are dimmed and screened in accordance with the regulations. You can get a leaflet giving details of these restrictions from any police station. No car or cycle will be allowed on the road at night until the lights have been dimmed in the way described in this leaflet. If you have a car use it very sparingly because the supply of petrol will be rationed immediately.'

As had happened in 1914–18, war cut the number of private cars on the road, though now it was mainly due to petrol rationing. By 24 July 1940 **The Motor** magazine was reporting that: *'Compared with a year ago the number of vehicles on the roads has been reduced by a third, and even making allowance for the cars issued with supplementary rations it is likely that the average number of miles per vehicle has been reduced by at least 50 per cent.'* The article went on to look at the number of accidents over that period: *'With vehicle miles thus reduced to little more than a third by June, 1939, it might be reasonable to expect a very considerable reduction in road accidents.*

It is, therefore, the more disappointing to note that, although the numbers have fallen they have done so by less than 5 per cent., the total figure being 479 as compared with 493. Analysis discloses that pedestrian deaths are almost the same, although there has been an increase for children under 15 years of age (59 to 63), and a slight decrease in those over that age (127 to 120).

The fall in drivers' deaths is also small, being only 32 to 28, which is counterbalanced by the

number of motorcyclists killed from 87 to 91. These figures seem to show that as the density of traffic has fallen so has the degree of care exercised by pedestrians and drivers alike. So far as the pedestrian is concerned, we have commented often upon the quite astounding carelessness with which many walkers place themselves in front of moving vehicles not only in daylight but also during the black-out.'

That month it became illegal to buy a new car without a licence from the Ministry of Transport – none would be issued for private cars until June 1945. News of this caused motor traders with new cars in their possession to rush to register them, after which they could sell them as used cars. The market in second-hand cars, particularly those that gave good mileage, boomed, while big, heavy petrol consumers lost favour. One way to get rid of them without losing out was to have them bought or requisitioned by the government, or for civil defence purposes, for which the owner would be paid compensation, authorised rates being 7s per week (today's equivalent £8. 50) for cars over 14 horsepower and less than three years old, and 5s per week (£6), for all others. In addition, the government paid any expenses incurred by the owner and would have to make good any damage to the vehicle. Civil defence workers at the beginning of the war tell of being offered Rolls-Royces and the like for knock-down prices.

However, you did have to be careful. The **Daily Express** War Time Lawyer warned, *'In this connection it may be added that the loan of a car to a Local Authority for civil defence purposes does not absolve the owner from his ordinary duties, such as insurance. In fact one owner who lent his*

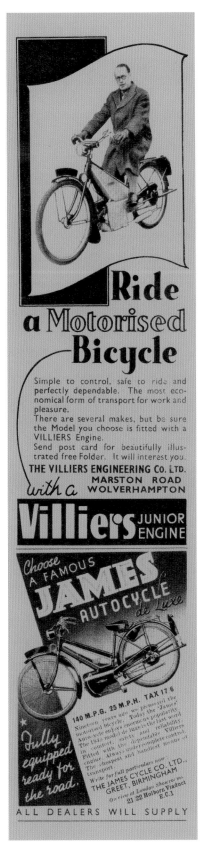
car to a Local Authority when it was only insured for himself was fined for allowing a person not covered by his insurance to drive it. He was fined also for not seeing that the driver complied with lighting regulations, although at the time of this offence the car had passed completely out of his control.'

Motorcycle sales also soared, and by mid-1940 there was a fashion for the 'autocycle', a sort of moped, which could be pedalled downhill or along the straight, or driven uphill, thus giving over a hundred miles to the gallon. At this time the Rudge autocycle sold for £26 (about £675 today).

Bicycle sales boomed, especially after the cessation of the basic petrol ration in 1942. A man's bike costing from 30s to 90s (£36–£108) in mid-1941, and a lady's up to £5 10 (£132).

One obvious alternative to the car was the horse. Douglas Macdonald Hastings, writing in the **Picture Post** in April 1940, said: *'A good horse, well driven, will go twenty-five miles a day; a twenty horsepower car, petrol-rationed, will do two hundred miles a month. So a hackney, travelling at a top speed of ten miles an hour, will go three times as far as a month's petrol coupons. The war has discredited the horseless carriage and made the highway fit for a carriage horse again.'*

Before the war you could have bought a carriage for little more than its worth as firewood. At the outbreak of war, however, seeing their potential, dealers began to buy up old carriages, quickly followed by members of the public, and prices rocketed to up to twenty-five guineas.

Left
Petrol rationing meant that autocycles became attractive; advert from March 1940.

Above Right
Bicycles were the perfect answer to petrol rationing, but they too became difficult to find.

In their rush, many failed to consider the draw-backs of horse-travel; driving a horse-drawn vehicle looks easy when you see someone else do it – you shake the reins and cry some variation of 'Gee up'. In reality of course there is far more to it than that, and even should you manage to master the art, there is the problem of stabling it, pasture for it to run in, and the not inconsiderable time it takes to prepare the horse and carriage, both before and after a journey.

Above all there was the need to feed and water the horse. The **Girl's Own Paper** of May 1941 wrote about the problem of feeding a horse in wartime: *'It is always cheapest to keep your pony out at grass . . . he must have some hay and there is no reason why you should not manage to make a bit of extra hay yourself . . . so make friends with* someone who has a patch of disused lawn.' The National Horse Association of Great Britain produced a leaflet, **Feeding Your Horse in Wartime**, which, in December 1944, recommended garden and house scraps, but mainly potatoes, raw, 5 to 6lb, mixed with chaff.

Of course, the blackout and air-raid regulations applied here as well. An ARP circular of September 1939 stated that: *'When the air raid warning is given drivers of horse-drawn vehicles should unharness their horses, and if possible lead them to an open space. Horses should be tied by a halter lead and not by the reins. In no case should horses be tied to lamp-posts or railings. If it is necessary to tie them to the vehicle, they should be secured to the rear of the vehicle which should be anchored with skid brakes, chains or other means. The halter should be fastened below the hub of the wheel.'*

With all the problems of keeping such large animals, many who bought horses and carriages in the first rush were soon selling again, and prices fell to around fifteen guineas for the carriage, and the whole outfit, carriage, horse and harness, for forty or fifty guineas.

From April 1942 tyres became a problem for the few remaining car drivers, but equally for bike riders, as the Malayan rubber plantations fell to the advancing Japanese forces. They were now available only for authorised use, and each new tyre had to be exchanged for an old one. Once again the government stepped in with advice.

How Every Driver of Motor Vehicles Can Help the War Effort.

90% of the world's natural rubber resources are now in enemy hands. This places a heavy responsibility on every

MINISTRY OF SUPPLY

WHY WE MUST DO A **100%** JOB OF **TYRE CARE**

It is important to remember that synthetic rubber cannot entirely replace "crude" (i.e. natural rubber). Supplies of crude are required in varying degree to mix with synthetic.
The Allied Nations reserve of crude must, therefore, be more jealously guarded than ever. Heavy duty tyres already in service — those fitted to lorries, buses, etc. — represent by far the greatest bulk of that reserve. The manufacture of new heavy duty tyres consumes by far the greatest amount of rubber.

100% TYRE CARE INCLUDES:

WATCH YOUR SPEED — not exceeding the legal limit for a commercial vehicle : not over 40 m.p.h. for a car.
NEVER accelerate fiercely : never brake hard : never bump or scrape the kerb : never drive on a flat tyre.
AVOID overloading. Always "spread" the load.
DIG OUT flints, glass, nails, etc., daily.
CHECK air pressures regularly and often.
CHECK wheel alignment regularly.

CHECK brake adjustment regularly.
CHANGE round wheels and tyres (including spares) properly and regularly.
PAIR, space and change round twin tyres properly.
REMOVE stones trapped between twin tyres after every journey.
WIPE OFF oil, grease and paint.
KEEP tyres and tubes in good repair.
TAKE expert advice regularly on tyre care and maintenance.

SUBMIT TYRES FOR REPLACEMENT WHEN SMOOTH

driver of motor vehicles. For the most effective way to conserve Britain's rubber stocks is to take the care of the millions of tyres still in daily use.

18 Points for Drivers

Have tyre pressure checked every week.
Submit tyres for replacement when they are smooth.
Never drive a commercial vehicle above its legal speed limit.
Avoid driving a car over 40 m.p.h.
Never corner at speed.
See that wheels are in proper alignment.
Never accelerate fiercely.
Drive slowly over rough roads.
Remember that fierce braking wastes rubber.
Never scrape or bump the kerb.
See that brakes are evenly adjusted.
Remove stones and flints from treads after every journey.
See that tyres are changed round properly and regularly.
See that tyres and tubes are kept in good repair.
Avoid overloading.
Spread the load evenly.
Avoid driving a vehicle on a flat tyre.
Take expert advice regularly on the care and maintenance of tyres.'
(from the Highway Code)

Synthetic Rubber Inner Tubes

ARE NOW BEING MANUFACTURED

"S"

You will recognise an inner tube made of synthetic rubber by the letter 'S' stamped on it, at least half-an-inch high.

and demand special care in repair if the best results are to be obtained. Cycle tyre patches of existing makes may be used, but it is important to prepare the place to be repaired with an abrasive material, such as sulphur remover or sandpaper, before proceeding. In every case solution must be used to secure good adhesion to the tube.

DUNLOP

Left
Rubber shortages after the fall of Malaya meant that tyres had to be carefully looked after.

Above
The answer to the rubber shortage, synthetic rubber inner-tubes, August 1944.

Below
In the end there was always shanks's pony – but notice, even supplies of shoe-polish were short! June 1943.

By now bicycles too were becoming harder to find; in 1942 bicycle manufacture was down to 25% of its 1939 level through strict limitations placed on the manufacture of all goods for the civilian market, and old, rusted bikes were hunted out from sheds and reconditioned. The booklet **1001 Household Hints** suggested that you *'Rub the enamelled parts of your old bicycle with black polish, working it well into rusted parts. Polish it smartly and the machine will look like new.'* This, of course, assumed that your bike was black originally; don't try it with a brightly coloured one!

Travel of any sort became limited: *'At present Ireland, the Isle of Man, parts of Scotland, the Isle of Wight, and the South and East Coasts of England are out of bounds to tourists, but other areas are*

likely to be declared prohibited from time to time, and therefore enquiries should be made before planning a tour.' (**All You Want to Know on Cycling**)

Petrol rationing meant that ever more people were forced on to public transport, because all transport was prioritising war needs, such as the movement of troops and ammunition. Increasing numbers of people were using a decreasing amount of transport. The result was inevitable: queues and crowding. The government sought to cut this down with

BUS STOP
AND SAVE TRANSPORT

WALK *but use*

CHERRY BLOSSOM BOOT POLISH

and keep your shoes fit for walking

USE SPARINGLY-SUPPLIES ARE RESTRICTED

No. CC 839755

THIS BOOK IS THE PROPERTY OF HIS MAJESTY'S GOVERNMENT

MOTOR SPIRIT RATION BOOK

FOR THE PERIOD: 23rd NOVEMBER, 1939 to 31st JANUARY, 1940

HP 8-9

Private Motor Car

Date and Office of Issue

Registered Number of Vehicle

TM 3335

The coupons in this book authorise the holder to purchase the number of units of motor spirit specified on the coupons for use in the vehicle bearing the number shown on the front of this book and must not be used for any other purpose.

This book must be produced whenever motor spirit is purchased and coupons must only be detached by the supplier at the time of purchase who must also fill in the particulars required.

The quantity represented by a UNIT of motor spirit is subject to modification and will be officially announced from time to time.

The issue of a Ration Book does not guarantee to the holder any minimum quantity of motor spirit and the book may be cancelled at any time without notice.

This book must be surrendered with any unused coupons when application is made for a subsequent book and no such book will be issued unless this book has been surrendered.

If for any reason the motor car ceases to be used, this book MUST be returned to the office of issue, together with the appropriate number of unused coupons.

various campaigns: 'Is Your Journey Really Necessary?', and 'Walk Short Distances'. One of the more effective measures was to iron out the peaks of the rush hour by the staggering of work hours. At the same time the Minister of Transport appealed to housewives: *'In the early mornings and late afternoons your husbands, sons and daughters – war workers – most need the buses, trams and trains. If you are crowding in, they are crowded out, so help them all you can. Please finish travelling by 4 o'clock.'*

Left
Hitch-hiking became a necessity during the war. Most drivers would pick up hikers, especially if they were members of the forces.

Above
Petrol was the first thing to be rationed. This book is from November 1939.

In spite of this, travelling on public transport became ever more difficult due to blackout restrictions, overcrowding, and deteriorating buses, coaches and trains.

petrol rationing

In the new mechanised warfare, petrol would be crucial, especially as neither Britain nor Germany produced their own, both relying on imports. On 1 August 1939 the British Government had announced petrol would be rationed immediately war broke out, and on 3 September the Motor Fuel Rationing Order was, along with many other new regulations, rushed through Parliament.

Rationing was due to start on 16 September 1939;

THE ONE BRIGHT SPOT

TAX UP 66%
TYRES UP 15-20%
PETROL UP 20%
LOCKHEED FLUID
no increase

NO SIR, LOCKHEED FLUID
PRICES HAVE NOT BEEN
RAISED. LOCKHEED ARE
BEARING THE EXTRA COST
THEMSELVES

Above
Lockheed fluid advert from February 1940; notice the Pool
petrol pumps.

Above Right
Petrol rationing meant theft boomed; locking petrol caps
became very popular.

Below Right
All forms of petrol-driven transport were rationed – this is a
motor-cycle ration book from 1942.

on the day before, garages were besieged by
queues of drivers trying to stock up, and it was not
only their tanks which they filled. People filled every
conceivable form of container, from milk bottles to
baths, in spite of the Motor Fuel Rationing Order
clearly stating, *'Motor fuel must be placed direct
into the ordinary fuel tank of the vehicle.'* In the

event, rationing was postponed for one week.

On the 16th it was announced that branded
petrol had been replaced by pool petrol: *'All the
petrol supplies in the country have been pooled by
the various distributing companies to form a single
brand known as "Pool" motor spirit, which is on sale
at pumps'*, with the price controlled at 1s 6d a gallon.

Rationing finally began at midnight on the
22nd. Car owners received their ration book by
presenting the car registration book at the local
post office or local taxation office from which they
normally obtained their road fund licence. The
ration received by each motorist allowed sufficient
petrol to travel about 200 miles a month – about a
third of the pre-war average. This meant that the
amount of petrol a motorist received varied with
the horsepower of the car they owned, as follows:
Up to 7hp – Four gallons per month.
8hp to 9hp – Five gallons.
10hp to 12hp – Six gallons.
13hp to 15hp – Seven gallons.
16hp to 19hp – Eight gallons.
20hp and over – Ten gallons.

Three-wheelers were given a basic ration of
three gallons, with a supplementary ration of two
or three gallons for those with car-type engines.

A supplementary ration could also be obtained
under certain circumstances. Additional petrol for
journeys between your place of business and your
home might be granted if you could prove that the
journeys were necessary and that no alternative
means of transport existed, or if your car was
'essential' for the *'prosecution of the war or
maintaining the life of the community'*. There were
also additional rations allotted to all *'genuine*

Padlocking   the Petrol

JUST introduced by S. Smith and Sons (M.A.), Ltd., of Great Portland Street, London, W.1, is a new petrol filler cap lock, which provides protection against petrol pilfering. It is secured to the wing and fitted as shown in the accompanying illustration. It is designed for the press-down release type filler cap, and the thick claw ends pre-vent this press-down operation being performed. Hence, the cap cannot be removed. Models are available for the Austin 8, 10, 12 and 14 h.p. and for the Rover 10 and 12 h.p. The price is 7s. 9d. complete with padlock and two keys. Models for other makes of car will be available soon, when announcements will be made.

commercial travellers who use their cars in the course of business'. This also varied according to horsepower, but was averaged at about 625 miles per month. Some drivers who used their cars for ARP work, such as for transporting what were called 'sitting case' casualties to hospital (that is those who did not need to lie down, and would therefore not need an ambulance), received extra petrol, not in the form of a supplementary ration, but directly from the local authority.

Under rationing it was an offence to receive or to supply motor fuel unless the correct number of coupons were surrendered, and only then to the vehicle whose registration number was on the ration book. The law also required that *'All reasonable steps to effect economies in the consumption of motor spirit and heavy oil, to prevent waste, must be taken.'* The Royal Automobile Club advised drivers to keep their sparking plugs clean, to get into top gear quickly, and to maintain an economic speed of 20 to 30mph. 'Free running' or 'coasting', with the engine in neutral, and the driver keeping control only 'by gentle brake pressure', was also claimed to save as much as a third of one's normal consumption on a long journey.

The motor industry tried to fight back by introducing new models with low fuel consumption but

by the middle of December half a million cars had been laid up owing to a combination of petrol rationing, blackout driving and heavy taxation. Laying up the car 'for the duration' meant more than just locking it up in the garage and forgetting it; once again the RAC gave advice: wash the car, reduce the air in the tyres to half pressure, then put the car upon bricks or blocks and remove the wheels altogether. (These, or at least the tyres, would later be requisitioned when rubber was short.) Take out the plugs, and pour a teaspoonful of oil into each cylinder, turn over the engine by hand and then replace the plugs. It said nothing about checking the garage – I came across one 1930s car during the '70s which had been stored in this way in 1940. However, when the owner tried to open the garage doors after the war he discovered

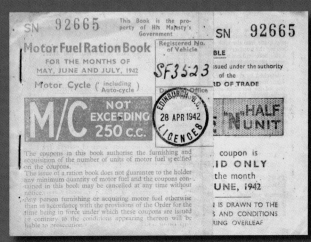

Right
Cycling needed no petrol and was therefore ration-free; many people took cycling holidays, encouraged by the Youth Hostel Association.

Far Right
Cartoon by Sillince; gas-power offered an alternative to petrol, but the bags were unwieldy and could make the car unstable.

Below Right
In the end many were forced to lay up their car 'for the duration' and go on foot. This advert is from June 1943.

that the garage had subsided into the ground and the doors would not open. Frustrated beyond measure he had once again abandoned it, only for it to be rediscovered in 1975!

In October 1940 the 'free lifts' scheme was brought in; window stickers were provided by the RAC and AA, and motorists displaying such a sticker were entitled to an extra ration. Another suggestion was for drivers to share the use of each others' cars, and under the government's 'Help Your Neighbour' scheme, introduced at the same time, 20,000 motorists who displayed a notice offering free lifts into and out of London received extra petrol. The war years were a golden age for hitch-hikers. The official view was that *'a vacant place in a car travelling to or from . . . Central London . . . called for an explanation'.*

In the meantime, the price of pool petrol had risen, first to 1s 8d a gallon, and then in England (London inner and outer zones) and Wales to 1s 11½d per gallon, and 2s ½d in other areas.

The black market first operated in petrol. Initially there were large supplies of coupon-free petrol available, at a price, of course – 6s 6d a gallon, about four times the legal rate, was about average. These supplies had been stockpiled by people in

the months leading up to war, but they were not infinite, and the supply soon began to dry up. To fill the gap came commercial petrol. A large proportion of the petrol for civilian use was set aside for commercial vehicles and soon some of this began to find its way on to the black market. To prevent this occurring, it was dyed red, and cars suspected by the police of using such illegal fuel would have their petrol tested. It is a sign of their ingenuity that black market operators discovered a practical use for the gas mask; passing the petrol through a gas mask filter was found to remove the dye! Forces petrol was also a good source, and in May 1940 it was announced that forces petrol too would be dyed red.

Almost from the very first forged coupons appeared, often printed in Eire. There was also the theft of coupons from Petroleum Offices; in July

1941, 500,000 petrol coupons were stolen in Morden and sold for £1 for 5 gallonsworth. And finally there was the still-used tactic of driving away without paying, or more importantly, without handing over coupons. A very popular means of making your petrol go further (illegal under the Petroleum (No.1) Order, 1939) was to add paraffin to it, or even to run your car on paraffin alone. Cars ran very well on it, but had a tendency to make a terrible noise and smell, and to produce dark clouds of smoke from the exhaust.

In spite of rationing, **The Light Car** magazine suggested in March 1940 that an Easter trip out in the car was not out of the question, if certain steps were taken. Starting the run at about 6.30 in the morning meant little traffic on the road. You could, therefore, keep to a steady speed of 20mph, thereby keeping your fuel consumption to a minimum. They also suggested short trips, either to visit your evacuated children if, as in many cases at that point, they had been evacuated to the nearby countryside, or to a picnic spot within 20 miles of your home.

Perhaps because of widespread avoidance of the regulations, there seemed to be plenty of petrol about, and there was an outcry when 5,000 cars were counted in the car park at the 1941 Derby. In October that year the basic ration was cut by one-sixth, giving a monthly average of 125 miles of travel.

" *Well, anyway, they must be able to carry a terrible lot of petrol in those things.*"

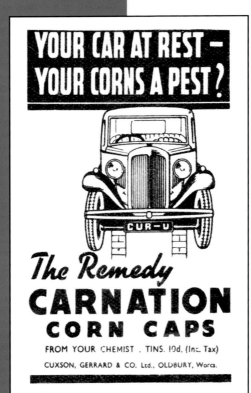

On 13 March 1942 it was announced that the basic ration would cease altogether as from 1 July; only the supplementary ration for cars which were essential for the prosecution of the war or maintaining the life of the community remained. Drivers who received such petrol had to travel only on the stated essential work, drive by the shortest route possible, and certainly not leave the engine idling – drivers could be, and some were, prosecuted for these offences. By May 1942, the average monthly distance travelled by the 700,000 cars remaining on the road was just 52 miles. The basic petrol ration was only restored a month after VE Day in June 1945; however, it would not be until May 1950 that petrol rationing was completely ended.

gas-powered vehicles

Petrol rationing led people to investigate alternatives to petrol. Probably the most successful and most bizarre of these was gas-power. During the first few weeks of the war, cars and vans were converted to run on ordinary (and most importantly, unrationed) household gas. The conversion was quite expensive – £30 (about £1200 in today's money) – and for this you got an auxiliary carburettor and gas bag in a wooden cradle 9ft long, 6ft wide and 4ft high, fixed on the car's roof. Sadly, the drawbacks soon became all too apparent.

After some initial interest, most drivers were reluctant to have the conversion done, as there were rumours that the gas would itself be rationed, prompting the Mines Department to announce in late October 1939 that the government *do not at present intend to ration coal-gas as fuel for motor-vehicles, although it would naturally wish to prevent any use of gas for non-essential purposes.*

It is not proposed either to prohibit flexible containers for gas from being carried on the roofs of motor-vehicles or on trailers; and no special restrictions are likely to be imposed on the use of gas in steel cylinders beyond those already enforced on grounds of safety.'

The Times of 25 October 1939 commented on gas vehicles, that: *'The balloon is easily installed and fitted, and does not add too much to dead weight. Its drawbacks are chiefly the small mileage it affords, the increased overall height of the vehicle necessitated by the bag, and its crate or container, and the inability of the apparatus to harmonize with the lines of the vehicle. It is possible to get waterproof material for the bag of the low-pressure coal gas conversion set which need not be stitched, and tapes can be tied to eyelets in tabs on the sides of the balloon in order to ensure that the bag will collapse in its crate without overhang.'*

Sadly, the drawbacks soon became all too apparent, the main one being the vast quantity of gas needed. The bag, likened by many to a barrage balloon, made even the sleekest, most aerodynamic car look lumbering. As the bag emptied, which it did alarmingly fast, it began to sag like a deflating whale, making the car much harder to handle.

The biggest problem, however, was that the entire bag contained the equivalent of only a single gallon of petrol, and thus required constant refilling; the gas companies set up a chain of supply points around London to enable drivers to refuel, but this still meant that every 20 miles or so, less in a large saloon, you would have to 'fill her up', a job which took about ten minutes. **The Motor** magazine reported that, to this end, *'certain garages are being equipped with stack pipes'.* In the end, events overtook the idea. As shortages of fuel began to bite, with coal and gas in particular, further conversions were banned in October 1942, while existing gas-equipped vehicles had to be taken off the roads unless they were employed on essential work.

A similar scheme using cylinders of pressurised gas was mooted, **The Times** commenting that *'the compressed gas cylinder gives greater mileage, since each cylinder may contain 350 cubic feet of gas – equal to over a gallon of petrol, but compressors at present are few, the cylinders are heavy and take up space, and they must be made of material more urgently wanted elsewhere.'* **The Motor** in July 1940 pointed out that *'the trouble is the shortage of high-pressure cylinders – and there is certainly little likelihood of any of these being produced during war-time. Filling bottles would be a job for the gas companies. There is an alternative that might interest you, namely, the use of Calor gas, which needs a special carburettor, and details of this conversion can be obtained from Arnott's Garages, Ltd., Grange Road, Willesden, N.W. There is apparently no objection to using this form of gas, which is supplied in liquid form in a small tank mounted either in the luggage trunk or outside the tail of the car. They have a car at Arnott's already equipped and they could make arrangements to demonstrate it to you.'*

One local council did take the pressurised gas idea into production. They used compressed methane gas, made in the sludge digesters during the sewage purification system, and compressed it into aqua-lung-type cylinders to power 30 council vehicles.

The most practical idea was using 'producer-gas', meaning that the gas was generated by the vehicle as it went along. This system was used mainly to power commercial vehicles. Once again **The Times**, in October 1939, described the process: *'More promising appears to be producer-gas. Producer-gas plants are now much more practical and economical than they were. Into a hopper or container charcoal, or anthracite, or low temperature coke or other suitable substance is put. This supply feeds down to a small fire, which can be started with a blower, or by the engine's being run on petrol for a minute or two, and kept going by the engine itself when running. Air is drawn in over or through the fire and the gas is then taken to boxes or cylinders where it is cooled and cleaned before entering the engine. With some systems the car or commercial vehicle motor can be started up on producer-gas. With others, petrol is first used and the change-over to gas can be made in a few minutes. Control of a machine is as usual, the only extra regulation being an air valve which can* *largely be set when the engine is running on gas and left. Filters are made to be easily withdrawn and cleaned.*

There is less power than there is from petrol, but with higher compression in the engine and by the fitting of a modified cylinder head a fair amount of the loss can be made up. An engine runs smoothly on producer-gas, and is free from "pinking", as it is not with Pool petrol. Rather more gear changing is needed, and as about 15½lb of anthracite is equiv-alent to a gallon of petrol the range is less. A gas plant of the type described can be fitted to most goods vehicles and to tractors, while on passenger-carrying machines and cars it can be housed in a trailer with a flexible supply pipe.'

The usual arrangement was for the vehicle to tow behind it a trailer containing a burner rather like a large dustbin. This arrangement meant that it was impractical for use with cars. The small amount of petrol needed to prime the system was allowed for under the rationing order; commercial vehicles fitted with gas-producer plants were allotted half the normal ration of petrol. Public service vehicles were allowed to draw a trailer fitted with gas cylinders or a producer-gas plant; however both cars and commercial vehicles pulling trailers were subject to a speed limit of 30mph.

By early 1942 seventy-five firms, including many bus companies, were making use of this method. It was supposed to give a vehicle a range of 150 miles, but London Transport soon found that in practice their buses needed stoking up again every 80 miles, and each converted bus got through a massive ton of anthracite every week. They were also difficult to drive, needed far more maintenance than a normal

bus, and were far less powerful, often finding steep hills impossible to negotiate. From 1943, petrol supplies for commercial companies improved, and most transport companies began to convert their gas-producing buses back to petrol.

Some interest was shown in the electric car, but as **The Light Car** reported in March 1940, *'Broadly speaking, it is true that 25 m.p.h. and 40 miles per charge represent the best that can be achieved'*, one of the main drawbacks being that recharging the batteries was an overnight affair.

I've got 9 lives YOU haven't LOOK OUT IN THE BLACKOUT There's danger on the roads

travelling in the blackout

The blackout regulations, including those for traffic, were brought into force on Friday 1 September 1939. The leaflet **War Emergency Information and Instructions** warned: *'You must not drive or cycle at night unless your lights are dimmed and screened in accordance with regulations.'* At first this meant that cars could use sidelights only, with their reflectors blackened, and the glass covered by two thicknesses of newspaper.

At the same time *'All street lighting will be stopped until further notice'.* Together these must have made driving all but impossible on any but the very brightest moonlit nights. With this in mind, the ARP Department issued the *'Memorandum on aids to the movement of traffic in the absence of street lighting'*, which listed the necessary requirements for aiding the movement of traffic under blackout conditions. These included screened traffic lights, where the red, amber and green lights were covered with metal discs with a small cross-shaped aperture. Alternatively, the lights might be sprayed with black paint masked to leave the cross shape. All other illuminated traffic signs had to be screened from above and dimmed, so that they would be *'legible, under black-out conditions, to drivers at a distance of 100 feet'* but *'inconspicuous at a distance of 250 feet'.*

Later, some traffic lights at busy junctions were fitted with hoods which could be brought into use at night. In **The Incredible City**, Mrs Robert Henrey describes how *'From Shaftesbury Avenue came a tall policeman riding a very small bicycle. He carried over his shoulder a long rod that looked*

PREVENT ROAD ACCIDENTS!

cross with the lights especially during the **BLACKOUT** *but look out for turning traffic*

Issued by The Royal Society for the Prevention of Accidents, (formerly The National "Safety First" Association Inc.,) Terminal House, 52, Grosvenor Gardens, London, S.W.1.

Left
Look out in the Blackout – the utter darkness made the roads dangerous at night, in spite of the fact that there were far fewer vehicles. (COURTESY OF THE ROYAL SOCIETY FOR THE PREVENTION OF ACCIDENTS)

Above
Another ROSPA poster, this one clearly showing the shields used over traffic lights. (COURTESY OF THE ROYAL SOCIETY FOR THE PREVENTION OF ACCIDENTS)

like a pike, and when he reached the first traffic lights of the Circus he jumped off his machine and with the help of the rod lowered the half-shutters that must dim the traffic lights before the blackout. . . . The police cycle round with their rods like the

Left
A white-line painting machine. These were used extensively to help motorists stay on the road during the blackout. (HMSO)
Below
Comic song from 1939. As with so many other wartime restrictions, the blackout was a constant source of humour.
Right
Advert from December 1942 for the Hartley headlamp shield.

lamp-lighters of our youth. Only they dim the lights instead of putting them on.'

The ARP memorandum went on to set out how, in order to improve drivers' vision, white paint, *'Quick drying glossy paint or enamel, was to be applied liberally:*

'(a) In lengths of 1 foot and with 1 foot gaps to the vertical faces (and, where considered necessary, to the horizontal faces) of kerbs at road junctions and intersections, roundabouts, bends and corners, and places where the carriageway width alters abruptly. The kerbs of refuges should be similarly marked.

(b) In lengths of 1 foot with 1 foot gaps, in roads

leading out from junctions – after an interval of 15 feet on the straight, and for a stretch of 10 feet on the near-side kerb.

(c) In horizontal bands 6 in. wide and 6 in. apart on trees, lamp-posts, etc., bordering the carriageway, from ground level to a height of 3 feet.

The vertical supports of pedestrian guard rails should be painted in a similar manner. On trees, lamp-posts, etc., bands of a white reflecting material having a higher efficiency than white paint may be used as an alternative.

(d) In the form of a continuous white line along the centre of the carriageway. Where broken lines defining three traffic lanes already exist, a central continuous white line should be laid down and all three lines maintained.

(e) In horizontal bands or strips 6 in. to 12 in. wide and a similar distance apart on fences, railings, etc., at bends and corners where the line of the road may thereby be rendered more easily visible.'

White paint had also to be applied to the bumpers and to the edges of running boards on cars, 'or to the equivalent positions on vehicles for night motoring'. These measures made little difference, and within a week the rules were relaxed to allow the offside headlamp, heavily dimmed, to be used. However, an ARP Circular of 18 September stated that: 'If an air raid warning is sounded at night all headlights must be extinguished except those of fire engines and ambulances on their way to the scene of a raid.' This was later widened to include all emergency vehicles.

Soon an official blackout mask for car headlamps was available. The **Daily Express** War Time Lawyer gave directions for its use: 'An official headlamp mask may be purchased, and its use is compulsory from 22nd January 1940. It may be fitted to either the off-side or the near-side head-lamp. The other must be shut off. The side-lamps must be screened.' **The Motor** magazine gave more detail: 'The mask is fitted to a head lamp in place of the normal glass for use if the car is run at night. It can be of the prescribed three slot, made as per official recommendation, or of any other type, so long as it does not exceed the requirements of the law. The mask may be fitted to either head-lamp (the other head-lamp bulb being removed), but there is sufficient lateral diffusion to illuminate the kerb at either side of the road. The idea is to illuminate as much of the road width as possible. Intensity must not exceed 2.5ft. candles at 10 ft. from the car. On certain cars, mainly American, which have built-in head-lamps, a special type of mask back plate is used. Alternatively, one could fit an entirely separate lamp to which the mask can be fitted.'

THIS WILL COME AGAIN

BUT IN THE MEANTIME
those who must drive at night
MUST DRIVE SAFELY.

The HARTLEY HEADLAMP DEVICE
V. & N. HARTLEY, WELLINGTON MILLS,
GREENFIELD. Near OLDHAM.

However, a police constable was entitled to direct that a fog or headlamp be switched off at any time if, in his opinion, *'conditions do not make its use imperative'.*

To show emergency vehicles in the blackout, special markings were used. Beside the regulation headlamp shield, the second headlight was used, but this time with cut-out letters to indicate the service as follows:

Air Raid Wardens –	W
First Aid Parties and Mobile First Aid Units –	FAP
Ambulances –	A
Rescue Parties –	R
Decontamination Squads –	DC
Repair Services, Roads, etc. –	RP/R
Water –	RP/W
Gas –	RP/G
Electricity –	RP/E
Messengers –	M
Stretcher Parties –	SP
Fire Service –	FIRE
Police –	P

Under these conditions it was important that what little light you had was used to its greatest efficiency. A Joseph Lucas advertisement of December 1942 asked: *'Is your lighting all it should be? Does it not only conform to the regulations made for ARP security but, just as important, is not over-dimmed or otherwise dangerous to road safety? Far too many motorists fall into this latter error.'* It went on to give instructions for adjusting your headlamp. *'Place the car squarely in front of your garage doors or a blank wall on suitable level ground. With the Lucas "Maxlite" one-slot mask, the beam distribution makes it necessary to adjust the head lamp mounting to ensure the*

CAR ON LEVEL SQUARE TO WALL. TOP OF MASKED BEAM SHOULD STRIKE WALL 12½ IN. LOWER, AT 25 FEET, THAN HEIGHT OF MASK APERTURE.

beam is projected below the horizontal. Also, further dip is needed to compensate for bouncing due to uneven road surfaces, extra loading in the rear or driving uphill.

Therefore a dip of not less than 2½° is advised, i.e. a one-inch drop for each two-feet of forward projection. The beam must not strike the ground nearer than 10ft. from the front of the car. If preferred, to suit local road conditions, slight compensation for road camber can be made by tilting masked lamp to the right a little. With a car particularly heavily loaded at the rear, extra dip may be needed. Shock absorber functioning should be watched to prevent excessive pitching causing undue rise of the beam.

The Lucas "Maxlite" complies fully with the regulations. With a clean reflector and standard bulb not exceeding 36 watts, this mask is designed to give the permissible of 2.5 foot candles at twenty feet.'

The use of a single unscreened fog lamp was permitted in foggy weather, provided that the lamp was completely separate from the headlamps, was operated by a separate switch and was fitted below the level of the headlamps, that its beam was directed downwards and towards the near side, and that it was extinguished immediately an air-raid warning was given.

A correspondent to **Autocar** magazine in December 1942 noted that *'We had quite a number of fogs in my part of the country this autumn. I was walking home in a real pea-souper one evening not so long ago when I noticed that most of the cars and nearly all the lorries had head lamps full on and unmasked. It was the first time I had noticed that some drivers seem to abandon the regulation mask in such conditions – an unmasked fog lamp may be used in addition to the masked head lamp "if progress is impractical otherwise". A policeman can decide whether conditions warrant the use of special lighting in fog. Also, if no fog lamp is fitted, an unmasked head lamp is permissible under similar limitations. In such conditions it is best to tilt the head lamp down and use the reflected light to get along.'*

Side and rear lamps were also covered. In 1940,

Left
Stretcher party car, clearly showing identifying headlight shield. (Courtesy of Lewisham Local Archives)

Above
Instructions for adjusting your headlights, from **Autocar** magazine, December 1942.

these were not to be more than 7 watts in power, no bigger than 2in diameter with the reflector painted matt black or otherwise rendered non-effective. *'The aperture through which light is emitted must be partially obscured by inserting behind the glass paper or some other uncoloured material having a density equal to that of two sheets of newspaper, or by applying a thin coat of paint to the interior of the glass in such a way that approximately the* *same effect is produced. The paper, paint, or other material must cover the whole of the portion of the front glass through which light can pass and must not be wetted, oiled, varnished or treated in any other way to increase its transparency.'* By 1942 *'Side lamps must be dimmed to be clearly visible at 30 yds., but invisible at 300 yds., the aperture not to exceed 1in. diameter.'*

A regulation came into force in January 1940, by which all road vehicles, including bicycles and tricycles, had to have a red tail lamp fixed at a maximum of 3ft 6in from the ground, except in the case of public service vehicles. By 1942, **Autocar** magazine reported that: *'Tail lamp restrictions were relaxed last year and the full aperture can*

LOOK OUT IN THE BLACK-OUT

REVERSING LAMPS PROHIBITED

NO INSIDE LIGHT

REMOVE IGNITION KEY WHEN PARKING

WINDSCREEN CLEAN

DIMMED SIDE LAMP

USE ONE HEAD LAMP FITTED WITH SLIT MASK

REDUCED RED REAR LAMP AND RED OR AMBER STOP LIGHT

DIMMED INDICATOR

DOOR LOCKED WHEN PARKING

MATT WHITE PAINT ON EDGE OF RUNNING BOARD

MATT WHITE PAINT ON BUMPERS

NOTE.
In addition; if the car is left outside, part of the mechanism must be removed, or a locking device applied, or the car must be in a locked garage or yard.

GOOD TYRES

GOOD BRAKES

FOG LAMP FOR USE IN FOG ONLY

SHUFFREY

now be used, dimmed by only one sheet of paper, yet many are still so dull as to be a great danger even on clear nights, let alone in poor weather or if not continually cleaned.'

Stoplights could be used as long as they were masked so that light was emitted from an area not exceeding 2 square inches. Reversing and number plate lights were prohibited, while dashboard and other interior lights were not to show outside the car, and direction indicators, or trafficators, might be used provided that the transparent panels were treated in such a manner that the light was emitted only through an arrow-shaped window having arms of width not exceeding ⅛in.

Strict blackout rules applied equally to cyclists. The **Daily Mirror** of 24 October reported that: *'People who ride bicycles with front lights that are too bright come within the same category as motorists and are liable to a fine of £100, said Mr G. Garrett-Pegge, chairman of Amersham (Bucks) bench yesterday.'* However *'Fines of 10s. were imposed on several offenders.'*

Lucas advertised its bicycle lamp as follows: *'For the Black-out. Many readers must have found by now how difficult it is to obtain satisfactory results from makeshift shields for torches and cycle lamps. As a rule, if the mask is effective enough to satisfy ARP regulations it is seldom possible to see more than a yard or two with the illumination given. There is a new Lucas shield and a special battery lamp, however, that are both efficient and reliable. The Lucas "Masklite" Cycle Headlamp Shield, which is patented and registered, consists of a mask obscuring the upper half of the front glass, and a shield round the underside of the bulb which renders* the lower half of the reflector non-effective. As the shield fits inside the headlamp case, the original condition of the lamp remains unchanged, and there is no unsightly outer shield or paint. It is available for all makes of cycle dynamo headlamps and cycle battery headlamps. The price is only 6d.'

All You Want to Know on Cycling spelt out the rules for bicycles. *'Cycles must carry a white front lamp, red rear lamps, and a white patch. Both lamps must not exceed 7 watts, and the upper half of the front lamp glass must be obscured, and the lower half of the reflector must be painted matt black, or otherwise rendered non-effective. All side or rear lampglass must be completely blacked out. Rear lamps must have one sheet of tissue paper behind the red glass, white patches must have an image of at least 12 sq. inches, at least 6 sq. inches of which must be on the off side of the machine's centre line. No part of a bicycle should project more than 20 inches, or on a tricycle more than 30 inches, beyond the white patch. A 6 inch length of white or white-painted mudguard will do, but aluminium or chrome is not legal.'*

In November 1939 it had been decided to impose a speed limit of 20mph in built-up areas during the hours of blackout, that being half-an-hour before and after lighting-up times (from one hour after sunset to one hour before sunrise from the third Sunday in April to the first Sunday in October, and for the rest of the year half an hour after sunset to half an hour

LUCAS N°68
A.R.P. LAMP

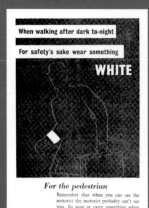

before sunrise), as brought in at the beginning of February 1940. This speed limit was enforced by police cars driving at the legal speed, and arresting anyone who overtook them. The first man to be convicted, at Croydon Magistrates Court in March 1940, was the driver of, believe it or not, a hearse, which was travelling at 34 miles an hour.

The virtual absence of air raids in the first months of the war meant that the blackout increasingly came to be seen by most people as a nuisance, and on the roads, a positive danger. **The Light Car** magazine, of March 1940, reported that: *'The total road deaths in February, 1940, was 416 compared with 619 for January, 1940, representing a decrease of some 33 per cent. This is the lowest total since the black-out was introduced. Most people will jump to the conclusion that the 20mph speed limit, introduced on February 1, was the deciding factor, but it must not be forgotten that the bitter weather experienced during the month kept many vehicles off the roads and that the intensive drive for safer walking must have had a big effect on the general result; moreover summer time came in on February 25. The total number of deaths on the road from the outbreak of war to the end of last month was 5,165, which emphasizes the danger of the black-out because 12 months ago statistics for the similar period revealed a total of only 3,439. Once again, many people will ask, "Is the black-out worth it?"'*

Above
Pedestrians were repeatedly exhorted to 'Wear something white at night'.
Below
Lucas cycle dynamo from 1944.

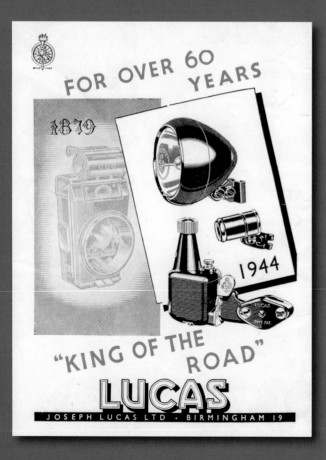

air raids

ARP handbook no. 8, published in June 1938, instructed people what should happen if you were travelling when the air-raid warning was sounded: *'People not within reach of home (that is, who cannot get there within 5 minutes) should be directed to the nearest public shelter, or other refuge accommodation. Vehicles (except those on official duty) should stop before the end of the 5 minutes,*

in a raid—

Motorists-park your car close to the kerb off the main highway. *AT NIGHT*, switch off head lamp. Keep side and rear lights on

and their occupants go to shelter.

Until the "raiders passed" signal has been given, no journey should be resumed. Likewise, if there has been a gas warning, until the all-clear is given by hand bells, remain in cover. Carry your gas mask with you.'

As with the blackout regulations, instructions for travellers changed. On 18 September 1939, an ARP circular pointed out that *'The principal change made by the new instructions is that drivers and cyclists who have good reason for going on should be allowed to do so. Police and air raid wardens should not therefore stop vehicles which do not pull up after the air raid warning signal has been given. If the driver or cyclist chooses to go on, it should be assumed that he has good reason for doing so, and he should not be required to justify his action.'*

Three days later, another ARP circular spelt out 'What Drivers and Cyclists Should Do after an Air Raid Warning Signal Has Been Given': *'When the air raid warning is given, drivers should stop as soon as they come to a suitable place at or near which they can find shelter, unless they have good reason for going on. Vehicles must be parked either close to the kerb or edge of the road or in a garage, car park or open space off the highway, if available.*

Vehicles must not be parked in any place where they will interfere with the free passage of emergency vehicles in either direction. At night, headlights must be switched off, but side and rear lamps should be left alight. In the case of cab ranks only the front and rear vehicles need be lighted.

Cars must be left unlocked, and any articles of value removed. Drivers of vehicles carrying petrol, explosives or other dangerous or inflammable goods, should park their vehicles in an open space away from the highway, if such place is available.

When the air raid warning is given, cyclists should stop as soon as they come to a suitable place at, or near, which they can find shelter, unless they have good reason for going on.

Cyclists, when they stop, must not leave their cycles in the road, but must place them where they will not cause obstruction. A cycle must not be left propped up by the pedal against the kerb, and must not be taken into a public shelter.'

Above

In an air raid, you had to pull your car over and make your way to the nearest shelter.

IN AN AIR RAID . . .

WHAT MOTORISTS MUST DO

BY DAY

● Park your car off the main highway, close to the kerb.

● Obey promptly any instructions from police or air raid wardens.

● Go to the nearest shelter, or take cover.

AT NIGHT

● Do the same as by day, but **SWITCH OFF YOUR HEADLAMP.** Leave rear and side lights on.

invasion

With the collapse of France in mid-June 1940, Britain was swept by invasion fears. New regulations for private transport were published. **If the Invader Comes**, a leaflet issued that month, contained instructions as to what to do in the event of invasion. These included *'Hide your food and your bicycles'* and *'Remember that transport and petrol will be the invader's main difficulties. Make sure that no invader will be able to get hold of your cars, petrol, maps or bicycles.'*

In the event of an invasion, no private cars or motorcycles would be allowed on the roads in the districts affected, only private cars or motorcycles engaged on services essential for the prosecution of the war, or the life of the community, might then use roads within the forbidden districts. All other private cars or motorcycles in the districts likely to be affected by invasion had to be put out of action by removing the distributor, petrol pump, steering wheel or other vital part, and the parts removed handed over to the authorities. It was stressed that should this order be disobeyed, drastic measures would be taken; in practice it usually meant that, on returning to the car, you would find your tyres let down and the distributor rotor arm missing. Elsewhere, on parking a car, it became compulsory to remove the ignition key and lock the doors, to remove some part of the engine so that it could not be started, or to lock the steering wheel, unless it was left in the charge of a person of fourteen or over. At night, except in the case of doctors and nurses on duty, part of the engine had to be removed in addition to locking the vehicle. The leaflet **Beating the Invader** of May 1941 gave instructions: *'Remove distributor head and leads and either empty the tank or remove the carburettor. If you don't know how to do this, find out now from your nearest garage. In the case of diesel engines remove the injection pump and connection. The parts removed must be hidden well away from the vehicle.'*

On 31 May 1940 an order was passed requiring the removal of any signs which gave the name of any place or the direction of or distance to any place. Signposts and milestones were taken down or painted out, but woe betide the lost motorist who stopped to ask a local the way; they might well find themselves arrested for being a spy or fifth-columnist!

If that did not make travelling difficult enough, from the end of May onwards roadblocks sprang up all over the country, usually manned by the recently formed Local Defence Volunteers, later to become the Home Guard. Drivers were warned that if called upon to stop (at night by the waving of a red light), you were compelled to do so; otherwise your car might be fired upon. The earliest roadblocks were most insubstantial, made from oil drums filled with earth or stones, and connected by lengths of wood and bits of barbed wire, or old cars, farm carts tipped on end, or ancient pieces of farm machinery.

From mid-autumn 1940 roadblocks became more substantial, taking the form of concrete cylinders, measuring 3ft by 2ft and weighing 9cwt. There were also small concrete pyramids known as 'dragon's teeth', and bent steel girders, 6 to 8ft long, which fitted into sockets in the road, which were called 'hairpins' because of their shape.

They sprang up everywhere, much to the annoyance of travellers who might be stopped every few miles of their journey, and asked to produce their identity cards and other documents. Tempers became frayed, especially as many regarded the Home Guard as 'not proper soldiers', arguments were common, and some drivers refused to stop, sometimes with tragic results as half-trained, suspicious, and jumpy Home Guardsmen opened fire.

Certain parts of the country were declared Defence, Banned or Protected areas. Entry was not allowed into defence areas for pleasure, recreation or holidays. Permits were not necessary, but documentary proof of the need for making the journey into the area was desirable. In June 1940 a strip up

to 20 miles inland from the Wash to Rye – the expected location of the German invasion – was declared a Defence Area. This was later extended to Berwick-on-Tweed, Dorset and parts of South Wales. In the banned areas the use of private cars or motorcycles was limited to those holding special permits, and those vehicles still in the area, but not permitted to be used, had to be immobilised. Protected areas, such as Portsmouth, contained many military installations. These were forbidden to non-residents unless in possession of a permit. At the same time the Minister of Transport empowered Regional Commissioners to forbid the use of any class of vehicle on any road in their areas. The primary object of this was to prevent roads urgently required for military movements being blocked by non-essential traffic.

Left
After the first few weeks of war these guidelines would be loosened – motorists who had good reason for continuing their journey were allowed to do so.

Above
Travel became more difficult – all sorts of direction signs and signposts were removed to confuse the expected panzers, and they had the same effect on the bewildered motorist.

"THE MOTOR," July 24, 1940.

ACCURATE STEERING

6d

The Motor

The National Motor Journal

Registered at the G.P.O. as a Newspaper.

WOLSELEY has national identity

epilogue

The war finished at last with the surrender first of Germany, then of Japan, in May and August 1945 respectively. Air raids, while severe, had been far less damaging than many had feared, and poison gas attacks non-existent. But the hardships of rationing and shortages had been far worse.

Few would have guessed that Britain would end the war exhausted and virtually bankrupt. The shortages, which people had suffered for the sake of the war effort, did not, as many expected, end with the conflict; they and the rationing they spawned went on for long afterwards, made worse by the cessation of lend-lease goods from America – no more powdered egg!

Indeed rationing became worse after the war; in May 1946, the cheese ration was cut to 2oz a week, and on 21 July 1946 bread rationing was introduced at 9oz a day, while in the worst year of shortages, 1947, even potatoes were rationed in December.

From 1948 Britain began at last to emerge from the shadows; on 1 June the basic petrol ration was restored – to about 90 miles a month – and furniture rationing ended. In July bread came off ration, followed in December by jam. In May 1950 petrol rationing ended altogether, along with points rationing. February 1951 saw sweets rationing abolished, at least temporarily, and October 1952, tea. In February 1953 sweets were taken off ration permanently at last, followed in March by eggs, in April by cream, and in September by sugar. The final year of rationing, 1954, saw butter, cheese, margarine and cooking fats off ration in May, while finally all rationing ended in June 1954 with meat and bacon, fourteen years after its introduction.

The experience of the home front had been a gruelling one for most who had lived through it, yet in many ways it had brought out the best of Britain, as people shared ideas and scarce items, and ingenuity and inventiveness managed to overcome some of the suffering, while a sense of humour helped them to put up with the rest.

I hope this book has given a taste of both.

Above
A VE-Day headband. After nearly six years of war the day so long awaited had at last arrived and Britain was ready to party!

ISSUED BY THE BOARD OF TRADE

Useful jobs that Girls can do—

TO HELP WIN THE WAR

Girls simply must be able to use their needles neatly in wartime —here are a few hints on sewing for beginners. But needlework isn't enough, in these days when EVERYTHING must be made the most of; see if you can't turn your hand to other jobs round the house.

BUTTONHOLE - MAKING

Step by Step...

: make the positions with pins placed vertically or with running stitch (A): then cut the slit very carefully along the thread of the material. It must be perfectly straight and long enough for the button to pass through easily. Insert needle through the slit and twist the cotton from the eye under the point of the needle (B). Draw with an upward movement, thus making a " knot " at the raw edge of the slit. Continue in this way, leaving space to equal the thickness of the cotton between each stitch, until the length of the slit is worked (C) For the rounded end, make overcast stitches (D and E). When the seventh stitch has been made, start to twist, the cotton round the needle again, thus making the first stitch on the second half of the buttonhole. Continue so to the end of the slit, then insert needle through the knot of the last stitch and bring out at base of stitches (F). Work one stitch the full width of the buttonhole (G). Work seven knotted stitches over this stitch (H). Fasten off securely at back. The round end of the buttonhole will take the pull of the button and should therefore be worked next to the opening (I).

An *EASY* renovation

When the sleeves wear out of a favourite frock and it gets too short for you, turn it into a slipover to wear with a blouse

and skirt. The neckline can be cut in square or V shape as suits you best and the armholes rounded deeply. Outline both neck and armholes first with tacking stitches as a guide to cutting. Allow ⅜" for turning and face with bias binding. Dart slightly at the waist, shorten to hip length and hem.

No need for a SHINY SKIRT

You can sponge away shininess if you take it in time, with a cloth dipped in a little ammonia and water. Use about a teaspoonful of ammonia to a saucerful of water. Very often light pressing with a warm iron over a damp cloth is effective if the shiny part, while still damp, is gently rubbed with a brush, preferably a rubber one such as is used for suede shoes.

SNUG SLIP[P] from OLD FE[LT]

Make yourself a pair of cosy slippers to save your coupons. Besides an old felt hat, you will [need] a little strong canvas and some gay scraps for [...]

First cut paper patterns—two heel pieces, one upper an[d] for each slipper. Use the diagrams as a guide to shape an[d] slipper as a guide to size.

Unpick and brush the hat and place the patterns as a & b. Cut out and, if you like, cut a simple openwork d[...] the upper fronts before lining.

Using the same patterns but allowing ¼" for turnings, linings. Any soft material will be suitable.

Join felt heel pieces with a flat seam, machined and back[...] Press turnings outwards and face with tape, for strength. [...] tape down on each side of seam (c). Do the heel lin[...] same way. Then join the linings to the felt (uppers and h[...] turning in the lining edges and slip stitching on wrong si[...]

Cut soles from an old piece of canvas as a foundation for [...] Prepare the plaited strands by cutting old stockings sp[...] (d) and plaiting (e). Sew these strands to the canvas (f) b[...] from outer edge and following the arrow.

To join uppers to soles, take the heels first and sew to [...] turnings. Use two needles (see diagram g) each of whic[h] enter the holes made by the other so that the stitches [...] even on both sides. Attach uppers in the same way, letti[ng] overlap slightly where they join the heels. Start from ce[...] and centre back.

Cut cardboard ' socks ' slightly smaller than soles and p[...] a layer or two of soft material. Cover with lining m[...] drawing this together on the underside and stitching [...] Attach to inside sole with strong adhesive.

TO AVOID 'seating A SKIR[T]

Prevention is bett[er] than cure—remember not [...] lounge about in a tailored ski[rt] Change it directly you come in, always hang it [...] when it's not being worn and keep it well press[ed] For extra precaution, put a rectangle of some str[ong] material—the best part of an old dress or coat linin[g] for instance, across the back. Cut this a sha[...] narrower than the back breadth and hem it to ea[ch] side seam. It should be attached to the waistba[nd] at the top and come well below the hips.

MENDING LACE OR NET CURTAINS

It's a simple matter if you have a piece of similar material large enough to extend well over the torn part. Put the curtain flat on a table with an ironing blanket under the place to be repaired. Dip the patch into rice-water, wring out well, spread it over the hole and press with a hot iron.

TO K[...]

is n[...] goes clea[...] and [...] of t[...] tak[...] pre[...] Qu[...] (n[...] ta[...]

Printed for H.M. Stationery Office by J. Howitt & Son Ltd., Nottingham. 51-4931

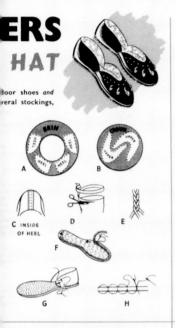

ERS

HAT

...door shoes *and*
...veral stockings,

A

B

C INSIDE
OF HEEL

D

E

F

G

H

Study your sewing machine

If you have a sewing machine, learn how to use it efficiently. Practise on paper first, without thread, until you get the knack of keeping your stitching straight.

Clean and oil the machine every now and then to get best results. Use only the oil supplied for the purpose and only one drop at each oiling point or point of friction (see diagram). Oiling parts marked with large ring should be oiled frequently —the others occasionally. After oiling, make a

few stitches on waste paper to remove excess.

To avoid breaking needles, do not attempt to pull or remove the material until the take up lever is at its highest point. Don't use too fine a needle for heavy materials.

Missing stitches are due to a blunt or bent needle or to thread that's too coarse.

Puckered seams mean that the stitch is too long for the material or that the tension is too tight.

...on't buy NEW for a

CUSHION COVER

...cushion needs a new cover, make one in patchwork, ...g odd bits from the scrap bag. Silk or velvet scraps ...ld be lovely and soft—but odds and ends of dress ...ollens will last longer. Trim your pieces to the ...pes you want and tack them to a square of news-...er cut the right size. Then machine or feather ...ch them together, taking care to ...the joins smooth and flat. Use ...best side of the existing cover ...back the cushion.

WASHING HINTS

*Mend **before** laundering — always make that your rule. Even a tiny run or hole is apt to grow bigger in the tub.*

Don't let things get too dirty before washing — the harder rubbing required will shorten their usefulness. Stockings should be washed after each wearing — not necessarily in soapy water.

Always use lukewarm water for woollens, stockings and coloured things. Hot water can ruin them.

Rinse everything thoroughly—soap left in a garment thickens and matts it. Never rub or twist your woollens or rayons.

Hang your clothes to dry carefully—put frocks and blouses on a dress hanger. Spread jumpers and cardigans out flat, patting them to their original shape.

...AND IRONING WISDOM

Don't iron clothes when they are too damp—it wastes heat. Get them nearly dry, then roll up in a towel for a little.

Never sprinkle Rayons. Use a moderate (not hot) iron on the wrong side of fabric.

When ironing sheets, tablecloths, etc., don't press in the creases ; just fold lightly. This will prolong the life of your linen.

Don't leave things damped down and rolled up for too long—this may lead to mildew.

FIX A LOOSE HANDLE

...vided the 'tang' (the bit that ...le) is at least 1½ in. long. First ... in the handle with a metal ...owder a little ordinary resin ...with it ; on top put a bit ... size of a pea. Heat the ...ill melt the resin and ...the resin-filled hole. ...he knife into warm ...Leave for a few minutes, ...off any surplus resin.

COLLECT WOOD ASH

—the clean white kind— to put in a jar near the sink. It makes a good scouring powder and helps to remove stains from metal and china.

Care of Brushes

Hairbrushes, of course, need regular washing in warm (not hot) soapy water, with a dash of ammonia. Rinse in warm water, then very thoroughly in cold, to stiffen the bristles. Shake well to remove as much moisture as possible and stand on end to dry slowly.

Tooth brushes will last longer if washed in cold water every time after use. Always stand with bristles upwards.

Clothes brushes and shoe brushes, too, need washing now and then. Use the same method as for hair brushes. Greasy household brushes call for soda as well as soap in the washing water. Put them away standing on end, not resting flat either on their backs or their bristles.

A SOGGY SPONGE

calls for a vinegar bath— use only a teaspoonful of vinegar to a pint of water. Rinse the sponge first, then soak it in the vinegar solu- tion for an hour. Squeeze clean, rinse again and dry outdoors if possible.

S.O.S. for a SCRUBBING BUCKET

An ordinary pot mender from the ironmonger's will stop a leak in a bucket. The discs should be fixed on each side of the hole and held with a screw and nut, the cork disc being placed inside the bucket under one of the metal discs.

WHEN A DRAWER STICKS

scrape its edges well with a chisel. Then rub the trimmed parts with candle wax.

Polishing Pads

for windows and mirrors can be made successfully from worn-out wash- leather gloves. First rescue any bits good enough for elbow patches or cuff-bindings ; then cut open the fin- gers, remove fasteners and lay several gloves flat on top of one another. Stitch a small circle in the centre of the pad to hold it together.

NATIONAL SERVICE

WOMEN WANTED

TO HELP THE CHILDREN

FROM EVACUATED AREAS

THE CHILDREN LEAVE FOR SCHOOL

A TALK IN THE VILLAGE HALL

EFFICIENT COOKS AND HELPERS PREPARE THE MID-DAY MEAL

PLAYING AFTER SCHOOL HOURS

THE AFTERNOON DARNING AND MENDING CLUB

DOMESTIC HELP TO KEEP THE CHILDREN HEALTHY AND HAPPY

THESE ARE JOBS WHICH WILL HAVE TO BE DONE. ALL WOMEN LOVE CHILDREN AND LIKE TO HELP THEM. OFFER YOUR SERVICES

APPLY TO YOUR LOCAL COUNCIL OR LOCAL BRANCH OF THE WOMENS VOLUNTARY SERVICES

index

OFFICIAL INSTRUCTIONS ISSUED BY THE MINISTRY OF HOME SECURITY

GAS ATTACK

HOW TO PUT ON YOUR GAS MASK

Always keep your gas mask with you — day and night. Learn to put it on quickly. Practise wearing it.

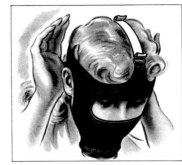

1. Hold your breath. 2. Hold mask in front of face, with thumbs inside straps.
3. Thrust chin well forward into mask, pull straps over head as far as they will go.
4. Run finger round face-piece taking care head-straps are not twisted.

IF THE GAS RATTLES SOUND

1. Hold your breath. Put on mask wherever you are. Close window.

2. If out of doors, take off hat, put on your mask. Turn up collar.

3. Put on gloves or keep hands in pockets. Take cover in nearest building.

IF YOU GET GASSED

BY VAPOUR GAS Keep your gas mask on even if you feel discomfort
If discomfort continues go to First Aid Post

BY LIQUID or BLISTER GAS

1 Dab, but *don't rub* the splash with handkerchief. Then destroy handkerchief.	**2** Rub No. 2 Ointment well into place. *(Buy a 6d. jar now from any chemist).* In emergency chemists supply Bleach Cream free.	**3** If you can't get Ointment or Cream within 5 minutes wash place with soap and warm water.	**4** Take off at once any garment splashed with gas.

AIR RAID PRECAUTIONS

VITREOUS ENAMELLED DIRECTIONAL AND LOCATION SIGNS

AIR RAID SHELTER DIRECTIONAL SIGN
S.D.101   26" × 12"

Enamelled both sides and supplied with brackets for attaching to Belisha Beacons, lighting standards, etc. Can also be supplied enamelled one side only. Right or Left hand for fixing on walls.

BLACK LETTERS ON YELLOW GROUND

FIRST AID POST DIRECTIONAL SIGN
S.D.110   26" × 12"

All as above but lettered— RED LETTERS AND CROSS ON WHITE GROUND as illustration

INDIRECTLY LIGHTED SIGN

A patented device with internal electric lamp (15w recommended) so devised as to indirectly illuminate the sign only. Direct light is not visible at any angle and no light is thrown downwards beyond the face of the sign.

AS SUPPLIED TO LEADING MUNICIPALITIES

ELEMENTARY CARE OF TOOLS

If you haven't a tool chest it is a good plan to make a simple wooden rack from odd pieces of old wood to fix to the wall in which to hang your tools.

Don't leave tools—particularly edged tools—lying about, or they may get damaged. Put them away as soon as you have finished with them.

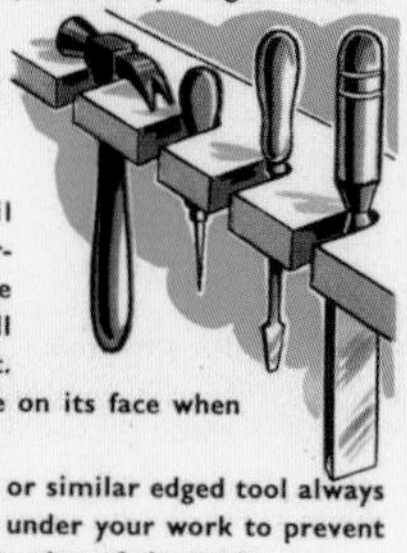

A thin film of oil smeared over the surface of tools before putting them away will keep them free of rust.

Never stand a plane on its face when not in use.

When using a chisel or similar edged tool always place a piece of wood under your work to prevent damage to the cutting edge of the tool.

Put a spot of oil on pliers, pincers, etc., where they cross.

How to Replace a KITCHEN CHAIR RAIL

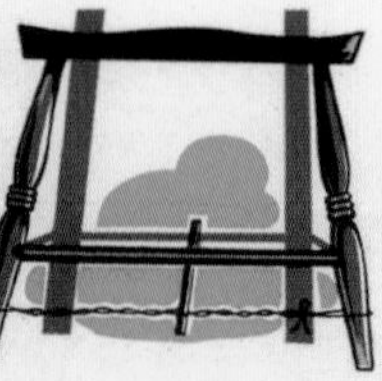

Once one of the horizontal rails on a chair has snapped, there's serious strain on a chair every time anyone sits on it. To replace the rail, cut a length from the handle of a discarded broom or any other circular rod, long enough so that it can just be forced into position. Taper the tips to fit tightly into the holes previously filled by the old rod. Then glue the holes, put the new rod into place, and draw the legs tightly together with strong string to hold while the glue dries.

How to put in a NEW PANE OF GLASS

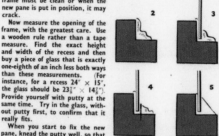

OLD PUTTY
1

First take out all remaining fragments of broken glass and every particle of old putty (Fig. 1). Wear old gloves while doing this to guard against cuts. The recess of the wooden frame must be clean or when the new pane is put in position, it may crack.

Now measure the opening of the frame, with the greatest care. Use a wooden rule rather than a tape measure. Find the exact height and width of the recess and then buy a piece of glass that is exactly one-eighth of an inch less both ways than these measurements. (For instance, for a recess 24″ × 15″, the glass should be 23⅞″ × 14⅞″). Provide yourself with putty at the same time. Try in the glass, without putty first, to confirm that it really fits.

When you start to fix the new pane, knead the putty well, so that the warmth of your hands will make it soft and pliable. Then, run a very thin line of putty all round the inside of the recess, to make a bed on which the glass may rest (Fig. 2). Next put the pane in position—better get another pair of hands to help you here. When the pane is in place, gently press it back against the wood frame (Fig. 3). If it will not go back, that's because too much putty was used to make the bed—take it out and use less. This is when the pane is apt to crack if any old hard putty has been left in the frame.

As soon as the glass is in position it should be held by three brads, about 4″ from corners, with one additional brad at the centre of each long side. Be careful as you drive these in—see that they go parallel to the glass but not quite touching it (Fig. 4). If they slant towards the glass, they may crack it.

Now run a fillet of putty all round the edge of the glass and give it a bevelled surface with the blade of an old table knife (Fig. 5). Imitate the surround of one of the existing panes as closely as possible. Finish off by trimming away from the inside any putty squeezed out of the recess.

HOW TO MEND A TABLE LEG

Where a table or chair leg has broken, diagonally below the level of the rails connecting the legs, a satisfactory repair can be carried out by warming the broken ends of the leg, well glueing the fracture and pressing the two pieces firmly together. Wipe off the surplus glue with a clean rag soaked in warm water and tightly bind the joint with string. When the glue in the joint has set (allow 24 hours undisturbed) remove the string, soak off if necessary, and clean the joint with a wet rag as before.

In cases where the leg has snapped off across the grain of the wood a temporary repair may be effected as follows :—

Turn the table or chair upside down in a level position, warm and glue the fracture, as previously described, then press the broken leg very firmly downwards until the fractured ends engage closely. Leave the joint undisturbed for 24 hours, then clean off the surplus glue. Prepare two tablets of hardwood or plywood about 4 inches to 5 inches long, ¼ inch thick, and of a width equal to that of the leg. Bore a suitable number of holes in each tablet and screw them on opposite faces of the leg. An equal number of screws should be inserted above and below the fracture and no screws should be inserted within one inch of the joint. The edges of the tablets can be smoothed off and the tablets stained if desired.

HOW TO SEW ON A BUTTON

Mark the exact spot for the button with a pin, and if much pull is likely, cut a small square of extra material to back the button ; or use another small button to take the strain. Start on the inside, having knotted your thread. Pass the needle through the material, the holes in the button, and so through the material again. Go backwards and forwards about ten times, leaving slack enough to form the shank, which should be longer on a thick material than on a thin one. Twist the thread round and round the slack to make a sort of stalk, and take a final stitch or two on the wrong side before cutting it off.

How to SOLDER a leaky vessel

Kettles or pots made of "tin," copper, brass, sheet iron or galvanised iron can be repaired quite easily by soldering. Get a stick of solder, some flux and a tinned soldering iron from your ironmonger's. Thoroughly clean the area round the leak by rubbing with emery paper or steel wool. It is most important to clear off every particle of rust and dirt. Smear with flux. Heat the soldering iron till it is really hot (but not red hot) and rub it over the area, using a small quantity of solder, until a film of tin has been transferred from the iron. Reheat the iron. Hold the stick of solder against the iron until a pool of molten metal drips off, big enough to cover the hole completely. Remove the iron, let the mend cool, and wash well with soap and water.

How to PATCH LINO

A worn or frayed place in the lino can be neatly repaired providing you have an extra bit to match. First, cut out the worn part with a sharp knife. Place this piece on the new piece—taking pains to match the design if there is one—and, using it as a guide, cut out a new piece exactly the same size. Glue the back of the new piece very carefully and place it in the hole, pressing it down well. It should scarcely show at all.

How to stop a WINDOW RATTLING

A wooden wedge between the meeting rails is simple and usually effective, particularly with windows of the sash type. With casement windows, look at the catch—it may not be tight enough. To overcome this, take out the screws holding the metal part that is nearest you ; then replace the fitting so that you can only just slide the catch arm into its slot. If this fails to stop the rattling, remove the two upright strips of beading at the edge of the window and fit them a little closer to the sash frame. A window so gripped will have no space in which to rattle. See that all catches are occasionally oiled.

How to clear a CHOKED SINK

Place a pail under the screw cap at the bottom of the U bend or trap and undo this cap with the aid of a strong bar —a screwdriver shaft, say. A rush of water will come directly the cap is off and it will bring accumulations of the choking matter that caused the stoppage. But if the pipe is still stopped up, poke it clear with a stick inserted at the sink end. Be sure to screw the cap on again securely.

Sometimes a sink can be cleared if the stoppage is not too stubborn by placing the palm of the hand or a swabbing cloth over the opening and rapidly lifting it up and down, causing suction.

HOW TO R... FAUL... DRAW...

When a drawer slides... the fault by first rem... entirely and then fitting... stops are small, thin... placed one at each side... the drawer opening. Th... left marks showing just... new ones, and two small... be sufficient to secure th... Put a chalk mark on... sticking is suspected. If... in action then rub th... paper or with a file, f... rub with a wax candle.

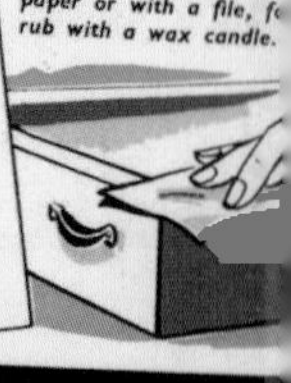

(F.2979). Wt.50848. 40000. 5/44. Gp.961. FOSH & CROSS LTD.

Simp... boys ... them...

jobs
n do
lves—

SO HELP

THE WAR

HOW TO MEND A FUSE

Open the fuse box and pull out one at a time the porcelain fuse bridges that carry the fuse wires. When you find the one on which the wire has melted and burned away, unscrew the two metal terminals that hold the wire and remove the broken ends of the wire.

Take a new length of *fuse wire of the same thickness as the broken one*, wind it a few times round the terminal and tighten the screw. Stretch the wire gently along the groove in the porcelain bridge and attach it to the other terminal screw. Cut off any surplus wire, replace the bridge, close the fuse box and turn on the main switch.

P.S.—Better find out now, before the lights go wrong, where your fuse box is. And make sure you have some 5-ampere fuse wire available.

How to put a NEW SPRING in a door lock or latch

Remove the little grub screw in one of the door handles, take off the knob and draw out the other knob with the spindle.

Unscrew the metal plate in the edge of the door. This will expose two more screws which must be taken out, when the whole lock can be pulled out.

Lay the lock flat and open it by removing the screw in the centre that holds the top plate on. Take out the broken spring and replace it with a new one of the same size and shape. Oil the moving parts and test the lock before replacing it in the door.

Occasional oiling, say once or twice a year, will keep the lock in good condition, and the spring will be less likely to break.

HOW TO REPAIR *A Frayed Flex*

The connecting leads for reading lamps, electric wires, etc., often wear so that the wire itself is exposed where it enters the plug. This is dangerous. Remove the plug from the socket. Get a length of electrician's tape and wind it spiral-wise round the frayed part, wrapping each wire separately first and then binding them together. Pay particular attention to the ends where they join the plug. To prevent fraying in future grip the plug itself when pulling it out, instead of pulling on the wire.

ow to do a DARN

e threads backwards and forwards across the
s closely as possible, beginning and ending an
sh side of the hole, leaving tiny loops at each end.
re-thread your needle and darn across these
, ewaving under and over, turning round and
back so that the needle goes under threads it
over the time before. Repeat until hole is filled
e loops at each end allow for stretching and are
important.

How to renew a COLD WATER TAP WASHER

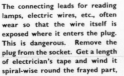

Turn off the water at the main—it's a good plan to know beforehand where this is—and let taps run to empty the tank. With a wrench or spanner unscrew and remove the top of the tap. Take out the worn washer and the metal seating to which it is fixed. Unscrew the small nut on the seating which holds the washer in place, pull off the old washer and put on a new one, then screw the nut tightly back into place. The new washer must be cut back with a sharp knife so that it does not exceed the diameter of the metal seating to which it is attached.

Drop the seating, washer end downwards, into the tap and screw the top of the tap on again. Tighten with a spanner and turn on the main again.

NOTE: Most modern taps have a smooth outer casing which must be unscrewed and lifted to give access to the large nut which unscrews the top of the tap. Protect this casing with a piece of rag. If you have no suitable spanner, the smooth outer casing itself can be lifted off by first removing the handle of the tap which is fixed by a small screw. To avoid twisting the tap itself, it is advisable to use two wrenches, one to grip the body of the tap, and the other to unscrew the head.

R A

R

correct
drawer
These
wood,
ttom of
ll have
ce the
ch will

where
d off
glass
light

How to look after PAINT BRUSHES

Since good bristles are scarce, every brush you own, paint brush, distemper brush, glue brush, etc. should be treated with care. Never put them away damp or dirty—don't leave them in the pot even at meal times but wash ready for use again. Hang them up in a dry airy place—never leave them resting on their bristles.

To clean paint and distemper brushes, use paraffin, working it well into the bristles, especially up near the handle. Then rinse, first in soapy water, then in clear. Oil-bound brushes should be washed in cold water. Glue brushes, too, should be washed in cold water and hung immediately.

HOW TO OIL DOOR LOCKS

Yale type locks themselves must not be oiled, but a film of oil on the catch bolts is a good thing. Ordinary locks should be oiled by putting just a drop er two of oil on the catch bolt, turning the handle until the bolt is inside the lock and then blowing sharply, to spread the oil inside the lock.

How to refix a LOOSE BROOM HANDLE

Take the handle out and saw off an inch or so where it is worn or split. Insert this fresh end into the old hole and nail firmly in place.

How to Refix HANDLES ON FURNITURE

It's because the holes of the screws which hold them have worked too large that drawer handles, etc., come loose. Take off the fitting and plug these holes by inserting bits of any hard wood—an old wood penholder would do—sharpened to points and snapped off to suitable lengths. These can be hammered in to make a really tight fit. Put the handle back into position and replace screws, which will now hold firmly.

How to Refix LOOSE CASTERS

Shaky casters on chair or table legs are usually due to loose screws. The cup caster type should be taken off and replaced so that the screws will go into new holes. (The old holes can be filled up with plastic wood.) To deal with a pin caster —the kind which has a single screw that goes in the centre of the leg —take the caster off and fill in the screw hole with a mixture of sawdust and glue. Allow this to harden and then replace the caster.

Sabrestorm Publishing

Other titles available – for a complete list visit

www.sabrestorm.com

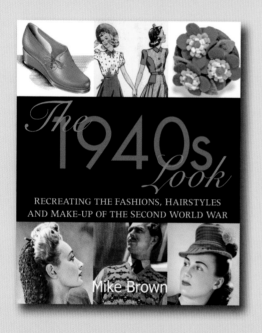

The 1940s Look
Recreating the
Fashions, Hairstyles
& Make-up of the
Second World War
ISBN 9780955272318

The 1950s Look
Recreating the
Fashions of the Fifties
ISBN 9780955272332

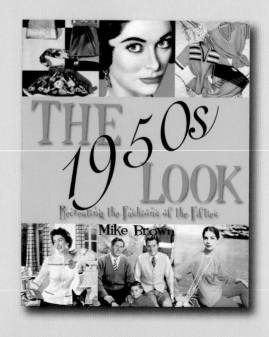

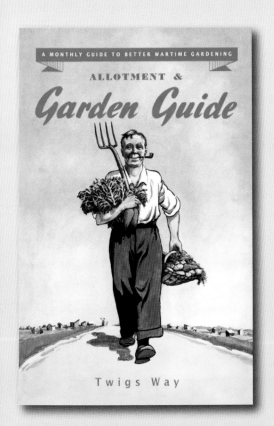

Allotment & Garden Guide
A Monthly Guide to Better Wartime Gardening
ISBN 9780955272356

Make Do & Mend
Wartime Hints & Tips for the Housewife
ISBN 9780955272349

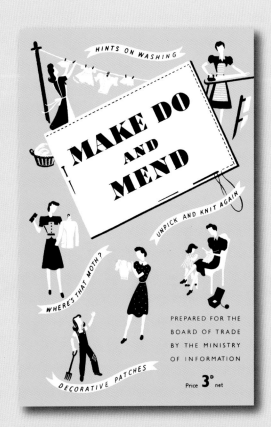

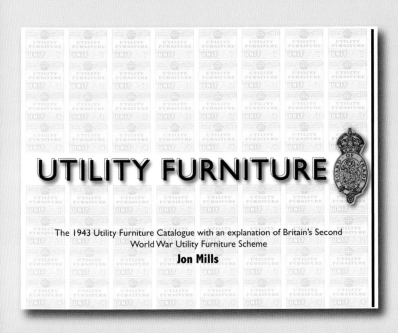

Utility Furniture
A Complete Explanation
ISBN 9780955272325

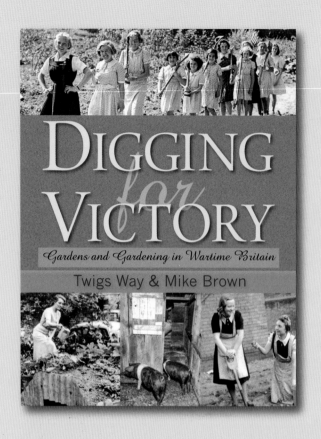

DIGGING
for
VICTORY

Gardens and Gardening in Wartime Britain

Twigs Way & Mike Brown

'Beans as bullets', 'Vegetables for Victory' and 'Cloches against Hitler': these slogans convey just how vital gardening and growing food were to the British war effort during the Second World War. Exhorted to 'Grow More Food', then to 'Dig for Victory', Britain's 'allotment army' was soon out in force, growing as many vegetables as possible in suburban allotments, private gardens, even the grounds of stately homes.

ISBN
9780955272370